ONE NATION UNDER SONG

My Karaoke Journey Through Grief, Joy, and America

ONE NATION UNDER SONG

My Karaoke Journey Through Grief, Joy, and America

KARAJOY
PUBLISHING

by L. Kris Gowen

Publisher: KaraJoy Publishing

ISBN-13 978-1-0879-3265-1

1 3 5 7 9 10 8 6 4 2

DEDICATION

To Molly, who helped me find my voice as she was losing hers

CONTENTS

I SKIP ONTO THE WELL-WORN STAGE AS I'VE DONE SO MANY TIMES before, and hold the microphone, still cradled in its stand. I am in my happy place. As the first few notes of my song begin to play, the bar audience nods in recognition, turning to their companions to share their thoughts and memories about what they're about to hear. Though I've never met any of these people before, I know them. They are my family for the night. They are part of karaoke culture—one small piece of a vast community where I felt at home while driving across America.

PREFACE

"WHAT BRINGS YOU THE MOST JOY?"

I was riding with a fellow academic, Seth. An intimate silence had nestled between us as we drove to yet another meeting meant to somehow make the world a better place. This time, we were getting together with fellow data nerds to consider merging two system-driven data sets in order to better track the outcomes of youth in foster care. As a researcher specializing in program evaluation, I was exposed to a variety of topics, from mental health to sexuality education to cancer prevention.

While the goals of this particular project were admirable, its execution and wider impact fell flat. I felt the futility of trying to get two large state bureaucracies to play nice with one another—no easy feat. I felt the hopelessness of wondering if anything I did would ever matter. Academics pursue funding, not passions; publications, not joy.

"Singing brings me the most joy," I said, somewhat surprised at my response, which came from instinct: a visceral response to his unexpected question. My inner self had taken the spotlight, giving my brain no time deliberate and come up with an answer I thought he would want to hear—or I would want to convince myself was true. My words came from my soul, which I rarely let have center stage. Overly educated folk are supposed to find joy in research, and the discovery of ideas, and the production of well-regarded articles lauded by peers. But the more time I spent in the academic world, the more I realized those things that brought me success in my work—research grants, publications, respect from fellow scholars—left me empty and wondering what was wrong with me. Still, I couldn't argue with myself: Singing brought me joy, and had for a long time.

As a child, I remember singing along to the radio's top hits—back when there was only AM, and Don Imus and Howard Stern dominated the airwaves of New York City. I knew every lyric, every note, every inflection to every song in *Casey Kasem's American Top 40*. I forced myself to sing every note, even if it was out of range. It didn't matter whether I liked the song or not, I sang everything I heard. If I didn't know the lyrics, I mumbled my way through the cadence and guessed at some words until I heard the tune enough times I could sing it with more confidence.

While my singing was seemingly indiscriminate, I did have my favorites. Billy Joel. Donna Summer. But in my eyes no one could compare to Olivia Newton-John. She was my first crush, entering my world with the 1978 movie version of *Grease*. Her stardom resulted in her picture being everywhere. I would cut out images from *Tiger Beat* and other teen magazines, and tack them to a bulletin board in my room, creating a collage of contrasting images: soft blue eyes and pastel dresses juxtaposed with the curly hair, sultry looks, and leather of her more "bad girl" image. The second album I ever bought (the Beach Boys's *Endless Summer* had been the first) was *Totally Hot*, featuring long-forgotten hits such as "Little More Love" and the title track. I would play that album over and over and sing along, at first reading the lyrics off the record sleeve, then from memory. Eventually, I started harmonizing with her. Then, I would get my tape recorder out, put in a blank cassette, and record Olivia and me singing a duet. I'd dream that our collaboration was real.

My singing wasn't reserved for private moments. Whenever a song came on the radio, my response was more of an involuntary reaction than anything else. If there was music, I contributed my voice to it, no matter who was around. Friends and family were subject to my home singalongs. Retail workers listened to me as I provided my own personal soundtrack while trying on jeans. I sang in our church choir in middle school, and during senior year was cast as Snoopy in *You're a Good Man, Charlie Brown*. In that role, I had two solos—my first experience of singing alone on a stage while others listened. The feeling was intoxicating; when I sang "Suppertime," I didn't need to hold back my voice . . . or anything else. I sang loudly; I danced wildly, as a cartoon dog is wont to do.

At Stanford, I sang in the glee club for a few years; I auditioned for the more prestigious a cappella groups, but never quite made the cut. I often made callbacks, just delaying the bitter disappointment when my name wasn't posted among the chosen. I resorted to befriending or hooking up with various a cappella members instead. I'd get invited to their parties, and after a bottle of Yukon Jack was passed around a few times, song would break out in four- or more-part harmony. Get more than three singers together, add a little booze, and singing is inevitable. Intoxication made any flaws more forgivable. But to me, in those moments, there were no flaws. The harmonies were as perfect as the moment itself. During these slivers of opportunity to participate in the community of song, nothing was wrong in my world.

The one musical outlet I had that wasn't dependent on others, where rejection wasn't a risk, was my car. Windows up or down, radio or mix tape (or, later, CDs), I would sing as loud as I wanted to—which could be pretty damn loud. I belted out songs from *The Little Mermaid* and Fleetwood Mac's *Rumours* minutes apart, following them up with some Motown for good measure. Still, it wasn't the same as singing for and with others. I craved the community aspect of song.

After college, I dabbled in community theater and kept singing. But by the time I moved to Portland, Oregon—arriving Labor Day weekend of 2000, having been lured there by my best friend, Molly, who I met at Stanford and had moved there just a month prior to begin her career as a psychologist—most of my public singing took the form of karaoke. The other venues required too much of a time commitment, and my work as a researcher was too serious, too focused, too demanding. Karaoke was still manageable because it was spontaneous. Karaoke became my source of joy.

ONE NATION UNDER SONG

My Karaoke Journey Through Grief, Joy, and America

CHAPTER 1

CHANGE

I DON'T REMEMBER WHEN I FIRST ARTICULATED MY GOAL OF SINGING karaoke in all fifty states, but by the time my partner of nine years and I had split up, this goal was all I had. The dog that had become the only thing holding us together had died two weeks before. That furry, bear-nosed, 110-pound loyal companion and consoler of eleven years died in my arms. At the vet, without any fuss, Brody allowed the needle to push into a body too tired to fight the bone cancer anymore. I stroked his velvet ears and whispered songs of gratitude for our time together, until his eyes closed and there was nothing to do but walk home with an empty collar and hollow heart.

My human relationship had been a struggle for the three years preceding, never quite recovering from accusations of infidelity. Perhaps I did cheat, but not in the physical sense. My relationship with Seth changed from a professional one into one with an emotional intimacy I never had with my partner. And when my partner discovered the time and soul I had shared with Seth, nothing could convince him there hadn't been more. He left me on a Super Bowl Sunday; neither of us bothered to watch the game that year.

Seth had said it was soccer that gave him the most joy. So I wasn't the only academic who saw my career and passions as separate entities, despite being groomed to believe that my work would be the thing that defined me (one of the things that grad school teaches you is that you are nothing outside of your research accomplishments). The result: We both had set aside happiness in order to do what was expected of us. While we both knew there was something fundamentally wrong with this, neither of us knew what to do about it.

That Super Bowl Sunday, I went to sleep alone, believing there had to be a different way. I was by myself for the first time in what felt like a thousand forevers. I had faced the truth by screaming for him to get out, my grief still raw and spent, and he complied by driving off in his pickup truck without a word, sleeping in a place that was no longer my concern. I stared at the wall, and breathed in the solitude. There was no one left to care about or care for. The only one left in my life was me. Without rules to follow or a dog to walk, I was forced to figure out what was next. I had to ask myself what I wanted to do, why I wanted to do it, and what the hell mattered anyway.

I was lucky. I had a counselor who was a perfect fit for my combination of stubborn resistance to change and my desperation to be happy. She challenged me through every step of my process—my excuses, my failure to see life patterns that were obvious from the outside. From our sessions, a pivotal question arose: "What goals do you have?" The only one I could think of was singing karaoke in all fifty states. I had no idea what I wanted in a relationship, where I wanted to live, or what I wanted to do with my career. The only thing that brought me the joy I was so desperately seeking was the idea of singing in all fifty states. As to why, I never had an answer. The idea's origins weren't linear, like a math equation; there was no starting point that logically led to a next step and then a next until an answer could be filled in (be sure to show your work!). Life goals are much more complicated than that, and I was still in the process of understanding mine.

Of course, I loved to sing, but that was only a small part of karaoke's allure. When I revealed my sole desire to my counselor, I had only sung in nine states. But in those nine I'd had the privilege of witnessing people in their communities. I had seen an old red-headed lady named Ginger crooning 1940s tunes as a former naval officer served as the karaoke host in Maryland, and stuffy men in grey business suits letting loose thanks to beers and microphones in Missouri. It wasn't just the idea of singing across the country that excited me; it was the chance to see little slices of America as I visited each state that made me smile. For while karaoke has a common script no matter where you are, each place and night offers something new for everyone—an element of the unexpected. When a person is called to the stage, you never know what they are going to sing or how well they are going to sing it. I've seen "Love on the Rocks"—that slow, stately Neil Diamond tune— performed by a young African American man wearing a "Kiss me, I'm Irish" t-shirt; a frumpy middle-aged white woman in pajama pants rap a mean Coolio; and a heavyset, unshaven guy belt out Tori Amos's "Cornflake Girl" in perfect falsetto. Karaoke has taught me you can't judge a person by their looks. Each of us has the power to surprise the world.

Emboldened by my disclosure in my counselor's office, I began sharing my life goal with others. People—especially those I worked with—were none too impressed with the general goal and the relatively small number of states I had already sung in, but that didn't matter. In my heart, I knew my goal was one of the few things I cared about, and that I was going to do it, slowly, steadily, when life offered chances. Some work travel and a soul-searching road trip over the next two years got that number up to fourteen, plus the District of

Columbia. Then my new partner and I took a weekend road trip to Montana to inch the total up to fifteen.

I had met Dave online. He was born to travel, and it was that aspect of his online profile that drew me to him. I wanted to know more about visiting the world, and his life stories thrilled me. Over a beer on the back patio of a local pub, I listened to him describe close encounters with bush fires during his motorcycle trip around New Zealand and Australia, and his experiences teaching English in South Korea and Saudi Arabia. Here was a man—a cute one, with bushy eyebrows, thick dark hair, and a kind face—who not only had traveled, but was about to go off again. Perfect. When I had first looked at his profile, I saw him as someone who could teach me about traveling overseas, and maybe provide some much-needed sexual release. Then, after a few months we would both go off and experience our separate corners of the world. But things don't always work out as planned. After our first date, I wasn't smitten, exactly. But I was drawn to his odd combination of bravery and clumsy shyness. I wanted to know more about him, his oversized leather gear, and his undersized motorcycle.

I got that chance. One date became two—our second time together at a run-down restaurant known for its taxidermy displays, where we talked for a long time about seeing the world. We admired the stuffed bears, cougars, and rhinos with tropical drinks in hand, and I couldn't get enough of this setting or this companion; everything seemed so natural, despite all the oddities. Months later, Dave and I took that trip to Montana, driving 547 miles one way on a Saturday through high desert snow, just so I could sing a song in a bowling alley—only to turn around on Sunday to get home in time for work.

Our relationship blossomed, and I grew to love not only him, but his family—especially his mom, Milly Rose. Milly Rose always smiled, and had a soft spot for anything sugary; I think that her consumption of See's Chocolate was what made her so sweet on the inside. Over the years, Milly Rose would email me to let her know how things were going with her, and never failed to ask about my well-being. She signed each correspondence with "Love."

Over the years, traveling became a way of life for Dave and me. We lived in South Korea, where he returned to teach English and I continued my research. Then we got ESL certifications in Vietnam, and that allowed us to live in Oman for a year. Expat living stalled my karaoke quest, so after Montana, my fifteen-state total held steady for a couple of years, temporarily losing its dominance in my mind and heart.

Then my best friend died, and my half-hearted conversation piece of a goal was suddenly a driving need.

C H A P T E R 2

MOLLY

MOLLY. MY SINGING BUDDY, MY ROAD TRIP BUDDY, MY SPORTS FAN buddy. The reason I moved to Portland. She was the person I turned to first when I really wanted advice—the real stuff that didn't sugarcoat my stupidity, the futility of a potential path, the fact that I do look better with shorter hair even though I like to wear it long. Molly could tell me what she saw and deliver tough news with matter-of-fact kindness. When I didn't follow her suggestions (an inevitable artifact of my stubbornness) she never said, "I told you so." Instead she treated my repeated problem as if it were something brand-new, patiently doling out the same sage words as before, without a hint of irony or snark. She enjoyed rolling down the windows while we were driving, and letting my less-polished alto take the lead as she harmonized. We sang Crowded House tunes on a road trip through the Deep South, and Shawn Colvin cruising through Oregon and Washington before Portland became our home.

Dave and I were teaching English in the small Middle Eastern country of Oman, a land so different from the US that a typical day never failed to bring surprise. Going to the bank, the grocery store, or class—nothing was how I thought it would be based on my experiences of going to the bank, the grocery store, or class in America. Living overseas brings a sense of surrealism to the everyday that is both exhilarating and mind-numbingly dull. It was in this setting in January 2015, when the heat was still tolerable and the second semester just under way, that I got the email from Molly. I read it over a million times, understanding the words, knowing what they meant, but still wanting them to somehow magically change into something else. The news had to be different:

Hey—I hope you're doing okay over there in the heat.

This is a very hard email to write, but I'm going to have to send something like this to a lot of people so I guess I'll start with you.

Around Thanksgiving, I noticed some mid-back pain that stuck around and didn't seem to get better, despite lots of stretching and rest. After about a month of this, I saw my doctor, who didn't notice anything, but to be sure she sent me for a chest X-ray. The X-ray was abnormal, and showed something unusual in the left lobe of my lung. I went on for a chest CT and visit with a pulmonologist. The chest CT found the same thing—something like a mass in the upper left lobe, but also lymph node swelling and small nodules in both lungs and my liver. We hoped it was sarcoidosis, a chronic disease that often heals itself without treatment. But the pulmonologist recommended a bronchoscopy, in which he would put a scope down my throat to see how my lungs looked and take some tissue samples to biopsy the nodules and the lymph nodes.

He called me yesterday when he received the pathology results and unfortunately, the news is very bad. I have lung cancer which has already spread to both lobes and my lymph nodes and likely to my liver, which makes it metastatic stage IV. (If you're feeling nerdy, it's actually non-small-cell adenocarcinoma.) Because it's metastatic,

7

this is not considered a curable illness, but may be treatable. Prognosis varies widely . . .

Molly had lung cancer. Molly had lung cancer. My best friend had stage IV lung cancer . . .

Molly wasn't supposed to get lung cancer at age forty-two. She didn't smoke; she'd recently started running and had completed three half-marathons while I was overseas. She had two young sons who inherited her love of fantasy football (but not her devotion to the Vikings) and a caring husband who changed careers from Fortune 500 accountant to high school math teacher with the goal that no student of his would ever rent furniture. She had a job she cared about, helping people with mental health challenges get the services they needed, and embraced Portland for everything it had to offer. Molly wasn't supposed to die a year later, leaving her family and friends behind. She had too much giving left in her.

I got the call in Portland on Super Bowl Sunday, about three hours before kickoff; Molly's mom telling a few select friends to get to the hospital quickly. It was time to say goodbye. I somehow managed to drive to Krista's house, where she somehow managed to drive us to the hospital parking lot and then find Molly's room. There was our friend, lying very still, surrounded by her sister, mother, husband, and countless machines searching for small signs of life. That morning, when her children came to visit, she managed to sit up and give them hugs, letting them know she loved them before slipping into the unconsciousness she would never recover from. I sang the Beatles' "Here Comes the Sun" to her softly—her favorite—while holding her hand, as her shallow breath let me know she was still there. I let her know it was all right.

Molly died in a hospital bed five Super Bowl Sundays after my longtime partner had left. She died before she knew the Broncos had beaten the Panthers. She would have been pleased, but she also would have felt sorry for Cam Newton. He didn't deserve the amount of blame he took for the Carolina loss, she would have said. We never got a chance to talk about how sports radio host Dan Patrick covered the result. We didn't slump into her couch to watch the game, lazily critiquing the overproduced and overhyped commercials. We didn't see Beyoncé's halftime show, with its costumes inspired by the Black Panthers. There would be no Super Bowl viewings or debriefings—about the game or other life events—with her again.

We also would never sing together again. Singing was a huge part of both our lives—she took it more seriously than I. Then again, when she committed herself to something, she always did it with a level of dedication that surpassed my drives and passions. And she always excelled at whatever she set out to do. Her exquisite soprano voice was good enough that she made it into one of the a cappella groups that had denied me at Stanford—good enough to make several choirs and choruses (once she even sang backup for Kenny Rogers!).

Occasionally, I could persuade her to sing karaoke, though it was never her thing. I never asked her why. When Portland opened up a private-room karaoke venue, it was easier to get her to join in. A group of us would go there, after her diagnosis, and sing wonderfully horrible songs by Air Supply, Barry Manilow, and Neil Diamond. On those days, Molly's signature song became "Wrecking Ball" by Miley Cyrus; she could belt out that melodramatic chorus with the perfect balance of vocal purity and teenage angst, punching every syllable with flair and sarcasm.

We sang karaoke together in those rooms until she could no longer draw a breath deep enough to share a note.

After Molly died, I tried to continue my life as best I could, but it wasn't working. I tried to go over to her house—now Ted's and the boys' house—but I couldn't. I didn't want to see the low-hung coat hooks, or the awful light pine furniture I helped her pick out when we first moved here, even though I personally preferred darker wood tones. I couldn't sit on the blue couch, across from the oversized chair she had sat in, bald and collapsed, too tired to do much of anything when I visited. In her last few months, she would save whatever energy she had for the kids, and that was fine by me. We would talk about nothing in particular, and often just resort to secure silence in each other's company. Even though she was the one who was dying, she remained the rock I clung to. In her presence, my life was simply better.

Without her, I had nothing. Dave had taken another overseas job in China. I hated my new job—I knew I would when I accepted the offer, but the position had been a way to get back from the Middle East as quickly, but practically, as I could after getting Molly's email (even in extreme circumstances, I did things the practical way). Oregon was still in the throes of its rainy season, which slid me further into depression, further into the folds of my couch, further into myself.

Yet even after her death, when I needed her most, Molly was able to guide me, help me move through my aimless life in a way I couldn't see on my own. I had one thing left: my karaoke goal. Molly's diagnosis showed me that, despite my tendencies to do things purposefully and practically, the best time to pursue a dream was actually *right now*, while it was still possible. It was time for me to go. Time to hit the road, see the country, and sing.

And so I did—four months and six days after Molly was gone. Though I had already sung karaoke in some states, I wanted this journey to include the entire Lower 48, as if I had pushed a reset button on my goal and life. I was going to witness the whole country through karaoke. I was going to experience joy in every state. (Well, almost every state: Alaska and Hawaii were going to have to wait.)

CHAPTER 3

GROUND ZERO: OREGON

PORTLAND WAS NOT THE FIRST PLACE I SANG KARAOKE, BUT IT WAS where I first paid attention to the role it played as an outlet, a community, and an important part of my life. The very first time I sang karaoke was in Arizona, visiting a friend from high school who had moved there for law school. She drove a red Ford Galaxie 500 that was as big as my then-apartment in California's Bay Area. We bar-hopped our way through Phoenix, and at some point stopped to meet up with her friends.

The place happened to have karaoke that night, and though none of her friends seemed interested in participating, I certainly was. I had more than enough liquid courage in me to think singing a song I had never rehearsed in front of a bunch of people I didn't know was a great idea. I picked up a huge black tattered binder that listed thousands of choices on its laminated pages. It was time to make a decision—what would be my first karaoke song? Back then I didn't have a sense of how to choose a song and whether it (or I) would be well-received.

Fueled by the rush of the unknown, the chance to sing, and alcohol, I got up and sang Heart's "Alone." For the record, this song is not a good karaoke choice. It's slow and sappy, and meat markets disguised as bars do not appreciate an amateur bringing the mood down. To make things worse, I missed the climactic high note, coming in horribly flat after the interlude. I could feel my voice grind against the musical backdrop, but didn't know how to fix it on the fly. Still, I had a great time. The rush of singing with a microphone, in front of a crowd, was enough for me to want to do it again. And again. And again. But it took a while before that happened.

I began singing karaoke regularly in 1993, when I moved to Boston for a year to attend grad school. I knew no one, and sought company in a local bar. (I wasn't going to meet a lot of people in my studio apartment housed in a four-story brick walk-up.) At first I went to the bar to watch my beloved Phillies lose the World Series. And then I just started going to escape the grind of my program, the loneliness I felt in a city not known for welcoming strangers. I became a regular, met other regulars who became casual friends, and mastered the one pinball machine in the back of the bar. One day the bartender let me know that starting next week, there would be karaoke on Wednesdays at nine. I was beyond thrilled, and from then on planted myself at the same table every Wednesday at eight forty-five, huge binder of songs and a beer in front of me. There was another regular, a guy named Chris, who also frequented karaoke night, and we would often get confused over whose turn it was. To avoid the mix-ups, I signed up instead as Kristi. I now had a stage name, albeit an uninspiring one.

As Kristi, I showed up every Wednesday and sang songs by Pat Benatar, Billy Joel, and any other artist who moved me that day. I also coached one of the servers there on her performance of "I Will Survive," her chosen audition song to pursue her dream of being a Bud Girl. As a pretty hardcore feminist, studying progressive inclusive sexuality education at one of America's top universities, I had mixed feelings about helping a fellow woman reduce herself to a billboard in revealing clothing. But help her I did, and when she came running to me one night with a huge smile on her face, I knew she had gotten the part. Being a Bud Girl was her joy, and I wasn't to judge what makes someone happy.

While my time in Boston showed me how community played a huge role in karaoke, singing in Oregon allowed me to see fellow karaoke singers as family. Through the years, I became a fixture at various venues in Portland. First, a sketchy Vietnamese restaurant known for bar fights and a bathroom often occupied by people more interested in snorting cocaine or getting it on than actually peeing amid the graffiti and wads of toilet paper on the floor. Then, a Chinese restaurant in the north part of the city. I loved the mix of people there: hipsters, older African American men dressed in pinstripes and ties, residents from the trailer park up the road, truckers staying at the nearby self-proclaimed "Classiest Truck Stop in America."

Then I found my karaoke home: the Local Lounge, a gay bar around the corner from my house.

Sadly, karaoke only happens there on the second Saturday of every month, but that date continues to be circled on every page of my calendar. It's the time when Nikki Lev, the gender-fluid host dressed in a tulle skirt and corset, welcomes everyone in the small crowd. It's the time when Luke, the lumbersexual from Alaska, queues up the songs. The TVs are muted but continue to show either softcore gay porn or old episodes of *The Golden Girls*. An attractive young man takes over pouring drinks from the bartender/owner—who lingers for the night, socializing outside, where the smokers are. Then, it's time to sing. At first, Nikki and Luke announce the theme of the month and encourage everyone to follow along. For example, one April, the theme was "fools," and "Fool in the Rain" by Led Zeppelin, "Fool on the Hill" by the Beatles, and "Foolin'" by Def Leppard were among the tunes. Some singers got more creative with their interpretations of the theme, offering up "Crazy Little Thing Called Love" by Queen and Paul McCartney's "Silly Love Songs." I put in my selection, "What a Fool Believes" by the Doobie Brothers. When it was my turn to sing, I realized the range was pretty darn high, as I strained to mimic Michael McDonald's nasally falsetto. I had never sung that number before, and I never will again—and that's okay. This bar, this space, makes room for risks, screw-ups, and imperfections. Everyone is welcome.

Aside from theme week and the amazing hosts, I'm drawn to the karaoke at this bar on this night for other reasons. It's close to my house, so I can worry less about drinking, wherever it may take me. The drinks are strong, and the draft prices are pretty cheap for such a good selection. The number of singers is about perfect—not so many that you can only hope to be called up at some point during the night, but not so few that the lack of participation creates a sense of loneliness among those who choose to take the stage. Instead, there are times to sing—and in between, there is time to relax and enjoy the entertainment given by others.

I love hearing what other singers choose to perform: wide-ranging, yet familiar. There are '80s mainstays, traditional country tunes, classic rock selections, and a good dose of songs from musicals. People sing whatever they want here, and it all seems to fit in. The same way, the singers create a patchwork of Portland: people of all genders and sexual orientations, all shapes and sizes. A regular in a wheelchair. A Mormon couple newly breaking away from their church. Me, a woman unhappy for reasons she doesn't always understand. We all come together to sing, cheer each other on, and escape from whatever the hell else is going on in our worlds. When I'm ready to call it a night, I sneak out of the bar as the performances continue, and walk around the corner to my house, knowing I get to do it again in another four weeks.

The second Saturday of June 2016, however, when I left the bar, I knew I wouldn't be returning for a while. Instead, three weeks later, I would be singing somewhere else, in a part of the United States I had never sung in before, but at the same time familiar in its community of karaoke. Like lovers who vow to wish upon the same star when forced to be miles apart, I knew that when I was singing somewhere else, Nikki and the gang at the Local Lounge would be singing along with me. I would never be alone.

CHAPTER 4

WASHINGTON

June 10, 2016

L EAVING PORTLAND GAVE ME A SENSE OF RELEASE, AS IT HAD ALL the other times I'd left. Since 2013, each journey had taken me to continents and cultures I never imagined I would dare visit. I went to all these places because of Dave; I was grateful for the ways he had pushed me into the unknown. Our experiences in other countries lasted several months at a time. South Korea, Vietnam, and Oman were all places we called home for at least a while; Dave and I would debate whether a stay of that length made us tourists or something else. The scenery of a twilight-lit mosque, an open-air market full of dragon fruit, or small children coming home from school at 9 p.m. as we sipped beers outside a convenience store made me believe we were, indeed, tourists. Yet the familiarity I felt made me doubt that label. But what I knew for sure was that each time I returned to Portland I didn't get a sense of being back home.

My heart would empty as the reality of my life settled back around me, and I would dream of leaving again.

This newest trip was in some ways more mundane, since I was staying in the US, but also more thrilling, as I wouldn't be staying in any one place for long. My plan to sing in the Lower 48 on one summer trip guaranteed I'd be in a new place every few days, with little time for lingering. It also meant I would be spending a lot of time in my car—a black cherry 2009 Scion tC, a modest two-door I bought after returning from the Middle East. I was drawn to its deep sparkly red, it was reliable, and I could afford it. But most important, the car fit me. The seat was comfortable; I could easily reach the glove compartment, rest my elbow out the driver-side window, fish my sunglasses out of the middle console. On my dashboard I stuck a plastic cartoon Buddha I'd bought at the Chengdu airport that April. When I pressed his head down, he would wear one of four expressions: angry, confused, content, or joyous. I clicked him into this last position as I prepared for departure at 10 a.m. on June 10. At that moment, my car became my home. It would be my sole source of continuity until Dave joined me on my journey in a month or so. But for now, my car and I rolled out of my driveway—together and into our future.

I headed northeast to Spokane, the first stop on my journey: estimated travel time of five and a half hours to cover the 351 miles. The start of the trip was familiar to me: Interstate 84 west, passing the Bridge of the Gods and Hood River, before veering north into Washington. I had driven this route many times before, through the Columbia River Gorge with mountains all around me. As much as I looked forward to leaving it, I still admired the area's beauty.

Muhammad Ali's memorial service was on the radio from a sports arena in Kentucky—a state I'd visit in a little over a month. Those he left behind spoke to spread his messages of love, bringing cultures together, and hope. With the presidential election in full swing, there was a lot of tension throughout the country, the policies and characters of the candidates more different from each other than ever before. There were the usual white male politicians who spouted their party's familiar rhetoric, of course. But there was also one of the few women to ever try to become America's leader, an older man with shocking white hair and an even more shocking progressive agenda, and an orange-toned businessman who was used to getting everything he wanted. Ali's death brought their supporters together to celebrate the passing of someone who wasn't afraid to fight for others when he wasn't actually fighting others. Billy Crystal captured Ali's power during his eulogy:

> Muhammad Ali struck us in the middle of America's darkest night, in the heart of its most threatening gathering storm. His power toppled the mighty foes and his intense light shined on America and we were able to see clearly: injustice, inequality, poverty, pride, self-realization, courage, laughter, love, joy, and religious freedom for all. Ali forced us to take a look at ourselves, this brash young man who thrilled us, angered us, confused and challenged us, ultimately became a silent messenger of peace, who taught us that life is best when you build bridges between people, not walls.

Listening to Crystal's speech, I was hit hard with emotion. The year wasn't even half over yet, and already we had lost so many icons: Ali, Prince, David Bowie. People whose identities some, in intolerant times, hung onto for dear life. Whereas Ali represented courage in expressing religious beliefs and racial equality, Bowie and Prince challenged gender norms, saving the lives of many young people just by being themselves.

And of course I had lost Molly. Too much loss in too short a time. I wasn't ready for it, and it didn't feel like the country was, either. For those months, when news about a celebrity was posted on social media, everyone took a collective gasp. When news about the primaries came, it was about hate and fighting and lies. All the good in the world was slowly dying away, right when I was trying to breathe purpose into my own sense of self.

Though I was traveling solo on this first leg of my journey, I wasn't going to be alone. On this first stop, I was staying with friends I had met in Portland, and who had since moved up to Spokane to be closer to family. Kathy and her husband, Mick, were excited to host the first guest in their new home, and Kathy's mom was excited to join us for a night of singing. My hosts had a karaoke place all picked out for me, which required an early dinner at home before officially kicking off my list of states. Karaoke started at 7:30 on a Friday night, which seemed a little odd to me but made perfect sense once we got to the bar. All the parking spaces at the entrance to S.O.B.'s (the lounge portion of Sweet Old Bob's diner) were full up with larger American cars, including a two-toned rose-and-red Buick with a license plate that read "HOTMAMA" and a van declaring itself the "Lil Love Shack" through both its vanity plate ("LILLVSK") and airbrushed paint.

Once inside, I pegged the average age of the patrons at seventy-two. Music touches the lives of everyone, and karaoke is one way to make not just listening to but participating in music accessible, no matter who you are. Karaoke is also extremely social, and while older generations will always have their bridge clubs and bingo games, singing is another way to bring people together.

We had arrived right at the starting time, and the room was almost full—the low, cafeteria-style seating already taken. I put a song in before the server had a chance to take my beer order, placing me far down an already-deep rotation. A quick scan of the older crowd signaled to me that a song from the 1960s might fit in with the rest of musical selections. Kathy told the "KJs" (karaoke jockeys)—a couple who turned out to be the owners of the Lil Love Shack—about my karaoke quest. The female half immediately sat down at the largest table of regulars to spread the news. They looked in my direction—some clapped, others nodded and smiled. A few got up from their seats to wander over to other friends; more people looked my way, whispered to each other, and pointed. Minutes into my quest, I was already the source of gossip before I'd sung a note.

Crooners dominated the stage, singing with intense heart and dedication, seeming to acknowledge that, in the golden years, every minute counts. I recognized Anne Murray, Johnny Cash, Hank Williams, and Willie Nelson, as well as Chris Isaak and America's "Sister Golden Hair." The lengthy rotation scrolled across the bottom of the prompter along with the list of weekly venues the KJ duo worked, and an advertisement letting everyone know they also sold fresh eggs—three dollars a dozen.

Finally, "Kristi" was called to the stage. I put down my Kokanee and sang the Ronettes' "Be My Baby"—and with that, the first step toward my goal was complete.

A woman with a little plastic surgery and a lot of rhinestones came up to thank me for bringing back memories. Mick whistled his approval until another patron told him the frequency was killing their hearing aid. I was proud to have guessed my audience, finding a song that hit the spot and moved the evening along in a direction that pleased the crowd. Kathy's mom was clearly in her element, belting out "King of the Road," but substituting "Queen" to make it more personal. (When not singing, she was the most enthusiastic dancer in the room, though she was far from alone.) And Kathy and Mick's relatively modern picks—Pat Benatar, and Bruce Springsteen's classic "Born to Run"—were cheered as much as everyone else's. There were no S.O.B.'s at S.O.B.'s, friends and strangers welcomed equally.

I was moved to tears when a man sang "Take These Chains from My Heart" by Hank Williams, the microphone trembling in his weakened hands. The unintended warbling effect made the performance that much more poignant. While that song is all about heartache, for me, it was about hope. It showed that people will come out and sing until they can't anymore. I was comforted, knowing a person can't age out of karaoke, and vowed right then and there to make sure I never did.

CHAPTER 5

IDAHO

June 11, 2016

K ATHY AGREED TO JOIN ME FOR A QUICK TRIP INTO IDAHO FOR A
second night of karaoke. We chose a place to sing in
Hayden—about thirty-five miles one way—because it was non-
smoking. Idaho allows different regions to regulate its smoking
laws, and for now most allowed the practice. I had grown
accustomed to being able to breathe in bars since 2009, when
Oregon outlawed smoking in public places. I still remember
the clouds that would hang over the stage at Grandma's, a
basement bar where I liked to sing back in Oregon's smoky
era. It would get so bad in there one guy wore a gas mask,
pushing it aside when he sipped his beer, but keeping it on as
he danced solo around the singers in a creepy haze.

Rusty's Bar was housed in the back of a strip mall, its exterior decorated in shiny new neon signs. Nothing communicated
the history of the place—possibly because there wasn't any.
The karaoke started at 8 p.m., but a late dinner in Spokane

made it so we didn't arrive until over an hour later. There were only two singers in the rotation. After a woman with blue hair and a cardigan decorated with skulls rocked some Pat Benatar and an older man wearing an AC/DC hat sang "Wild Thing," I sang Hall & Oates. No one clapped, except for Kathy and me. The KJ, Madam Karma Karaoke, wiped down the microphone with hand sanitizer after each singer.

By ten, a good-sized crowd had come into the bar, but still the singers were few and far between. Here, karaoke was an afterthought—as indicated by the awkward setup. The well-lit bar was split into two gigantic halves separated by large wooden columns that sported posters of drink specials and keno advertisements. On one side the drinks were served from a long, wooden bar, and people sat on stools or in tall booths, leaning in close to hear each other. *American Ninja Warrior* played on the televisions that hung near the ceiling. The karaoke was on the other side of the bar, along with a couple of pool tables and a free-throw machine (those were always occupied). One tiny monitor stood in front of Madam Karma Karaoke, forcing singers—unless they knew the words perfectly—to serenade her and turn their backs to the pool players and the rest of the crowd. Any attempts at connection were doomed.

Madam tried to engage the rest of the patrons by playing several songs in between the singers: "Who Let the Dogs Out" and "Baby Got Back" failed to entice anyone to take the dance floor. The twentysomethings gathered round the bar were more interested in flirting and posturing than getting their groove on. A group of young guys ordered beers and the bartender asked if they were paying for the ladies as well. She motioned to a group of casually dressed, heavily made-up women sipping pink-and-blue cocktails in martini glasses. None of the women had started a tab. The guys said no, and paid cash for their own drinks. "Yellow beers" were three bucks, according to the bartender, and the "fancier beers" were four. I saw one guy give her three singles after his pour. Another guy chose a darker beer with a skull-and-crossbones tap, gave her a five, and told her to keep the change. At least one of them tipped.

Kathy sang—and again, I was the only one who clapped. "Definitely awkward," she said as she sat back down and gulped the rest of her beer. Madam wiped down the microphone before putting on some more dance tunes and going outside for a smoke. We took her departure as our cue and left as well. In the parking lot, there was a pickup truck with a large Confederate flag, lolling in the soft breeze.

We easily could have headed back to Spokane, but Kathy didn't want such a subpar experience to be our whole night. So we headed off to Coeur d'Alene, an additional twenty minutes out of the way, for a second karaoke destination. As soon as we walked into the Silver Fox Saloon I knew it was more my kind of place—except that everyone had a cigarette either dangling out of their mouth or resting in an ashtray. On the stage, a skinny white guy was singing Chef's innuendo-laden "Chocolate Salty Balls," from the brilliant, boundary-pushing animation series *South Park*, and sung by legendary soul artist Isaac Hayes.

He was followed by an African American man who did a great rendition of "New York, New York," leaving the stage with a cordless mic, visiting tables, serenading women and men alike, making each feel special for a stanza or two. The KJ, positioned at a table onstage, poured himself a drink from a full pitcher of beer—probably not his first, going by his slouched posture and slightly garbled speech. He also sanitized the mic between performers, just as Madam Karma Karaoke had done. I guess that's a thing in Idaho.

I ordered a pint of Montana microbrew; it came in a frosted glass and only ran me three seventy-five—a far cry from the prices of Portland. Kathy and I sat down at a table made from a cross-section of a large tree trunk. The walls were hung with snowboards decorated with hypersexualized women and Warner Brothers cartoons, and advertisements for sweet drinks such as a house-made "Whipped Margarita" and "Straw-Ber-Ritas" from Budweiser.

Soon we were joined by a young man with dreadlocks named Walter. He had just finished singing "Wild Thing"— the same song we had heard at Rusty's. Walter said he couldn't remember if that was the first or second time he had sung that song that evening. He blamed the potential repetition both on his intoxication and on the KJ, whose collection lacked "Three Pigs." The guy who ran the show on Thursdays had that song, Walter moped, but he liked coming on Saturday night because he didn't work on Sundays. The other six days of the week he was outside, trimming trees—except on the days he took off to play video games. This had happened the previous Monday and Tuesday. He also didn't go to work if it was too hot: on those days, he came to the bar to hang out because it was cooler and darker. But then the next day he was too hungover to work so he didn't show again. It was all good, he continued—his boss was a decent and understanding guy.

There were several more singers here than at the last place, but still plenty of room to get into the rotation. The crowd loved Kathy's "Sister Christian" and were equally appreciative of my "Summer of '69." An air guitar accompaniment came from a table of bikers who gave me enthusiastic thumbs-up, and as I walked back to my table I received some high-fives. If we had made the one stop, the mission to sing in Idaho would have been accomplished, but a lot would have been lost. Instead, we found a place with character, even if we had to sacrifice our clothes to the stale smoke.

The owner of the bar interrupted the rotation from the back of the room, demanding to sing a song. He wore a Silver Fox t-shirt and was too drunk to stand up and make his way toward the stage. The KJ passed the mic to a regular, who marched it to the slumped man. "Fly Me to the Moon" was queued up, and then began playing—but the owner/singer was only semi-aware, and he never moved from his barstool. He did his best, I gather, but was one or two lines behind the beat the whole time.

Ten minutes later, when Kathy went up to get some water, he was passed out at the bar.

CHAPTER 6

MONTANA

June 12. 2016

THE NEXT MORNING, I WAS ABLE TO WASH MY CLOTHES CLEAN OF the night's cigarette smoke before heading off to Montana at around noon. I felt a nicotine hangover and a tightness in my lungs as I waved to the places Kathy and I had sung at just hours before.

The drive back through northern Idaho and into Montana was beautiful. Hills full of green with smatterings of purple, mauve, and violet—blended yet distinct—provided a soothing backdrop for the occasional splash of bright yellow wildflower. I pulled into a rest stop for lunch, fetching food from the small cooler I had packed. I ate two boiled eggs and some fresh cherries I had bought from a farm stand that advertised via a hand-painted plywood sign. The rest stop smelled like pine and apple tobacco—the latter thanks to a kid sitting on the lawn with his friend, smoking a pipe. Their license plate said they were from Texas.

That morning, I was preoccupied with news of the Orlando shooting: forty-nine people killed in a hate crime the night before at a gay nightclub. The outpouring of grief was on every radio station—even the sports stations that often kept me company. When I had heard enough of the tragic news—I knew more information would unfold as the days passed—I turned to baseball games for the rest of the drive, when there was radio reception. When there wasn't, I thought about the eulogies for Muhammad Ali I had listened to on Friday, and how quickly the Orlando tragedy had happened after that. Friday I had been full of hope; upon a great man's passing there were so many speeches about love and respect for diversity. Two days later, hate prevailed. I looked out at the beautiful landscape, the snowcapped mountains and the quiet, and wondered how a country so breathtaking could sustain so much ugliness. It wasn't just the Orlando shooting, either: the highway was fraught with pro-life and anti-meth warnings, and graphic pictures of car accidents reminding people to "drive safe." It was hard to see the good in humanity. Numerous blinking construction signs let drivers know that sixty-eight people had died so far that year on Montana's highways. Several handmade roadside memorials reinforced this message. They all looked recent.

I had arranged to sing in the capital, Helena—mostly because it was home to one of Montana's few Sunday karaoke establishments, Hap's Depot and Laundromat; in fact, Hap's hosted karaoke every night. The venue was connected to a laundry facility, which added to its charm. When I got to my hotel, I was pleased to learn it was only a mile away, and so I stepped out into the fresh cool air and walked to my destination. I passed through a residential area of trailers and manufactured homes. It was after 8 p.m., but many folks were still out and about, mowing and watering lawns; scratching their heads over the opened hood of an old car; or chatting on the front porch, watching the world go by.

It didn't take long before I realized I was lost. That wasn't surprising—my sense of direction has never been good. Even though I'd written down the street names and basic turns given to me by Google, I'd somehow managed to miss a left and end up in a dead end near some run-down houses and an auto mechanic. I asked a couple standing around their rusty blue pickup truck for directions to the street I had missed. Their two dogs barked protectively from behind a chain-link fence, and the woman told them to "shut the hell up," to no avail. The man let me know I had overshot by about six blocks; I thanked them, and turned around.

Three blocks later, I noticed my scarf lying on the sidewalk. I had bought that scarf in Cambodia, and was quite fond of its creamy white with blue unidentifiable flowers. I picked it up, dusted it off, and brought it to my face. Then I looked up to the sky, a combination of faded blue and wispy white, and expressed gratitude for getting lost and having to turn around, so I could be reunited with my beloved possession. I made the proper turn, crossed the railroad tracks, and headed over a bridge to Hap's. I passed an old man carrying an empty fishing net. I said hi—and he looked away, nervous.

Inside Hap's, I didn't feel heavy dryer air or hear the spins of active machines. Customers had to make their way through a cluster of video poker machines (all taken) near the front door before reaching the bar. To the right was a larger room that included not only the laundry facility, but also three pool tables (also all taken). Lots of people wore short shorts and tank tops; I was wearing jeans and carrying a jacket and my retrieved scarf, since the weather reports had said it might dip close to freezing by the time I walked back to the motel. I ordered another local beer, a honey rye, and again the price was three seventy-five; the ale was a tad sweet, but pretty darn good. The sign taped on the mirror in front me stated that the

Happy Hour special from four to six was either blackberry brandy or schnapps.

The guy sitting next to me made polite conversation; he was a day-shift bartender at a different place, making a hundred dollars a day in tips. He would have made even more if he had worked nights, but he didn't like to deal with the crowds and the level of intoxication that happened during the later hours. The man with the fishing net wandered into the bar and we made eye contact. I said hello again, and although he pulled up the stool next to mine, he still seemed nervous and didn't speak. He sipped something out of a coffee cup he'd brought along with him.

The KJ leaned against the bar and worried her left eyebrow. She and the bartender talked about exes, bills, and some employee drama. When she got back to her station, I put a song in and we chatted. She told me she was walking around in a daze; her best friend had died from cancer the day before. I asked why she had bothered to come that night, given her grief, and she explained that this was a small town, and there wasn't anyone available to sub, and a lot of people paid "good money" to drink in order to sing. Sure, some were more focused on pool, but some really needed to sing. I let her know I understood—telling her about losing Molly in February and saying that I, too, sometimes needed to sing.

The singing started at 9:20, an hour and change after the posted time. People didn't seem to mind: no restlessness, no clock watching, just understanding. The KJ leaned into the microphone to say, "I appreciate everyone's patience today," and opened the night with Journey's "Lights," and its admission of loneliness and longing.

A pair of twentysomethings abandoned their pool game to sing "I Love Rock and Roll" together while holding their cues and giggling. Then I sang Fleetwood Mac's "Dreams," and a couple of people—including one of the pool players—came up to me while I was singing to tell me how much they love that song. It felt weird to be interrupted mid-song, but it fit with the laid-back atmosphere of the place. I was extra touched by their compliments, because ever since I was that age when one slowly begins to realize that childhood and adolescence are two completely different things, Stevie Nicks's voice always rang true to me. I'd been told before that I sing her well— somehow I was able to mimic her earthy, sultry tones—and every time I do, my aim is to honor her as much as it is to share a tune.

Fishing-Net Man followed me with "Pink Carnation," as I retook my seat. I thanked the bartender for watching my purse, and she asked what brought me here. I told her about my forty-eight-state karaoke goal, and she said her goal was to drive around Montana and try the top-twenty pie slices in the state. The KJ handed her the mic, and she stayed behind the bar to pour two stiff Jack and Cokes while singing "Blame It on Your Heart" by Patty Loveless, with sassy bitterness.

A local inebriated lady with a bloated belly barely covered by a thin white t-shirt pinched the KJ's ass and then tried to slur her way through Elvis's "Don't Be Cruel." It was hard to tell if she was feeling the effects of alcohol, meth, or a well-crafted cocktail of both. Her table of friends seemed pretty messed up as well. Earlier, her husband/boyfriend had put her down, and her response had been to march over to the station and put in a song. She glared at him as she wrote her slip, confidently handing it over with an unsteady hand. She chose to sing to show him up, but after the first few notes she and everyone else in the place knew she had failed. Her face fell into sadness as she tried to keep up with the music—tried to read the words scrolling across the monitor. She just couldn't do it.

Next, the KJ called up someone named "Jo,"—to no avail. Then she wandered over to me and the bartender and said she wasn't sure whether Jo was a he or a she. "Maybe Jo is still

31

figuring it out," I suggested. No response. I was heartened by the idea that a gender-fluid person might live in this town. The KJ started to look annoyed, but instead of skipping to the next singer, ran around the bar, to the pay phone near the restrooms, outside to the smoking area, and then out front to look for Jo. Finally, they surfaced, still on a phone call, hanging up just before taking the stage and singing a melodramatic song—slowly and off-key.

I sang one more song before I left—"No Souvenirs" by Melissa Etheridge. I was pretty sure no one would know it, but chose it anyway, though this was unusual for me. I like my contributions to fit into where I am, but here I felt safe. I felt any choice was going to be okay. During the second verse I looked over and saw a couple in Hawaiian shirts by the gambling machines, singing along. They were my age, and I smiled.

As I got up to leave, I told the KJ to take care of herself, and to take all the time she needed to honor her friend. She held back tears and gave me a hug.

I exited the bar, and noticed a guy following me out. I immediately tensed up—looking for witnesses, searching for pockets of safety. "Hey, lady," he yelled—and I jumped as he gently placed his hand on my shoulder. "You dropped your scarf."

It was my turn to tear up as I thanked him and resumed my walk back to the hotel.

C H A P T E R 7

NORTH DAKOTA

June 14, 2016

THE SCION AND I WERE BECOMING FAST FRIENDS. MY CAR WAS much more than transportation, a way to get from one song to the next. It provided me with relaxation, and a safe space to grieve, think, and ask the questions I couldn't ask anywhere else. It expected nothing in return. Climbing into my car, I felt like my whole self. I could experience excitement, fatigue, peace, sadness, and desire. I could go anywhere I wanted to— both inside and outside myself, and even if I didn't always know where that place was or would be. The car wasn't perfect—marred by glaring white scratches along its dark red paint. But then again, neither was I.

En route to North Dakota and growing tired of my own thoughts a mere five days into my journey, I turned on AM radio for company, settling on a station whose DJ was reading the want ads. Most available positions seemed to be in the restaurant or healthcare arenas. Sometimes, an administrative job would be announced. All the details of each position were broadcast—the hours, the wage, the qualifications needed. I listened for at least an hour. Then again, Montana is a big state—so big that static eventually overtook the station as I drove farther from everything.

Eventually, I crossed into North Dakota. We had never met; it was the only state I had never been to before, other than Alaska. It gave its best first impression. I was lured in with a beautiful, bright welcome sign, and soon I passed exits for towns named "Home on the Range" and "South Heart." I drove through the National Grasslands. The local radio informed me of several livestock auctions, and the fact that one company was no longer able to offer hogs; they apologized for that. Then, the radio stations and grasslands disappeared, and I heard and saw nothing but highway. The state had gone into a complete stillness.

Then came the record rainfall. Part of I-94 was closed near Bismarck, and I was forced to exit. I circled around fast-food restaurants and gas station three times before I found a business loop that would get me through. I finally got back on the freeway, but the rains never stopped until I reached Fargo, well over 400 miles later. My legs shook as I got out of the car. The drive had been too long, but the rains made it hard to get out to stretch.

The Upperdeck, my spot for karaoke that night, was both a bowling alley and a bar, and seemed to be the only place in Fargo that had karaoke on a Tuesday. That I could find karaoke at all on a Tuesday in North Dakota was probably a miracle in and of itself. The venue reminded me of a place where I used to bowl that also had karaoke Thursday through Saturday nights. One Christmas Eve a small group of us bowled a few games there and then sang—after eating Chinese food, of course. When it came time to sing, we were the only ones in the place, so we took it upon ourselves to sing the songs no one

34

should ever sing in a karaoke bar: "Come Sail Away" by Styx (with its unending interlude); "Somewhere That's Green" from *Little Shop of Horrors*; "We Are the World," with its many voices and infinite chorus fade-out. Three of us sang that last one together, and actually sat down early, boring ourselves with the continuous lyric (*"We are* still *the world, we are* still *the children. Here we are,* still *singing this song . . ."*). Sadly, that bowling alley was later sold off, becoming a hardware store, its long alleys transformed into aisles of toilet seats, bolts, and pesticides.

Settling in at the Upperdeck, I felt at home with the sounds of crashing pins and celebrations in the background. I waited for Dave's friend's cousin—someone I had never met before, but whose kindness and love of karaoke brought her out on a weeknight to greet me, even though she had to work early the next day. The call to sing is strong in those of us who love it. I waited for her the way I would meet a blind date—a little nervous, assuming the relationship was only going to last one night, but still wanting to make a good impression. It wasn't hard for us to find each other, despite not exchanging pictures, because it's pretty rare that females show up at bars by themselves. Kristen had long brown hair, a large smile, and a cute flared skirt—her eyes shone with excitement. She shook my hand firmly, making direct eye contact, before plopping down next to me. I liked her immediately. She was much younger than I, but that didn't matter. It was nice to chat with someone after a few days of solitude.

The beer choices were Bud, Bud Light, Miller Light, and Coors Light. I was clearly not in Oregon anymore, and even the craft beer options of Idaho and Montana were long gone. Kristen ordered Coors Light, insisting that Bud Light gave her hangovers. I had no idea there could be a difference between the two, but followed her lead. Throughout the evening, the bartender kept leaving his post to make sure our red plastic cups remained full. Almost as soon as we were served, the karaoke host sat down at our table, asking if we were ready to sing—unless, of course, we needed two or three beers beforehand.

We said we were fine singing sober and happy to take requests: he asked for Stevie Wonder, and I obliged with "Superstition," something I had never done before. As I sang, I watched the rollers below, and offered a bit of commentary during instrumentals (gutter! 10-pin!). It made me miss being on the lanes—something I hadn't really done since I started traveling four years before. Kristen kicked off with an upbeat musical number unfamiliar to me, but it showed off her vocal training. The KJ kept coming by the patrons as the night wore on, making sure songs were constantly lined up, successfully keeping the evening moving.

It was nice being with someone who also really liked to sing. Even back home, when I went out to a karaoke bar, I often went with folks who just liked to hang out and would never consider putting a song in. Or I had friends who were content just singing once. Kristen was more like me, putting in a song right away to establish herself in the rotation, and then reliably putting in more choices until the night was done. Our conversations came easily, revolving around her career as a music teacher and my summer plans as a bum who would sing in the Lower 48. She used old-fashioned phrases like "knee-high to a grasshopper" and cussed prolifically. It's a lot more fun to sing when you're not alone.

"Anything goes" was the genre of song selection here. Sure, there was the predictable slant toward country, but I also enjoyed listening to Disney selections, Elton John, Ricky Nelson, Otis Redding, and Blue Öyster Cult. For my second song I chose another first for me, something I'd been humming to myself over the past few days: "Thing Called Love" by Bonnie Raitt. I thought about Orlando as I sang the verse about acting out of hope instead of living in fear. Striving for peace, crying for love.

For a while, I found it hard to focus on the words, the sights, my presence on stage. I was in a fog, processing the words I was singing, the ones that called to me, while trying to stay in the moment. My moment. This sensation was unusual for me. Usually at karaoke, I thought of little other than the selection and singing. It was a time to de-stress, put my emotions aside, and mingle with friends and strangers around song. While I did experience those moments of escape that night, there were times when I just sat there and felt an ache over what had happened in Orlando. Sometimes, without even knowing it, a song allows you to sing what you cannot say.

C H A P T E R 8

SOUTH DAKOTA

June 15, 2016

THE NEXT MORNING IT WAS STILL RAINING, BUT AS I CROSSED THE border into South Dakota, the sun began to shine. I had made it far enough east that the states had begun to shrink and I was able to take secondary roads instead of the interstate and still stay on schedule. As soon as I hit Highway 81, my drive was much more relaxing. I went slower. I saw more things, could roll down the windows and feel the warm air, and smell the smells of the state: the grasses, the farms, and the freshness. I filled up at stations named Superpumper and Gas N Goodies. I drove by a lot of lakes, whose water levels were high from the storms of the past few days. Blue waters, pink rock, and white-tufted grasses.

The AM dial offered up agricultural radio, something I listened to every chance I got: cattle auctions, newscasts on soy and corn futures, long-term weather reports. I heard experts talk about soil conditions and offer their predictions on wheat prices. With each segment, I heard about something I had never given thought to before. As a city girl, I was so far removed from this reality that I became completely fascinated with every detail—that farming takes not just a green thumb and some heavy-duty equipment, but savvy business sense and a good science base to understand what to grow, and how to grow it.

Eavesdropping on this world made the scenery of corn fields, rolling hills, and soy farms more real. I felt a spiritual bond with the land around me, knowing I was driving through people's lives, families' futures, and the sources of my meals in the days to come. I tried to imagine the people who were tuning into these shows along with me, listening carefully to what the experts had to say—I envisioned a father nearing retirement and his adult son, taking a break from the toil of working the land to listen; I saw a stern and sun-worn woman riding a tractor, tuning in as she plowed the fields, getting them ready for the next crop. For some reason, in my imagination all these people wore overalls.

As the farm reports faded into the brash hiss of static, I turned to a religious radio station discussing sex. As a researcher who often has addressed sex education—in fact, it was one of the topics I enjoyed working in the most—this was a topic I could relate to more directly. I anticipated the worst—a diatribe about sin and filth; shame and judgement. Instead, the guest author spoke of love and care. His main message was that it was essential and godly to be connected to your sexual desires as long as they did not harm or objectify others. According to the speaker, the Bible said nothing about masturbation. He believed masturbating was okay in the eyes of the Lord, as long as the images in your mind honored, and did not degrade, another person. I listened with openness and hope; perhaps these were the messages of common ground in such a contentious arena as sex. As I rolled into Sioux Falls, I passed a huge fireworks store with all seven of its flags at half-mast in honor of those lost in Orlando. I checked into a nearby hotel and took a nap, as the singing didn't start until 10: late for an old bird like me.

Once again I arrived at the karaoke bar alone, but wasn't alone for long. I met up with my friend's nephew and his girl-friend on their second-year-dating anniversary. Neither of them sang, but they were up for keeping a stranger company, and I was grateful for that. Sweet of them to share their time with me. We all agreed to get there an hour early to keep up our momentum; I arrived first and managed to save three seats at the corner of the bar. Given that it was a strip mall, it seemed pretty packed for a Wednesday. The crowd was very young and very drunk. Women dressed to be noticed: lots of cleavage, short jean shorts, and skimpy floral dresses with high heels. The men seemed to put less effort into their looks—a uniform of unkempt beard/ball cap/t-shirt—but for all I knew they thought about their images as much as the women did. While the men seemed to echo those I had left in Portland, the women looked completely different—except for those who dared to dress down by donning baseball caps.

It was twofer night, so ordering one beer meant walking away from the bar with your hands full. I ordered a shandy and two were placed in front of me. I was already seeing double and the drinking hadn't even started. I asked if I could wait until I finished my first before getting my second, but that was not part of the deal, though it did explain the lack of sobriety in the place. Sipping my drink, I felt old. This place was clearly a pickup joint for those barely out of college. Or maybe they never went to college—who knows? Young men with pool cues, leaning over tipsy women in low-cut dresses balancing them-selves on barstools. Two guys yelling at each other in good fun—until it wasn't, and a third came in to break the tension.

The karaoke started promptly, and given the crowd size, I knew enough to put a song in early. I was called up to sing

"Working for the Weekend" soon enough, and it was a suitable choice for the venue, a perfect balance of the familiar but not often heard at a karaoke bar. A woman in a bright-orange cap declared the bartender "the best human ever" for placing a lime in her drink. In the smoking area, a fight broke out between two women, taking the main focus away from the stage for a while—until people came back inside, returning to their drinks, pool games, flirting, and listening. I felt like I'd crashed a college party, especially when a clean-cut dude got up to sing "Total Eclipse of the Heart" in the style from the movie *Old School*, complete with profanity: "I fuckin' need you more than ever . . ."

Part of me wanted to leave, but I wasn't done people-watching, and my company was great. Conversations about how they met, the Cubs' chances of winning it all, the differences between the US and Canada, and what a pain in the ass their dogs could be all came easily. I put in a second song, not knowing if it would come up before I left or not; either result would have been fine with me.

Many stereotypical karaoke tunes—"Don't Stop Believin'," "Pour Some Sugar on Me," "Picture," "Folsom Prison Blues"— were sung. A stringy blond guy stepped onto the stage to perform a heavy metal song. A man in his fifties with a ratty red-grey beard and covered in amateur tattoos came up next to me and explained that the blond was auditioning to be the lead singer in his band, and wanted to know my opinion. I had no idea why he thought I would be a good judge, but I listened more critically anyway. Usually, I'm not a fan of judging a karaoke performance; karaoke is for release, fun, and amusement. Its entertainment comes from song choice and singing with soul, not necessarily talent. For me, the ideal karaoke singer gets up there, sings a song the audience can relate to, and manages to leave a part of themselves on the stage without taking their performance too seriously. Karaoke is more about the shared experience than gaining the admiration of others.

As I looked at this performance with a newly critical eye, I saw that the auditioning young man lacked confidence; he was trying too hard to impress, looking nervously about the room, trying his best to win the audience over. He played with the microphone stand awkwardly yet defiantly—like he thought that's what a metal singer should do. It looked like it was his first time. He was trying to be a rock star. I was honest in my assessment as I reported it to my bar neighbor—and he agreed. I felt bad contributing to the failure of this poor kid for a band I was never going to see, but I'm not one to lie.

I was about to leave, when the KJ called my name and I got up to sing "Hit Me with Your Best Shot." People sang and danced along, shouting the chorus in accompaniment. Performing such a stereotypical karaoke number was the only way I felt I could fit into this crowd, and for that brief time I was no different than the fighters, the judgers, or the flirters. As I stepped off the stage, I knew it was time to go. I hugged my companions good night and headed out, the music still audible as I got into my car and drove off.

CHAPTER 9

WISCONSIN

June 16, 2016

I WAS ABOUT A WEEK AND FIVE STATES INTO MY TRIP, AND I WAS settled into my car and routine. I was much happier off the interstate, instead passing from small town to small town with a more manageable agenda; all I needed to do each day was get to the next singing destination: a minor but essential task that required so little of me. I purposely passed through Minnesota to get to Wisconsin; I would be doubling back later, disrupting my schedule slightly in order to spend time with friends. Signs in support of Trump dominated the landscape, placed on the very top of front lawns for all passersby to see. I also saw some support for Bernie Sanders, and a few scattered signs supporting Ted Cruz. But it was Trump capturing the hope of Americans—at least in this region.

I passed a sign that read "Bunnies for Sale or Rent" and wondered what circumstances would lead a person to rent a bunny.

Weeks ago, when I had mapped out the first few stops on my schedule, I had planned to sing at Scooter's, a gay bar in a small college town. Driving on that day, I was sort of afraid to do so. Though I passed many flags at half-mast at rest stops, auto dealerships, commercial and state properties—all showing support for the tragedy that had happened on the other side of the country—I wondered: is it respectful to invade a sacred space at this time? What if I wasn't welcome? Still, despite my reservations, I resolved to walk into that bar with an open heart and kind soul. I didn't want fear to stop me. A bald eagle flew overhead as I crossed the Mississippi River into Wisconsin.

Eau Claire put on its best show for me. The weather was perfect at dusk, which arrived blissfully late, and since the college was on summer break, things moved slowly, peacefully, warmly. The campus buildings were rustic brick and covered in ivy. The downtown streets were lined with colorful sculptures, and jazz was piped through hidden speakers, making the whole town feel like a professor's living room. I let my mind wander to a place where I became that college professor, bundling up in the dead of winter to walk along these art- and music-lined streets, heading out to watch a Packers game at the bar. I convinced myself it was a good idea to move to a small college town in Wisconsin.

I could have walked the town all night, and part of me wanted to instead of sing. I took a deep breath, and walked into Scooter's. A grizzled older woman was tending bar—the kind of woman who seems damn tough, and probably is, but underneath there's a softness that draws you to her. Her name was Pat, and my blood pressure immediately lowered in her presence. She poured me a Spotted Cow—a local lager she recommended to all newcomers. The bar special of only a buck for domestic pints made the suggestion a no-brainer. I munched on some peanuts and placed the shells in the empty bowl as I pretended to watch a show starring David Duchovny. The Cavaliers and Warriors' Game 6—possibly the final game of the NBA season—was nowhere to be found. A rainbow-colored poster advertising Jägermeister proclaimed it a "proud shooter." A sign at the base of the bar read, "Do it now or forever wish you had."

The place was relatively empty, except for a group of men who occupied one corner of the bar. A young African American woman stumbled in and took the seat next to mine, mumbling something to Pat about the stupidity of relationships. Pat removed a full plastic tumbler from her hand and poured out its contents while listening. Unfazed, the woman slid off the barstool, said she'd be back, and swayed out the back door.

Around 9 p.m. the place began to fill; a large group of women came in, ordered drinks, and adjourned to the back patio. A couple pulled up stools next to me, engaged in focused conversation. I was hurting—because of Molly, but also because of Orlando. To my surprise, no one else seemed to be. There was an air of comfort, not fear or sadness. I slowly learned it was okay to be here. People struck up conversations with me about allergies, the weather, and recent breakups. Everyone was simply getting on with their lives as if nothing horrible happened in Florida, or anywhere else.

Jake, the KJ, ordered a drink from Pat, then turned to me, an obvious newcomer, and warmly shook my hand. He was a former computer guy who'd hated the cubicle lifestyle and now managed to make a living as a KJ and by being in a band. He said he was a lot happier, and working nights was okay since there was "no man in my picture"; his shoulders fell with that statement as he briefly looked away. Pat's shift ended— she worked days, and was thankful for not having to deal with the "drunken riffraff." She placed her hand on my shoulder and wished me good luck. A young man in a tight white t-shirt and glorious smile took her place. It was time to sing.

The song selection was as diverse as the crowd: though 80s alternative dominated the night, classic rock, heavy metal, and country tunes were also shared. I was uncharacteristically nervous as I got up to sing my first selection, "The Logical Song," a late-'70s hit by the oft-forgotten Supertramp. My anxiety washed away as soon as I began. I felt at peace, allowing myself to feel as happy as everyone else seemed to be.

The line of singers was long, and the crowd appreciative. A tiny young woman left her group of friends to talk to me. Her words slurred as she asked my sexual orientation; her eyes didn't quite focus on me or anything else. I let her know I was straight, but felt the need to defend myself, saying I sat on boards of LGBTQ nonprofits. I told her I was an ally in the fight for inclusive sexuality education. *It's okay that I'm here*, I repeated to myself.

She wasn't as interested in my story as in her own. She was straight, too, but her mom was a lesbian, and she was so proud of her mom and her path to coming out. I thought about Molly's mom, who had a similar story, but kept it to myself. The woman said she was here every week, and sang as much as possible. She said she knew she wasn't great, but still loved karaoke because it was fun. As long as she sang on key, which was about half the time, she felt her performance was a success.

A man stumbled up to the mic (stumbled all over the bar, really), and tried to sing Elton John's "Don't Let the Sun Go Down on Me"—a long, drawn-out, melodramatic number better suited for the shower or car than this energetic crowd. About a minute in, he sort of gave up and instead swayed to the music, only occasionally picking up his vocals during the chorus. Jake wandered over to me and said the singer did this every week: "Throughout the night," Jake said, "people get up to do their thing, and my job is to let them do it." I noticed my dollar bill was the only one in his tip jar, which didn't make sense for such a friendly place.

CHAPTER 10

MINNESOTA

June 18. 2016

J ON, ONE OF MOLLY'S BEST FRIENDS FROM HIGH SCHOOL, WAITED for me in his large suburban home outside of Minneapolis. I was greeted with a warm hug as his dog and daughters hovered around the entryway, peering at me curiously. I had first met Jon in California, when he was lured there by the mid-90s tech boom. Molly and I were already there for college. She and Jon reunited, and I fell for his roommate. Though that romance lasted only a few years, in Jon and his wife, Kristin, I found friends for life.

Jon and I had just seen each other a few months ago at Molly's memorial, but the time before that was at her wedding, twelve years prior. It's simply too easy to let years go by in between visits. Intentions are there, ones with true heart and affection, but I've been shocked to learn how easy it is for me to slip into that "some other time" mentality, allowing what is right in front of me to take charge, demanding immediate attention the way a screaming tea kettle or flat tire does. Meanwhile, the things that matter most—deep relationships, squeaky brakes—are left to wait another day, until it's too late to mend either.

Singing wasn't going to happen until the next night, so Jon and his kids took me to the Mall of America for a true tourist experience. We visited the Lindt shop, where I stocked up on a variety of dark chocolate truffles in crinkly, shiny wrappings— I'd savor them on my trip, extracting one from my cooler when I needed sweet comfort. Then it was off to the Lego display— larger-than-life sculptures made of the classic building blocks.

Outside of that, there was nothing here for me. Chain stores and large crowds aren't really my thing. Besides, my car was packed so perfectly, my suitcase so tightly, I had no room for unanticipated purchases.

On Saturday, we went to a "revival baptismal" to celebrate the rebirth of Jon's uncle as he faced death. A hard life had transitioned into Parkinson's followed by a cancer diagnosis, and there was no more time for healing his body, only his soul. I put on my nicest dress and joined the family, walking into a place I rarely set foot: a church. I couldn't remember the last time I had been to a religious service.

The building smelled old, like a little-used library. The pews were simple, the carpets worn. The priest and the uncle's brother both said words about the importance of life, of finding the meaning of life, of coming to peace before you are no longer able to walk this earth. "Make every minute count," said the uncle, his voice weak and scratchy as care-fully stepped into the tub, hidden by a large wooden frame engraved with a cross. His wife held his hand as he walked in and eased himself down into the water. They both knew he was dying, and this was their way of accepting, of getting ready, of letting go. But on this day, she never let go of his hand. Today was not the day for letting go completely. Those who gathered were completely silent—no cheers, no cries, just silence. Then, it was over. The uncle was helped up and he exited the other side of the tub, where he was met with a robe and immediate family, both covering him with comfort. We all got up to leave.

After dinner, it was time to go to Otter's Saloon. When Kristin called to make sure there was actually karaoke that night, the bartender suggested we get there early. But when we arrived, no one was there except a guy wearing a Twins jersey yelling at the ballgame on TV, and a couple of other locals. The bouncer wore all black, including his hat. His name was Donovan. The tables were sticky, the floor's hex tiles chipped, and the cheap beer wasn't cheap. I ordered a Redd's Apple Ale simply because I had never had one before. One sip of the horrible sugar water, and I knew I'd never be ordering it again.

When the karaoke kicked off, there were only four singers: me, Kristin, the KJ, and Donovan (Jon skipped the karaoke). We all took turns singing whatever pleased us. After a couple of rounds, the KJ took a smoke break, and Donovan stepped in to cue up Kristin's song so there was no delay. Then he and Kristin dueted "Jackson," and he celebrated their fun rendition by buying us a round. After another half hour went by, I wondered why we were encouraged to arrive early—Otter's had a reputation for being one of the most popular karaoke bars in Minnesota, but it sure wasn't showing it. Then, in the span of fifteen or twenty minutes, as if through some sort of magical summoning, more than a hundred people filed into the place. Everyone pressed into everyone, and there was no space to move, no space to make my way up to the bar to order another drink.

It didn't take long after that for me to learn what made Otter's so popular. People come here to *participate* in karaoke—whether to take the mic, sing along, or just watch. A guy sang "Sweet Child of Mine" and though he was wildly off-key the bar went nuts. Talent matters little in karaoke when there is plenty of enthusiasm. The energy continued to grow with Billy Joel's "You May Be Right" and the heavy metal of "Bodies," from a heavyset, badass woman who nailed the gruff screaming voice perfectly. The crowd cheered so loudly, I could barely hear my name being called to sing next. The KJ, used to the crowds, patiently waited for me to push my way through.

After "Why did you do that?" the most common question I get asked about my trip is "What was your favorite place?" That question can take on a lot of different meanings: a bar, a city, a landscape. But if I think about the best singing experience, that would have to be when I sang 4 Non-Blondes' "What's Up" at Otter's in Minneapolis, Minnesota. While karaoke is almost always fun, there are a few times when I hit the sweet spot—a perfect combination of song choice, timing, and crowd support—and the experience becomes magic. I feel ecstatic, comfortable, floating, happy to the point of tears. I'm in a zone where sharing my passion is enjoyed by the rest of the crowd. All of that takes a perfect balance of so many factors—the people in the bar, my level of inebriation, and whether I'm "on" or not vocally. And at Otter's that night, it all came together perfectly.

First, it was the song. Sometimes choosing a song is easy, other times not so much. I tend to be pretty good at it but can still get it wrong. I think about where I am: a country bar? A college town? The sketchiest of dive bars? A suburban strip mall? Then I pay attention to the people I'm sharing the evening with: how old are they? What are they wearing? What are they singing? What did the KJ open with? You don't have to choose a song that blends perfectly with what everyone else is doing—but it's good to select something that at least would be played on the same radio station as the other choices.

Finally, and this is where it can get tricky, is the question of when you think you will sing. If the night starts out quiet I like to open with something mellow, but upbeat and catchy.

Slower stuff can be saved for the end of an evening, because it's not bracingly loud. People will be drunk—and many will be way beyond any semblance of sobriety. Their poor ears and hearts probably don't need to be filled with grunge at that point—or maybe they do, if that's what the crowd has been about all night. If I'm lucky enough to get my name called at the peak of the evening, that's when I hope I chose a song everyone knows, and can dance and sing along to.

At Otter's, the place was packed, the crowd pleasantly buzzed and still enjoying each other's company when I got up to sing. People cheered, swayed with lighters held high, took videos of themselves singing along, or pictures of me with the microphone. While I was still the star, we were all singing together: karaoke as group sport. The right song, the right time, the right place. I'd hit karaoke gold. It's one of my favorite feelings, right up there with the euphoria of laughing super hard with dear friends or sharing an intense moment with someone I love more than I thought possible. I belonged there, and for those few minutes, nothing else mattered.

When I was done, there were high-fives all around, and the crowd was somehow even more energized than before. So much so, in fact, that when the next woman came up to sing "Bohemian Rhapsody," the crowd erupted with glee and continued to sing along, though this time to the point where you couldn't tell who was holding the mic. It was too loud to hear the star of the moment, and I felt bad for her. Maybe she didn't care. Maybe she was relieved. Whatever she was feeling, it couldn't have been the center of attention. Either there was no singer, or we were all singers; it was too hard to tell.

It makes me wonder if there is a time when karaoke isn't really karaoke anymore, or if there is such a thing as too much of a shared experience. While in theory I would say no, I pondered this question in the back of Jon and Kristin's SUV, still glowing from my perfect karaoke moment.

CHAPTER 11

IOWA

June 19, 2016

THE NEXT MORNING (BUT NOT TOO EARLY), I SAID GOODBYE TO JON and Kristin and headed south to Iowa. We vowed to try harder to see each other in the future. A friend's death is both a typical and an unacceptable reason for old friends to reconnect. After an hour of resettling into solitude, a wave of sadness came. For a while I tried to force a cry—one I felt rumbling deep within, one that begged me to allow myself the chance to open up and grieve. But it simply wasn't there. As I continued down the road, the sobbing stayed crushed in my throat, unable to move, stubborn against coughs, fighting my willingness to feel. Maybe there was no cause for my lack of tears, or maybe it was all the causes piling on top of each other, preventing a cry from breaking free. Molly wasn't there. Dave wasn't there, and I missed him. Dave was coming, but I wanted to take this trip on my own. Racism and hatred were rampant in America. I had no idea what I wanted to do with my life.

Times alone were when I missed Molly the most, when I would beg for her to come back just once more so I could talk to her about what the hell was going on with me. I'd do anything for that chance: I'd listen to stories about potty training. Go to a David Wilcox concert and not fall asleep like I had the last time. Spend too much money on a dinner I would forget a week later but she would remember for years to come.

Iowa wouldn't be the only time I'd experience fleeting, mysterious sadness. I tried to find a pattern to these dark clouds, but there was none: the radio could be on or off, the scenery just as majestic or banal as it had been for miles. Despair would just be in the crosswind, smack me suddenly from just beyond my peripheral vision, and then continue on its way as if nothing had happened. Moments later, I would still be alone in the car, staring down streets I had never seen before and would probably never see again, driving toward my next town, my next chapter, sadness no longer keeping me company. Instead, there was a peaceful solitude that tended to linger until my next destination.

Still basking in the glow of Otter's, I was soon confronted with the reality that not all nights in all states would have that magic. I arrived at the Des Moines bar I'd picked out just as the sky was getting dark, summer solstice two nights away. Two bunnies hopped around nearby. Seeing them was the most exciting thing that would happen to me in Iowa that night.

The bar itself was pretty empty, maybe it was because it was Sunday (Father's Day, to boot). The weather—not too humid, especially for the Midwest—made it the perfect night for bar-becuing outside. Or maybe no one was here because Game 7 of the NBA Finals was on, and this wasn't really a sports bar. Two screens featured the game, but the sound was devoted to music (mostly '80s rock) provided by the KJ, Kit-T-Kat. She was raring to go, dressed in leopard print and matching cat ears. A couple shot pool, their backs to the screens. Another couple sipped beers outside, enjoying the cooling breeze. Three men took over the corner of the bar, arguing about nothing in particular. They littered their comments with homophobic remarks. At first I was uncomfortable, and then I was ashamed I didn't speak up. A sign on the cooler behind the bar featured a cartoon Scottie dog, and read, "Hi Ladies, I'm AJ! You are safe and sound. I'll chase away the hounds." All talk and no action.

I took a seat a healthy distance from the men—the perfect balance between still being able to hear but not signaling a wish to join in—and ordered a club soda. I'd planned to have a beer, but nothing about the place suggested it was worth it. I was already bored. The bartender was grateful I offered to pay for the soda. Normally they don't charge, she said, but since I wasn't getting anything else . . . she looked up in the air, and decided to charge me one dollar and fifty cents—same as she would for a soda. I tipped her a buck and thanked her again.

The men at the corner chatted up the bartender, and began an animated discussion over where they would want to bartend if they could do so anywhere in the world. "Here," she replied without so much as a brief glance toward the ceiling. "I like it here." One of the patrons insisted she was wrong: A beach in Florida or California was a much better choice. He was pretty insistent, but he got pushback from one of his companions: Hawai'i was a better option. Personally, I think I'd want to bartend in Toronto. Or possibly Vietnam. Or Eastern Europe somewhere. Day shift only, like Pat the bartender in Wisconsin, so I didn't have to deal with the "drunken riffraff."

As the conversation continued, the man who favored Florida and California got more and more animated in his need to prove the unprovable. The bartender reminded the two of them to use their "inside voices," and when they failed to do so she told them to leave until they could calm down. The two stopped their debate and walked out without protest, as if this were a usual thing.

It was well past the posted karaoke start time, but Game 7 was close, so I didn't mind. Plus, the bar was still empty. KJ Kit-T-Kat kept wandering over to the few of us to see if anyone wanted to sing yet. She wandered around the entire space, speaking into her headset, letting people know karaoke is fun and you don't have to be a great singer to do it. She proved as much by performing an off-key, somewhat breathless rendition of the Who's "Squeeze Box," singing into her headset and wandering through the bar.

When she finished there were still no takers. She put the background music back on and sat down to eat a Subway sandwich. When "Funky Town" played, the old man in the corner held up his hands to "raise the roof," and started to sing a bit to himself. The arguers decided they could behave themselves and rejoined him, sat down, and exchanged back massages. I was the only one paying attention as the Cavaliers, who had come back from a three games to none deficit, claimed Game 7 to beat the highly favored Golden State Warriors—the first time a team had ever been down that far and crawled up to victory. The fact that it was Cleveland, a city often equated with failure, made it that much sweeter. An incredible finish to a dramatic series, yet no one here seemed to care. I had pegged the male half of the couple playing pool as someone who would have at least stopped to watch the final minutes, but nope. Sports history was made in silence here in this small section of Des Moines, Iowa. Before the nets were cut down, the old man asked if the TV could be switched to the World Series of Poker. I took that as my cue to sing.

I chose "Only the Lonely" because it didn't require a lot of energy; instead, its success relied on being sultry and soft, melancholy and hopeful. Plus, the title seemed more than appropriate. I held back my vocals because everyone seemed pretty relaxed and interested in their own conversations, pool games, or poker watching. Still, I felt powerful as I embraced the simplistic beauty of the song. When it was over, I stepped down to mild applause. No one sang after me. The KJ went outside to hang out with the couple chilling on the patio, and I went to my hotel, never knowing if anyone else sang that night.

CHAPTER 12

NEBRASKA

June 20. 2016

I WOKE UP EVERY MORNING LOOKING FORWARD TO DRIVING RURAL roads. I enjoyed driving through the unending roads of farm country, seeing the towns that served as stopping points along the way. Many of the towns were all but shut down, probably because everyone but me was using the interstates to rush from point A to point B; I often went more than an hour before seeing another car, and was comforted by this solitude.

I stopped in Griswold, Iowa, for a break and a walk. It was a dying town. There was one place to grab a beer, and two gift shops—but the only place to buy food was the gas station. There was a small grocery store, but the painted letters of "Going Out of Business" and "Everything Must Go" on its windows were chipping away with time. A restaurant had closed due to water damage. I walked around the residential areas and saw two places for kids to play and a stage barely big enough for two performers. I imagined everyone coming out to hear a local musician—mayor by day, violinist by night—as the sun set and families spread out blankets to picnic on the park lawn. In the late morning, the town was really quiet. People must have been tucked away at their jobs in neighboring towns, or perhaps farther. There was no industry here that I could see. With kids out of school for summer, I thought I'd have heard more laughter in the parks.

I arrived at a bar outside of Omaha, Nebraska, at nine thirty, a half hour after karaoke had started. The singing was going strong. The bar was in a strip mall and looked divey but well-kept. Wooden walls, cheap pleather-and-wood stools, dartboard off to the side. The place was pretty full; some folks sat at the small round tables near the dance floor, some at square tables farther back, and some at the bar solo, like me. Most were wearing business attire and looked middle-aged, also like me. I felt at home almost immediately. I sat at the bar, my back awkwardly facing the stage, and ordered a Bud Light to nurse; I think I was supposed to get a Coors—in North Dakota didn't Kristen tell me Bud Lights gave her hangovers? It had only been a week and I'd already forgotten. My bottle arrived, and tucked underneath was a cardboard Budweiser coaster letting me know it was "Proudly Serving Omaha, Nebraska" in red, white, and blue lettering. I absentmindedly watched a baseball game on TV.

The KJ was a little older than me, a current/former hippie with dark-rimmed glasses and a grey beard. He wore a tie-dye t-shirt and rope necklace: he looked like a skinny Jerry Garcia, with kind blue eyes. He had a beautiful voice, and throughout the night sang slow country love songs unfamiliar to me. One couple sat at the front of the stage, right off the small polished dance floor. It was hard to tell if they were on their first, fifth, or two hundredth date, but like everyone else they were dressed as though they had come straight from work, and their lack of sobriety suggested they'd been here since quitting time. One of them sang "Hit Me with Your Best Shot" horribly off key, but everyone clapped anyway. Her companion, also looking drunk, clapped the loudest.

As each name was called, the singers walked up a couple of steps to the microphone stand resting on worn black carpet to share a part of themselves. A solo customer in a white cowboy hat and tan flannel shirt sitting next to me sang "Lady" by the Little River Band, and it brought me to tears—not because it was done particularly well (he wasn't bad, though), but because it reminded me of when a dear friend sang it at my goodbye party, her first time ever singing karaoke. An African American woman with tightly styled hair and a crisp grey suit sang a powerful rendition of "Voices Carry" as her companion watched, sipping a red concoction out of a martini glass. Two friends grabbing a drink after work? A couple enjoying a night out? The other woman never sang, but paid close attention every time the one in the grey suit went up. Then again, many of us did. Her second song was an amazing Aretha Franklin work—an understated homage true to the Queen of Soul.

Some singers left just after ten, and others replaced them. It was a small but steady crowd with almost everyone either singing or there with someone who was. One by one, the singers continued to deliver hidden gems from my past. An attractive young man—round face, dark skin, flashing smile, and a body that belonged in a weightlifting club—sang "Smooth" while filming himself. A tall skinny white woman in torn jeans and cowboy boots performed the '60s folk-rock tune "Everybody's Talkin'" by Harry Nilsson, and brought an attentive peace to the boisterous crowd.

For the most part, everyone here was pretty good, but not everyone was heard. When I sing, I have the benefit of a naturally loud voice, and can use it as I please. I chose to do so during my rendition of "Gloria" by Laura Branigan, following in the footsteps of those singing less-obvious but familiar songs from the '70s and '80s. When a short, heavyset woman with cropped hair and a nose ring sang "My Way," people talked loudly over her soft voice. No one was listening. Maybe it was the slow song choice, or because she was singing it cautiously and an octave higher than it was written. She made faces reaching the high notes and seemed disappointed in herself when she forced some of them. I felt bad for her, because it still sounded on-key—just an odd interpretation of a classic. I thought about those horrific yet darkly comical stories of people being shot in the Philippines when they didn't sing that song well enough. To me, it all pointed to the need for karaoke to cater to the familiar so that others can share in the moment. Even though it's your time up there, you aren't singing just for yourself.

The woman up front got progressively drunker as the evening wore on. While her companion brought over glasses of water on occasion, he also continued to order more cocktails. I watched as she increasingly struggled to stand up to make her way to the bathroom or outside for fresh air. By the time it was her turn to sing her second song, "Total Eclipse of the Heart," she had gone over the edge. Her name was called, and she used both hands to push herself up out of her chair as she wobbled toward the KJ to take the mic. She knew better than to get up on the stage, opting to sing from the dance floor. As the music started, she swayed back and forth and stared intensely as the words of the song went by on the monitor. Every once in a while, she would catch up to what was happening and participate. After one chorus, gravity got the better of her and she fell over onto the steps behind her, stood up, handed the microphone back to the KJ and sat back down. Her partner took her back out to the patio. End of song.

I asked the KJ if she was a regular, and he said no—he had never seen her before, unlike most of the crowd that night. As we continued to talk, in between his announcing new singers and queueing up songs, he described his affection for this place. He had previously been a KJ at a karaoke bar, but he preferred it here because this place was more of a bar that had karaoke. Sure, lots of people came to sing, but they also came to do other things; unwind, shoot pool, watch baseball, and live their lives. I saw what he meant, and it put a different spin on my observation that no one was listening. This was a comfortable place to come and sing, have others sometimes tune in, sometimes tune out; overall there was an atmosphere of enjoyment and relaxation. It was a great place to be oneself.

CHAPTER 13

KANSAS

June 21. 2016

I'D ONLY BEEN ALONE FOR TWO DAYS SINCE LEAVING MINNESOTA, but it didn't take too long before I began closing into myself, allowing myself to be enveloped in a quiet solitude. As I drove through a series of small towns, I considered the essay, "Hiding," by David Whyte, which describes hiding as a means of survival, a way to protect oneself until strong enough to shine forth in the world. A caterpillar in a cocoon, a bear in hibernation, a tulip bulb all hide until the time is right.

With those thoughts, I remained invisible to the world, stopping only to pee or refuel. In the early afternoon, I pulled into Beatrice, Nebraska. The number of churches amazed me; three on one Main Street corner, with others blocks away, all of them built in the 1910s or '20s, with pale bricks and impressive steeples. Back then, people had to come from miles around to attend every Sunday, using cars that didn't exactly move so fast, on roads that weren't exactly smooth. It must have taken hours.

As I drove out of town, I passed an old barn that was now the home of Uncle Mike's Guns. It didn't take long before I was staring out into very little. A few signs were scattered along the road, and they all carried one of two messages: support of Trump or condemnation of abortion. Many signs were handmade: "The ABCs of abortion: Another Butchered Child," "Jail Killary," or "I See a Future Where America is Great Again." I hadn't seen anything warning me about the dangers of meth since I left Montana, though I was informed that depression is the number one cause of suicide, at least in these parts.

I arrived in Overlook, Kansas, in the late afternoon, so I had some time to kill. For some reason, I used Yelp to look up the bar I was going to; maybe it was because I was looking to see if they served a decent dinner, or if I was going to have to go back into the hatch of my car for snacks. Normally I don't look places up on Yelp if I can confirm their hours and options in other ways—but it happened, and I immediately regretted it. The reviews discussed how dirty it was, the fights that happened there, staff harassing customers, and people getting robbed. Reviewers advised parking under streetlights and not walking around the area alone. For the first time, I was hesitant to be by myself. I messaged Dave about my reservations. He was in China, but I felt better knowing someone knew where I was in the world.

Despite the reviews, my desire to maintain my schedule, my desire to sing, and my general stubbornness outweighed my reservations. I drove into the strip-mall lot a few hours later. I parked close to the bar, under a light, and hoped for the best. The front entrance was painted dark and a sign above it claimed karaoke happened "eight days a week." A guy sat smoking on a bench right outside; his t-shirt read "Whores, Sailors, and Tattoos."

I opened the door and was hit with a loud burst of heavy metal. The top of the wooden counter was sticky. The walls were decorated with dark wood paneling and a thick layer of dust. I was nervous. Normally I'm okay in dive bars, but this one bled into seediness. I took small comfort in the fact that the bartender looked like a big goofball and wore a Hawaiian shirt with only one button done up over his large belly. He tossed a coaster my way and frowned, saying that no one else got the memo that it was luau night. I wasn't sure if he was kidding or not. The other bartender wore a shirt that said "Go Fuck Yourself." She clearly didn't get the memo.

I ordered a club soda with lime and it was plopped down in front of me in a red Solo cup. The woman sitting next to me was wearing a pink tank top and smelled of humidity and sweat—she'd probably been out in the heat too long. I put a coaster on top of my drink before I went to the bathroom, making sure to memorize the position at which I had placed the cardboard square—one corner toward the bar edge—in case anyone decided to tamper with my drink. One of the toilets was clogged and looked like it had been that way for days. I vowed not to go back in there unless I really had to.

A group of four women came in to sing and order a round of Fireball shots. Another group walked in, and the luau-shirted bartender (who, it turned out, was also the KJ) yelled, "Holy shit!" into the microphone—loud enough that I jumped. As people streamed in, he hugged pretty much everyone—clearly this was a spot for regulars. He started the night off with "Under the Boardwalk," and the women in both groups started dancing. I hopped off the bar and sat at the tables to be closer to the action (and be comforted by the presence of others).

The man who had been smoking outside came back in to sing, first announcing, "Sorry, I'm really drunk and this is what happens." He screamed into the mic, appropriate for his heavy metal selection. I followed him with "Voices Carry," inspired by the woman I'd heard in Nebraska the night before. The song was more haunting than I realized. Singing it for the first time made me focus on its lyrics more than I normally would; reading its words forced me to face its theme of domestic violence, and sent my mind into memories of loved ones who had survived. Unexpectedly shaken, I sat back down as a guy approached me, saying he "took notice of me," because of my "interesting song choice." It soon became clear that he mostly took notice of himself, regaling me with stories of his punk rock past in 1980s Houston, before sharing his philosophy on karaoke.

Normally I might have been intrigued, but this man didn't care about anything outside of himself. He spoke incessantly, never stopping to see if I wished to contribute to the conversation. Karaoke, he maintained, was about making a song one's own, taking it to a level beyond the original. Although I smiled and nodded, I silently challenged his opinion. A song too distant from the familiar can detract from the shared experience, so I'm hesitant to stray too far from the original. I thought about how the woman who had sung "My Way" the night before was lost in the crowd.

I got some reprieve from Mr. Interesting's monologue when he got up to sing "his version" of "Comfortably Numb." Ironically, I liked it because it was actually highly reminiscent of Pink Floyd, as opposed to innovative. His idea of performing it "his way" was to sing a little angrier, and to put his foot up on the railing—casually, yet deliberately. When he finished, he took a bow and sat back down across from me, asking if I would consider singing a song if just one of its notes was out of my range. I said I would; he would not. I remembered the time I sang "Forever in Blue Jeans" in Portland at the Local Lounge; though I cringed as I pushed through the notes that were too low for me, the moment still brought me joy. It's a happy song, sweet and simple in its love. It also brought memories of growing up listening to my parents and their friends laughing and drinking wine in front of a living-room fire, while Neil Diamond albums played in the background.

The next singer was one of the regulars. She went by the stage name Loretta; she wore comfy fleece pants that could have doubled as pajamas. When she finished, the in-between music kicked in and the KJ/bartender got down on his hands and knees to fix the pool table—he was a brave man to experience the bar's carpet that up close. It was too loud for conversation, which provided me another welcome break from Mr. Interesting.

Loretta must have sensed my need for rescue, for she came over and asked me to join her table. I jumped at the chance. Her companions were a mix of generations—a man of retirement age, a young woman just out of college, and the rest in between—but it was a gathering of my people. I never quite got what brought them together outside of their love of song, and I'm not sure there needed to be anything else. I struck up a conversation with Daisy, the college grad, and soon found out we had Stanford in common. She was taking the summer off, trying to figure out if she wanted to go to med school or law school, having been accepted to both. She'd gone to Stanford on a volleyball scholarship, and looked the part— tall, beautiful, and lithe, with long blonde hair. We talked about travel, both of us having been to multiple continents. Her next dream destination was Cambodia, while I was still trying to figure out mine. I shared my experiences at Angkor Wat and the Killing Fields and encouraged her to go wherever and whenever she could.

Mr. Interesting wandered over to us and interrupted our conversation, claiming it wasn't safe in other countries and that lovely women like us needed to be more careful. Daisy and I let him know we felt a lot safer overseas than in the US, then turned our backs on him and kept dreaming.

Soon after, I was face to face with Loretta. She was a woman full of questions, and I found myself easily opening up to her. I shared my story of what had brought me there—Molly's death, a sense of purposelessness, a need to be on the road. With her next song, Loretta announced, "This next song is dedicated to Molly, who just passed from lung cancer." It was "Ironic," by Alanis Morissette. The Fireball women got up next and sang "Hopelessly Devoted to You" and then left, their shot glasses and Solo cups littering the table.

A gifted woman sang a version of "Come Sail Away," but not without critique from Mr. Interesting, who told me she was singing it wrong. He believed it wasn't gritty enough, and that it was too stylistically similar to musical theater. I replied that she performed the song technically well, just maybe not to his liking. Who are we to judge the proper way to sing a song? As long as karaoke brings people together, it should be celebrated, shouldn't it? He scowled at my challenges and said her performance lacked passion, retorting "What's the point of singing if you lack passion?" While I understood his point, I was past wanting to encourage further discussion with him.

As the evening wound down, Loretta let me know her posse was going to be singing the next day at a place in downtown Kansas City that was much nicer than this place: "They have a stage and a great sound system," she enthused. "Plus, it's in a different state! You can sing in Missouri tomorrow and we will be there to hear it!" I did like the idea of hanging out the next night with people who were somewhat familiar to me. I was ready to come out of hiding again.

CHAPTER 14

MISSOURI

June 22. 2016

I WAS TO MEET MY COMPANY FROM THE PREVIOUS NIGHT AT A PLACE in the Power and Light District, the "new" hip area of downtown Kansas City—a central square full of bars and restaurants and cut off from traffic. The area was revitalized ten years ago, but still looked clean. And fake—more like a city block you would find inside a Vegas casino, selling souvenirs and fifteen-dollar gourmet hot dogs, than one with actual residents.

The bar was huge: the front entrance required me to choose whether to fork right for more intimate dining, or left into the main bar area. I went left, into a brand-new, shiny space made to look like it was built in the '20s, with black-and-white hex-tile floor, a grand dark wooden bar, and high ceilings painted white. It was well-lit and designed for larger crowds, though attendance was somewhat sparse when I arrived, making it easy to see that I didn't recognize anyone in there yet. Of course I got there first, as I always did, bored in my hotel room and needing to get out before the evening lured me into feeling settled and complacent. I wondered if the gang from last night would show; I was slightly nervous that they wouldn't, but I also knew I would sing here either way.

Someone greeted me at the bar entrance and asked how many were in my party; I didn't know the answer to that. Maybe I would end up sitting here, by myself, at a large dark wooden table at this brand-new Irish pub. Together the hostess and I decided on a medium-sized table on the edge of the seating area. I wasn't sure why I felt nervous that the others wouldn't show. I had been in several bars by myself in several different states; why would it matter if I ended up solo again? Perhaps it was because I announced to the hostess that I would need a slightly larger table because I was expecting company, but deep down I wasn't sure that was the case. The truth was, I didn't want to be forgotten.

Another woman came in, looking as lost as I had moments before. I made eye contact, and she wandered over to me, asking if I knew Loretta. This woman was another solo karaoke aficionado Loretta had invited into her brood. We both ordered beers and I no longer cared what happened; I was no longer alone. Slowly, people I recognized started coming in—Daisy, the older man, and Mr. Interesting. The table I'd claimed wasn't big enough, so Loretta pushed another one next to ours, and as the night progressed we moved to an even bigger spot in the middle of the bar. People sat and stood around us—a small party comprised of those I had met before and new-to-me faces filling the large space, making it feel cozy. On this night, Loretta was dressed to perform rather than merely sing—wearing makeup, a beautiful flowy top, and super high-heeled sandals.

The KJ set up his sound system on the large stage in front of the bar. There were no public monitors to encourage sing-along participation—the only screen was small, tucked out of the way, and faced the singer. Karaoke singer as performer. Loretta let me know me there was a speaker onstage that allowed you to hear yourself so you could tell if you were on key. "This is high-class karaoke, where you can be a real singer," said a man who hadn't been there the night before. Isn't being a real singer sort of the opposite of being a karaoke singer, though?

The large stage, the professional sound system, and the polished bar were all strange to me. I connected more with the KJ, an amiable, dumpy guy with a torn concert t-shirt. He managed to bring the karaoke vibe amongst all the polish. When it was time for my first song, I walked up the seven steps and across the large stage, past the inward-facing speaker, and to the microphone. The intro to my song was cued, and it all went back to normal. I didn't notice the extra speaker, or the improved sound system. I've always been the kind of person who was happy to listen to her favorite song on a tin radio. But it was clear this setup—and the environment it was in—was a lot classier than where we'd been the night before: classier by a country mile and a flushing toilet. I missed the cozier feel of a dive bar, but since the people I was with were pretty much the same, even the formal stage felt like home.

My song choice was "Say Goodbye to Hollywood"—a song I thought I knew cold, so I allowed my eyes to stray from the monitor, something I rarely do. Somewhere along the way, I missed or added a line, so when I glanced back at the monitor I found myself in the wrong spot. My gaff lasted only a second before I got myself back on track. I smiled to the crowd, laughed at myself, and moved on. In a way, messing up like that made me want to keep going—not try harder, but continue to enjoy myself. It was okay to make a mistake. In karaoke, it doesn't matter. Or at least it didn't to me.

Mr. Interesting's companion got up to sing "Go Ask Alice" after I was done. As the song neared its climactic end, the audio totally cut out, and it was clear she was upset and the KJ could tell. He started her song over, apologizing and saying nothing like that had ever happened before. I believed him. As the song cued up again, she didn't seem as into it. Her shoulders slumped—her heart less connected to the lyrics. Her performance was still flawless, but there was a slight hesitation in her voice, as if she'd lost faith in the song, and in karaoke itself.

A woman wearing all black (including her lipstick) followed with "What's Up." Despite the black, I found her stage presence a little too cheery for song about praying for a revolution. But when it came down to it, she sang the song her way, and enjoyed her time with the mic. That's how karaoke should be.

Fueled by "What's Up," I got into a political discussion with Daisy; she was afraid for the future. She had been a Bernie Sanders supporter, loving his stances on education and helping those in need, but now that he wouldn't be the Democratic nominee, she didn't know what to do. She hated Trump—his disrespect for women, for people of color, for everyone but himself—but believed he would keep us safer from ISIL. That, to her, was the most important issue facing America right now. "My generation is going to be responsible for World War III," she lamented as she stared into her vodka tonic. "I don't know if I can handle that."

I searched for a way to ask her why she believed Trump's approach was better than Clinton's when it came to foreign policy. Nothing came. I was forced to settle with her unsatisfying response that foreign affairs were Trump's number one priority, while Clinton was more about gun control—which Daisy was also for. Ultimately, she felt it was more important to feel safe on a global level than an individual one. After Orlando, she said, she thought fighting terrorism was the main thing we should be doing. I asked if she was going to vote for Trump. She didn't know, and was thinking of not voting, but admitted that was the same as voting for Trump, which she insisted she didn't want to do, and yet . . . she stared into her drink again.

I was rattled. Bewildered. How could someone so smart see the world so differently than I did? We had gone to the same school. Sat in the same classrooms. Visited friends in the same dorms. Eaten frozen yogurt by the same central campus fountain. Yet here we were, generations apart, worlds apart. While karaoke, our love of travel, and our alma mater had given us a connection, we were different in so many ways. Focusing on song seemed the best solution at that moment, and so I turned back to the stage to listen to someone from our group butcher a 1970s love song to the whoops of the crowd.

The KJ used a pure rotation, in that after everyone sings a song, they get to keep their place in line and give their song as they are called up to sing again. At most places, if you don't put in a song after you sing, you lose your place in the rotation. A KJ figures no song means no singing—either because the person has left, or they just don't feel like it anymore. A pure rotation like this signals that when people come here to sing, they are never really finished. My name was called for a second song, and I had no idea what to sing. I'd thought I did, but that was because I'd thought my second turn would happen much later, once I'd had a second beer, when the song choices around me would have been more upbeat. *Screw it,* I thought now. I needed to get lost in a song, in a silliness I hadn't experienced in forever. I belted out "MacArthur Park," a best-forgotten disco hit by Donna Summer, its lyrics so nonsensical it was impossible to know what they were about: leaving a cake out in the rain? Losing a recipe? And why green icing?

My company sang along with me, which fueled my energy and brought the song to the next level. As I left the stage, joy in my heart, I texted Molly's husband, Ted, to let him know I had sung the song he hated the most; any time we went out singing together, he would always beg me not to do it: "Sing anything but that damn cake song." It was the first time I had reached out to him in joy rather than grief. He responded, letting me know he was reading Molly's journal from her time in Asia, and missing her. By sharing my moment of joy, I provided him a small bright spot, and for that he was grateful. I missed her still, too, but for the first time in a while I felt less lonely, and not just because I was hanging out with others that night. I'd enjoyed being by myself for almost two weeks. I'd enjoyed the cocoon of my car, the companionship of the road and my thoughts, the AM radio and the sportscasters, as much as the singing, and as much as Donna Summer's nonsense. I was slowly starting to bloom into the first signs of feeling at peace, of feeling secure since I'd lost my best friend.

For my third and final song of the night, I asked the KJ to do a duet. We went with "Don't Go Breaking My Heart." As he cued it up he said, "This is all Velveeta, folks." I told him I used that phrase, too. He turned to me and asked, "Are we best friends now?" I said sure, at least for tonight, and we began to sing.

CHAPTER 15

A DOUBLE SHOT OF ILLINOIS

June 23 & 24. 2016

I PULLED INTO A DARK, RUTTED GRAVEL PARKING LOT BEHIND THE BAR in Peoria, Illinois. It had rained the night before, and I managed to step into a large puddle getting out of my car. My sandal was soaked, which should have been a warning of my evening to come. Still, my drenched left foot and I persisted as we walked through the back door of Pitch, an official karaoke bar, as opposed to one of those bars that happened to have karaoke—per the distinction made by the KJ in Nebraska. At Pitch, if the place was open, karaoke was happening. I went down a dark, narrow hallway and past the restrooms before I reached plush-red decor and a glass bar with highly polished red stools. The pregnant bartender chatted up a patron, telling him she was two weeks due from her fourth; somehow, she still managed to move around with great agility in such a tight space.

The patrons sat in small groups that looked like they went together in the same way different tables at a high school cafeteria are each part of the same class. Some art students sat just to the right of me, wearing all black fashions consisting of elaborate hats and flowy tops. Everyone, regardless of gender, wore bright red lipstick. The musical-theater actors sat at a side booth and wore skinny jeans and belted out show tunes when their names were called. A group of pretty people laughed as they sang, continually looking in the direction of their table for affirmation, but not getting any, as the rest of their party was too busy looking on their phones to give much notice to the world around them.

A lithe woman in a fedora; a black, bell-bottomed, backless pantsuit; one of those chain earrings; and strong dark eye makeup ordered a caramel whiskey with butterscotch schnapps on the rocks. One half of the cute lesbian couple sitting next to me said to her, "You're a strong woman to drink something like that," which seemed to please her quite a bit. The bartender told another customer they needed to make a drinking game for every time someone chose something from a musical. I remained invisible to her.

The KJ was a nonentity here. Singers input their songs into a computer on the wall, which also served as the catalog—no tattered, sticky black binders to thumb through for inspiration or distraction. All the KJ did was call a name, hand the mic over, and cue the song. The way he was running the show, his job could easily have been automated. He didn't encourage clapping or tell anyone they did a good job. Without a word, he would take the mic back from the singer and call the next name. A strange job for someone who seemed to just want to punch a clock and hide behind a desk.

The song choices were all over the map: grunge, country,

musicals, hip-hop. A mousy young woman wearing a tie-dye shirt sang ABBA in a strained whisper as she sat on her stool at her table, never leaving her boyfriend's side. A beefy balding guy with the theater folk sang "Let It Go" in Japanese. Though every song was welcome here, that wasn't the case for every singer. Clapping was reserved for friends and the truly fantastic, making me feel even lonelier than before. I tried to find the right song so I could be noticed, somehow fit into this disinterested crowd. I found myself wanting to please everyone to the point where it irritated me; still I thought hard about a song that would resonate with their detached presence. I went with Berlin's "Metro" for its old-school '80s techno vibe and angsty whine, peaking my performance during the line "I remember hating you for loving me," wailing into the mic with a balance of tone and snarl. Only one person clapped when I finished—one of the women sitting next to me at the bar, the one who had praised others for their drink choices. The KJ remained silent. I felt discouraged; the community of karaoke was not there, at least not for me. For the first time on this trip, I felt as though I didn't belong.

The next day I drove to Chicago in silence, passing a series of signs that bordered a large field near Low Point, Illinois:

Thugs don't stop
To wait for a cop
Guns make sense
For self-defense.

I did a double shot in Illinois because the karaoke spot in Chicago was recommended on Reddit, and I figured I'd check out karaoke in the more urban part of the state. In stark contrast to Peoria, this place was clearly a bar first, karaoke joint second. Really, this place was a building first, as the entrance consisted of little more than a stone façade, an ordinary blue door, and a small, dimly lit beer sign. I didn't see the name of the bar anywhere except on a poster advertising an upcoming trivia event—it was the only thing assuring me I was in the right place besides the address.

The bar was full of people watching the Cubs game. It was the seventh inning, and the Cubs were up 1-0 with the Marlins threatening. On another screen, tucked away in the corner, the White Sox and Blue Jays were tied in the fifth; no one seemed to care about that. The talk around the bar was all about the Cubs. A red-faced drunk named Sully looked like he was going to pass out as he critiqued the Cubs' lineup, as a woman wearing an official Ben Zobrist jersey told him to "stick it." The interaction made me miss living in a sports town. The Marlins tied it up, but the Cubs came back to win 2-1 in the bottom of the ninth. (In a few months, the team would win the World Series for the first time in over 100 years.)

I nursed my beer and watched the changing of the guards— sports people out, singers in. The KJ had a crutch, and hobbled over to the bartender to ask for water and a tip jar. The bartender obliged with plastic for the water and a fancy pint glass prepopulated with a dollar. I asked her if she needed help bringing stuff over, but she said she's been managing this way for four years, and offered no further explanation. The first singer, a stocky man named Gerald, performed "Freebird" so softly that really the crowd was just hearing the instrumental. His mouth far away from the microphone, all his energy focused on a ratty stuffed animal lion he seemed to be serenading. When the song was over, everyone in the bar cheered loudly as he took a seat next to the KJ and placed the animal on his head. Gerald was the perfect example of how in karaoke, talent doesn't matter when there's heart and joy. I started to text Molly about what I had just seen, and then realized that wasn't an option. It never would be an option.

Unlike my experience in Peoria the night before, here the karaoke was what I'd come to expect—a night of total acceptance. Each singer was greeted with a warm hug by the KJ before they were given the mic. A gangly man in a Bulls cap and basketball shorts sang a touching Josh Groban. A heavyset woman belted out an off-key Pat Benatar. A man brought me to tears with his rendition of "Purple Rain." While a woman followed with a song about "the good old days" when "daddy's came home," the "Purple Rain" singer and the bartender talked about the peppers in their gardens, and how to plant them in the right places to get the best sun for different varieties, before the former ordered a sickly-sweet Redd's Apple Ale.

Nearly everyone in the bar sang a song. My opening contribution was Fleetwood Mac's "Go Your Own Way." Then it was Gerald's turn again. This time he whispered Jethro Tull to a stuffed black puma. As he finished, he grabbed three animals and headed to the bar to order a Jack and Coke. While waiting, he introduced me to Kitty and Kitty II, two black pumas, and the lion, Simba. It was clear these animals were well-loved and well-traveled, and hadn't seen a washing machine in years. Throughout the evening, Gerald would walk up to various patrons and rest his animals on their shoulders, where they would receive many scratches on their heads. No one looked phased or startled when it was their turn. Though Gerald took several trips around and to the bar, his home base was always standing next to the KJ, who spent a lot of time during songs petting Simba and listening to Gerald's every word.

CHAPTER 16

MICHIGAN

June 25. 2016

I FELT A LITTLE TIRED FROM THE MOMENT I HIT THE ROAD. WHILE I was still enjoying the solitude of my daily drives, I'd sung the last seven nights in a row and was currently gunning to get to Detroit, to sing in the afternoon sun for day number eight. I closed the door to my cocoon, turned on the ignition, and drove the four and a half hours on the interstate to get there on time. I cursed the mounting toll road costs; I cursed the slight soreness in my left hip; I cursed the lack of exercise options at the rest stops. The hiking trails and paths of the West were long gone, replaced by easy-on, easy-off jug handles offering toilets, a gas station, a McDonald's, and little else. It was impossible to tell what state I was in, but one thing was for sure: I was in America, land of convenience. I spent an hour of my drive redesigning rest stops from a public health perspective—walking paths, adult playground equipment. Signs to encourage exercise, telling travelers how many laps around a well-gardened path to get to 1,000 steps, or the benefits of stretching one's body to stay awake. I remembered seeing multiple exercise machines at parks and along the highway when I was in South Korea—stationary bicycles facing a city skyline or small hillside, set apart from the road by a small outlet pass. These options are not available in the United States, and that made me feel sad for our country—and sorry for me and my stiff calves.

Discouraged, I turned on the radio and listened to the latest on the water crisis in Flint, Michigan. Civil lawsuits had been filed against the water companies following the federal lawsuits against the city and the mayor. Everyone was covering their own asses, pointing fingers, and laying blame while thousands of people (over forty percent of whom lived in poverty) still didn't have access to safe drinking water in their own homes. Great efforts were being made to deliver bottled water to everyone, but few efforts were made to apologize for letting a whole community down, for placing the needs of a powerful few over the needs of those they were supposed to serve.

As I neared Detroit, I wasn't sure what to expect. I had never been there before, but outside of knowing the strong reputation of the Red Wings and their dedicated fan base, the only thing I knew about the city was that it was supposed to be failing. The auto industry was all but dead, and what was left of the city was a mystery to me, shrouded in a story of hardship, violence, and despair. During the peak of the 2009 recession, Molly sent me an email, telling me to search on online real estate sites for houses in Detroit that were $5,000 or less. I was surprised to see hundreds of options. A house, no matter how run-down—a house in a city, no less, with teams in all the major sports—should always be worth more than $5,000. But there they were—listings as low as $3,000, even $2,000. My heart had cracked a little down its center, as I'd read through the options. I was drawn to houses with "good bones," as I was able to overlook the plywood-covered windows and rotting siding to envision the potential of the porches big enough for chairs so I could watch the world go by as I sat outside in the shade under the weight of the humid air. I'd imagined buying up a block of Detroit and fixing the houses. From my rebuilt porch, I would wave to neighbors as they walked their dogs, or made their way home from work after a long day. I'm a believer in neighborhoods and the community they can bring. A sense of belonging that makes everyone matter. If you are a part of my neighborhood, you are part of me, and I am part of you. It all circled back to karaoke and my journey and the communities I'd been meeting along the way.

Because I took the interstate to get to my destination, there were no precursors, no hints as to what I was to encounter until I was almost on top of it. A sign pointed me to Comerica Park, where the Tigers play. Brown brick churches and apartment buildings. I took my exit, and drove into magic. I was in an area of Detroit that was indeed revitalized, dominated by a huge farmers' market that was just closing as I arrived. I quickly parked and wandered in. Local farmers were folding down tables and looking to offload their produce at ridiculously cheap prices. I got a pint of cherry tomatoes, some apricots going slightly bad, and a bag of green beans—for a buck each. I would eat like a queen for the next few days.

Then it was time to find the karaoke; it would be my first time singing during the day. The festivities had started at eleven that morning, and so had been underway for over five hours by the time I arrived. I had called the place twice the day before to confirm the early start. I never imagined there was such a thing as daytime singing, and needed multiple reassurances. In my mind, anything associated with bar culture happened at night—after a long shift, after the kids were done complaining—when people needed an escape.

I walked up to the address I'd written on my hand, needing

to ask directions twice. Out front was a grill the entire length of the establishment, itself two storefronts long. Ribs and corn as far as the eye could take in, two sweaty happy people constantly flipping everything with foot-long tongs. Speakers set up out front, piping upbeat, bluesy music to the people at the picnic tables on the sidewalk. Inside, a few people gathered around a bar, and a few more at tables—all eating ribs and corn. I asked if the karaoke was still happening today; a waitress with five orders up and down her arms swayed her head left: "Out back."

Down a shady alleyway I went, and on the other side was a huge parking lot full of people sitting on white plastic chairs at large round white plastic tables—all settled in for the weekly event. The smart ones brought portable white tents to shade themselves from the unforgiving sun. Two makeshift bars were set off to the side, selling bottled beers and a few select well drinks. The music from the speakers out front was provided by the karaoke talent in the back— yet I had mistaken it for a professional playlist. A woman was facing the hundreds of people in attendance, doing the most incredible rendition of "Shake a Tail Feather" from the *Blues Brothers* soundtrack. It wasn't just her voice that was amazing; her whole being was amazing. A gorgeous woman in her early twenties, with long, curly hair, and tight-fitting clothing that allowed her perfectly choreographed dance moves to show through. She sang this old song—I was surprised she knew it —with such confidence, style, and grace. I was in trouble. This was karaoke at a whole new level.

There was another reason I wasn't sure if I belonged there. I was the only white person in sight. No one made me think I shouldn't be there—no one started as I walked into the crowd, no one seemed to mind as I sat down at an uncovered shared table off to the side. But I felt I was crashing a family reunion, a space not meant for me. When I went up to the KJ to request a song, I felt like I had to explain myself; I said I was from

Portland, Oregon, that I was traveling around the country to sing in the Lower 48. I told her that I was honored to be there. That I had been in Detroit less than an hour and was already loving the place. She smiled a kind, sincere smile—not of someone who had a busy slate in front of them, but as someone who was truly listening, and truly cared about a stranger's tale. I chose a song, sat down, and wondered if I was ever going to get a chance to sing. In the meantime, I listened to the many people sharing their amazing voices with the crowd.

The KJ did call my name eventually, and when she did, she let everyone know I was new in town; I received a warm welcome of applause, and yells of "Hello!" and "Welcome to Detroit!" Then I sang, "Still the One" by Orleans, and people clapped along, stood, swayed, bobbed up and down. I was another singer in their group, another person who came here to share good music in the sunshine. I felt as though I was being hugged.

After I sang, I basked in a comfortable glow. I talked to a man sitting next to his wife; he was an artist, she didn't really say much until she announced it was time to go to pick up his mother. When they left, I moved into the shade of the alley for respite. My arms were red, and my skin burning. I shared the sun-free space with a man in his fifties—white hat, blue-collared short-sleeved shirt with white trim, white shorts. His friend, dancing a few yards away from us, wore an all-white linen suit. The man in the shade said it was his first time there, and I said it was mine as well. He was from the area, though—a stocker at the local large-chain grocery store.

When he asked what I did, I stumbled a bit. I never know how to answer that question in a way that brings people in. I landed on a partial-truth answer that I work in cancer prevention; it had worked with the artist, but this guy asked for details. I said I helped community cancer screening and prevention programs see if what they are doing is helping as much as we hope it is. Luckily, that was a sufficient response, and inspired my companion to share his own cancer survival story, and how he made it because he was a fighter. He spoke of enduring rough, draining treatments, and I said he could tolerate the strong treatments because he himself was strong and the people around him must have been strong, too. He agreed. His wife and kids stood by; he never felt alone. But now, he laughed, he had to stand in the shade all alone because the bright sun set his skin on fire—a side-effect of the treatments: "Here I am, one of the darkest people you'll ever meet, and the sun is now my poison."

As he talked, I thought about a former research project on primary care and long-term cancer survivors, and how we dedicate no resources and time to those who make it to the other side. I thought of Molly and how hard she fought—and how it still wasn't enough. I shared neither story with the man, who then asked me if I thought faith could help heal in these situations—situations like his. I chose my words carefully, not being a believer myself. I said that in some cases, yes: faith works if the person believes that their faith helps them fight. If the community stands by an afflicted person and prays, those prayers become strength. He said he fought his cancer because God told him he wasn't done with this life yet. I told him he was right, and that his hope and faith helped him live longer.

Silently, I knew sometimes hope isn't enough. I don't believe Molly ever lost hope, but at some point she realized it wasn't enough. She knew that she was dying and that it couldn't be stopped—not by faith, not by drugs, not by hope. I wonder when that was—on what day did she wake up and know her life was over?

After a couple of hours, the sun started to dip behind distant buildings, and the crowd got more diverse, but not by much. A white man with one arm got up to sing "Night Moves," getting the crowd to clap along by hitting his stump of an arm onto the mic. So many words describe this day.

Magic. Happiness. Comfort. Community. Joy. A large gathering of people in a parking lot—singing, dancing, laughing. Amateurs like me baking in the sun, until I found respite and wisdom in the shade of a building. People setting up the white event tents usually seen at weddings and then settling down, because they were there to stay. I went for a walk, then came back to hear some more music. When I left after 8 p.m., just as the sun was setting, everyone was still there, singing. I want to believe they are always there.

CHAPTER 17

INDIANA

June 27. 2016

I ARRIVED IN THE SUBURBS OF INDIANAPOLIS AND WAITED AT A
nearby shopping center for Kim, a friend I hadn't seen
since high-school graduation. Our meeting place was a large
shopping center that tried to be upscale but fell short. Com-
monplace chain-store offerings dressed up in new and polished
bricks: Party City, the obligatory Starbucks. Kim's dark SUV
blended in with the rest of the parking lot.

An attractive mom with a highly professional job at a large
respectable company, Kim represented success as Mountain
Lakes, New Jersey, the town we grew up in, defined it. All the
pieces had been there to lead me down a similar path, but for
whatever reasons got assembled differently. While I'm slowly
learning to accept the fact that what drives me is different
than what drives many with my background, I still feel a sense
of guilt knowing my feeling of completeness doesn't reflect
all I've been taught about money, status, and security. For

whatever reason, my utopia is driving around in a car singing karaoke. On good days, I am able to bask in the freedom this realization offers, and embrace the fact that my joy and sense of purpose come from a strange place that few understand, including me. On the not-so-good days, I question the life choices that got me to where I am—facing a reflection of my possible self.

I followed Kim to her parents' house to have dinner before we went out to sing. We pulled into a gated community centered on a golf course, wound around small streets of perfectly manicured lawns and pruned shrubs, and up a driveway that looked like all the others; no way would I have been able to find my way back to this particular location on my own. I entered a house larger than any I had set foot in before—a space more foreign to me than any of my apartments in Oman, South Korea, or Vietnam. The reality was that my car was as close to a home as I had that summer. I still feel more comfortable when I'm contained and my possessions limited, so I'm free to focus beyond a home base and into the unknown.

Kim's parents were warm and loving, offering sincere hugs to a stranger. Though I had been friends with Kim in high school, I had never met her family. Dinner was steak and salad, which we ate on their two-tiered outdoor deck. I sat facing the tenth hole, watching some golfers finishing up their round in the last hour of daylight. Talk of careers made me uncomfortable, since my own path was so ambiguous. Both Kim and her father worked for the same large pharmaceutical company and said they would hire me in a heartbeat—the industry needed more sharp minds like mine. Talk of politics brought a sigh of relief. Kim's parents leaned liberal, as I do, and spoke of the challenges of living where they did—among neighbors who had never lived anywhere but Indiana, and who supported Trump. Kim's parents simply didn't understand how "well-educated, rich people could watch Fox News at night and vote for a man like that." I had no answers, though I did think about all the Confederate flags I had seen as I drove into town, and felt that might be one reason. Then we discussed the bombing of the airport in Istanbul; friends I had met while teaching in Oman had been there the day before, catching a flight after visiting family in Turkey. They were just fine, but the idea of them being so close rattled me.

The sun was setting as we sipped wine. Soon it would be time to sing, but when I told my hosts where I intended to go, they looked nervous; they thought the area of Indy I had chosen wasn't safe, and I didn't know enough to argue. I didn't want to defend myself against people who had been so kind on a topic I knew nothing about. The part of me that would protest, let others know that I can take care of myself, had vanished inside a full belly and a warm Chardonnay glow. Kim's parents offered to have me stay two nights at their house so I could sing somewhere else the next day. Kim apologized that her home wasn't the best place to be. She was in the process of getting a divorce, and her soon-to-be ex was still living with her. I accepted her parents' generous offer with gratitude, and was led to the guest area—a whole floor to myself, complete with full bar. I fell asleep almost instantly.

I woke up a little later than usual, took a long walk around the golf course and saw a movie at the local multiplex. It was my first day off in a while, and I enjoyed escaping into mindless action and strong air conditioning. Kim got off work early and met me back at her parents' house, and I accompanied her on some errands, and then read a book at a coffee shop while she got her hair styled. Conversation came easily; we talked about life choices, partner choices, and the spotty memories of our lives in high school together. I remembered she was kind and made me laugh out loud. She remembered being at my house at various gatherings—watching movies and drinking beers. Kim treated me to dinner at a tapas place in a trendy part of the city, as she discussed giving half a million to her ex in their settlement, and the need to sell their 4,800-square-foot house to divide the proceeds. Those numbers made my eyes grow, and she must have seen it, for she immediately apologized if her talk of money made me uncomfortable. I said it didn't, it just caught me by surprise. I thought about how I was probably not going to have enough to retire, unless I moved to Vietnam—which, frankly, didn't seem that bad an option.

We arrived at the karaoke bar in another trendy area of Indianapolis, with streets lined with cocktail lounges and fusion restaurants, whose windows were opened, letting laughter our into the streets. The karaoke here, like in Michigan, was held outdoors. But the similarities ended there: whereas the karaoke in Detroit was held in the afternoon under the blazing sun, here I got to sing under the stars. The evening was significantly cooler than those in previous days, and the night had a soft breeze that made me want my jacket for the first time since I had left Montana. We sat on a smooth bench on a neat, clean patio made of Trex decking and faux tile tables. My Miller Lite tallboy ran me four dollars and fifty cents. The crowd skewed young, and most chose to sing in pairs or groups. Unlike the singers in Detroit, who sang with confidence and appeared to enjoy their time in the spotlight, the singers here needed the security blankets of company and alcohol. Beyoncé, Maroon 5, Celine Dion (covering Meatloaf), B-52s, Vanessa Carlton, and the Eagles—no singer was alone. Those who did brave being solo onstage at least brought their beer for companionship. Friends were supportive and clapped and whooped when the songs were done. But they did so from afar, in the area where smoking was permitted. The scent of cloves dominated the air.

One woman who did perform solo sang Tracy Chapman's "Give Me One Reason" in a more spoken-word interpretation than the original. Her quality of voice wasn't the best, running slightly flat, but she made the song her own. Each of us has a different memory of a song, and a different lens from which to filter it. That means each of us can sing the same song, providing our unique interpretation, and everyone else will hear it the way they experience it, creating a combination of infinite moments and memories. One song becomes a million.

Next, a trio performed "Man of Constant Sorrow," the only African American in the bar taking the lead, flanked by two sidekick harmonizers and dancers. When I'd first gotten there, I'd thought this bar was going to be pretentious. I'd been wrong; there was a warmth and heart present, because people were simply enjoying themselves and the others around them. Yes, the place was full of pretty young things, but it didn't feel as image-conscious as the bar in Peoria. Possibly because the talent wasn't consistently there—people here sang to have fun, not impress others. I suppose the singers in Peoria were having fun, too, but there was a much bigger sense of showmanship at the karaoke bar.

My name was called, and I sang "Heart of Glass," one of my standbys. It fits my voice well, is familiar to almost everyone, and has just the right amount of pop to get people swaying and singing along. I'm not sure if it was because of the beers, the tiki torches, the friendship, or just being in a good space, but I felt "on." I heard someone shout "Wow" as I began, which energized me despite the late hour. There is something about singing in the open air that feels freeing—more comfortable than I imagined. I didn't expect singing outside to be all that different, but it is. Summer karaoke has a special quality if you can sing to the light of the moon.

Next, an older Asian guy, beet-red from drink, walked up to the mic and said, "Sorry to bring you all down," before the first few notes of "Desperado" were heard. He was too drunk to sing, so a young guy carrying a beer came up to help him out. The result was two drunk men standing, mumbling words.

Two men there to take the fall. I guess that's why people don't karaoke alone. As they got off the stage and walked by our table, back to the smoking area, the older guy farted. "Ugh, we were crop-dusted!" I giggled to Kim. We were in high school again.

After one duet, a woman laughed at her partner into the microphone, "Nick, you're a fucking dick!" The bouncer came up to remind them, "No cussing outdoors." I'm sure those who rented or bought here figured on dealing with bar patron noise as people hopped from one place to another, but dealing with bad singing until 3 a.m. was a whole other ballgame. And as the night progressed, that seemed exactly what people were in for. Two hours later, I was still waiting for my second chance at the mic, and gave up. It was a Wednesday night, after all, and Kim needed to get to work the next morning. I wonder who among the others did as well. I had no idea with whom I was sharing this perfect summer evening. Who were young professionals? Whose parents lived in a golfing community? Who planned to vote for Trump? Who had never lived anywhere but Indiana? Who listened to public radio? Who flew Confederate flags? There was no way to tell, but I left satisfied anyway.

CHAPTER 18

KENTUCKY

June 29. 2016

Finding a karaoke spot from afar isn't always easy. First, a place needs an internet presence—a Facebook page, Yelp review, or, if you're lucky, an actual up-to-date website—to let the world know it exists. One of my go-to resources was a Facebook page called Karaoke Across America. When I first found it in my pre-planning searches, I was excited. I thought the page consisted of a group of like-minded people who were silly enough to spend their days wandering around the country singing in bars. I sent a request to join the group and learned from Steve Hess, its manager, that that wasn't the case. The site primarily consisted of KJs advertising their events, a stream of posts promoting shows happening that day: one in Phoenix; followed by another in Galloway, Ohio; followed by one in Fairfield, California; then Duluth, Georgia . . . I'm not sure how useful this is unless a person is somehow scrolling through the page while traveling to one of these cities. Then they can say, "Damn, that looks like fun. I'm in!" I don't think that happens very much.

Steve has also put together a Karaoke Across America website, with a search bar in which one can type a location in hopes of finding karaoke. You can limit a search by day of the week, start time, and even disc company used. (I have no idea who would care about such a thing, but you never know.) I would often start my searches here. When I found a place online, I called to confirm that karaoke still happened at that bar, at that time, and on that day. Sometimes the bar didn't even exist anymore. Steve did his best to keep the information updated, but this project was a labor of love for him. He had a wife, kids, and a day job. His hobby was collecting karaoke venues, and he was kind enough to share that with the general population, free of charge. It was thanks to Karaoke Across America that I found a karaoke place in Kentucky.

As I crossed the Ohio River, the number of trailers and manufactured homes increased, and their overall condition decreased. A pair of girls wearing dirty, striped t-shirts and brightly colored shorts ran out to the side of the road in bare feet when they heard my car coming. Each was holding two kittens, trying to sell them to passersby. Shirtless men sat on rocking chairs and weathered stools on their front porches. Small houses hidden along the side of the road were covered in dirt, hidden by battered couches and assorted metal bars—possibly once part of a swing set, or maybe just collected to sell off for cash as soon as a pickup truck could be borrowed.

I pulled into the low-level chain motel I'd booked, and immediately knew I had made a mistake. This was the sort of place where people lived, not passed through. It was dirty, its parking lot full of holes, old cars, and cigarette butts. A couple and their young daughter stared at me from the balcony above as I brought my belongings into a first-floor unit. As I unloaded my things—bright-orange suitcase, cooler of snacks, computer bag—the couple started screaming at each other. Such a public display of venom unnerved me, but I guess they felt comfortable venting their disagreement outside, because this was their home. Or perhaps it was so they didn't have to stop smoking, though I know smoking rooms were an option in these parts. Their toddler clung to the unstable white metal railings and stuck her head in between the peeling bars; pieces flaked off in her hands. She was peering down from the other end of the walkway, as far away from her parents as possible without venturing down the stairs. Her parents continued to yell as they walked back into their room, slamming the door behind them. The girl in her dusty pink-and-yellow dress and matted blonde hair continued to watch me. When I left to sing, I felt I would only be partly surprised if my stuff was still there when I returned.

The bar was housed in a strip mall, and although the address stated I was in Lexington proper, it read more like a suburb. A cheap Chinese restaurant and a mini-mart shared space with the bar. Kidnap someone, blindfold them, bring them here and ask where they were, and no way in hell would they have anything to grasp onto to make an educated guess. Maybe the price of gas would tip them off, though this summer it had been cheap all over. I was in Anywhere, USA.

The bar, though, put me at ease as soon as I walked through the front door. The room smelled of stale smoke that had been absorbed into the dark brick walls over the years. The bartender wore his long, dark hair in a ponytail, and a backwards navy baseball cap with his name, Pappa, embroidered on it in the same color, so it was only visible at certain angles in certain light. He had a soothing voice—and, as demonstrated when he disappeared behind a door and left me completely by myself, a trusting soul. The few others who had been in the bar went outside to smoke, leaving behind a phone and tablet.

I guess this was the sort of place where everyone assumes the good in others.

Pappa came back with a handful of limes. The smokers—an obese woman and a skinny dude named Bluebeard—came back in as well, this time with the KJ in tow. He began to set up, breathing heavily and steadily as he went up the set of rickety stairs and onto the stage. When he reached the top, he showed off a brand-new mic and stand, telling the smokers: "Hey! I ordered some new stuff for you to break."

The pool room, which was getting re-floored, was barricaded with plastic sheeting and masking tape. Pappa had said the renovation was going to be ready next week, but in the meantime it was slowing down business, which worried him. The four of them—Pappa, the smokers, and the KJ—talked about how to bring more patrons into the bar before the karaoke started. They talked about game nights, getting the pool tables back into commission, and starting Guitar Hero nights. It made me think Pappa was the owner, or at least a manager. But as I talked with him I no longer believed that was the case. He just really liked being there, and cared enough to have the place do well. He'd been coming to the bar for over twenty years, but had been working there for just over three. "I love music, and karaoke fits the bill," he said. "It's better than putting money in a jukebox." He wasn't much of a drinker or a bar person, he admitted, yet there he was, caring about the place and trying to think of ways to draw more people in. I felt like I was a guest in his home, sitting at his kitchen counter as he sliced the limes. He wore large, silver rings on several fingers. The one staring at me was a lone wolf.

The smokers continued to talk about getting customers into the bar, and the damn heat of the Kentucky summer. Pappa said Bluebeard was the bar photographer for Facebook for a while—despite only being able to see out of one eye—until he started freaking out patrons. Too many people asked,

"Why is this guy taking our picture?" so the bar decided to quit the idea of having a publicist. The pictures were all messed up and blurry anyway. At 9:30 the KJ asked the few of us there, "Who wants to sing a karaoke song?" All of us responded "me" in a hushed voice, not wanting to break the relaxed vibe.

Soon after, others began to filter in. Pappa hugged or fist-bumped most of them. His party was about to begin. Like most gatherings, it started out slowly thanks to those who preferred to be fashionably late. People sang Weird Al Yankovic, misogynistic rap songs, Norah Jones, and Red Hot Chili Peppers. One of the smokers turned on the disco lights and cranked up the bass so that the whole bar shook with adrenaline and beat. When it was his turn to shine, Pappa sang to the heavy rock beats of My Chemical Romance. I ended up singing some Killers and some Blondie, but neither song felt quite right. My voice felt strained, as I struggled to decide whether to land my performance and tone in my head or my heart. Still, I got a decent amount of applause each time; everyone was supportive of everyone here, and Pappa said I sounded good. His opinion mattered to me most of all.

I left the bar around 11 p.m., just when things were really picking up. I was enjoying myself, but I couldn't shake images of my room being broken into, and of what little I had disappearing. I'd felt a desperation among my fellow tenants that might have led them to take things if given the chance. I felt safe at the bar—everyone was very friendly while letting fellow patrons be; even the large crowd of young men that came in looked harmless, no creepy vibe off any of them. They were just there to drink, hang out, and sing. No reason for any of them to bug an old lady like me. Besides, I knew Pappa would take care of me if the need arose. I was just afraid for my stuff. With the party in full swing, I slipped off my stool and out the door. Part of me felt guilty that I didn't say goodbye to Pappa, but I reassured myself that he would understand.

I got back to the motel and my room was just the way I'd left it, and I chastised myself for being so panicked. Still, I felt better being back there. As I crawled into bed, I thought about how things were going at Pappa's place. The crowd had doubled in size just as I was leaving; I wondered if that changed the culture of the place, but somehow I doubted it. I drifted off picturing the bar just a little busier and a little drunker, with Pappa keeping careful watch over his brood.

CHAPTER 19
OHIO
July 1, 2016

O N THE AM DIAL THERE WERE TEN STATIONS: ONE SPORTS (ALL local talk), two music, two religious, and the other five were playing the same Rush Limbaugh show, seconds apart. I wondered how locals chose one station over the other if so many were offering the same programming. As I drove through Cincinnati and Columbus toward Cleveland, the number of religious stations increased. I searched the dial for more options, but to no avail. I thought about switching to FM, but opted for silence instead. Along the roads, I saw several pro-life signs and a farm whose owner displayed the Ten Commandments on the side of a barn. An hour later, I tried the radio again and managed to scrape up a faint signal for NPR. I had no idea what I would have done if I had lived in a place where access to public radio wasn't a given.

I arrived at the outskirts of Cleveland, in the middle of nowhere—or more precisely a small town with some modern amenities like a Rite Aid and larger grocery store, there to serve those who attended the small local college, where my good friend, Ellen, was a teacher. Otherwise, I doubt she would have lived in this area—when we were in graduate school I always thought of her as a city girl. I walked up the small cement steps of her small Tudor home and knocked. Ellen responded by swinging her front door and arms wide open. I felt at home in both.

We took a walk in the late afternoon sun, and Ellen talked to me about living in a "tiny historic town"—a place that's not a city, nor a suburb, and certainly not rural. These towns are all over America, she said, built as community centers as far back as the 1800s to bring people from the fields together for shopping, civics, worship, and other activities. This simple description of where we were standing brought it all together for me. In my weeks of driving, I'd seen several of these towns, and could never find a way to describe them. Light was shed on this integral piece of America's infrastructure. We walked through a park, and past several churches; I saw a few signs for designated horse crossings. The community was all around me.

Ellen's phone rang. Her husband, John, let her know his brother had had another psychotic break. With their parents vacationing overseas, the brother had boarded himself up in their house, waiting to be attacked. Convinced of his inevitable demise, he had called John to say goodbye.

Ellen and I rushed back to the house, and she and John jumped into the car to drive the four hours to the parents' house to talk to the brother—to try to convince him to let them in so they could take him somewhere safe. It had been a while since anything like this had happened. Ellen and I were disappointed our reunion wasn't longer, but I understood the gravity of the emergency she faced. As they drove off, I stayed behind in their empty house and got ready to sing, as a sense of betrayal and anger grew inside me. I was surprised by my reaction. Maybe it was because Ellen and I had bonded so easily again after a long time apart; maybe because I didn't want to be alone. I tried to remind myself that I did have some time with my friend, and her house was within walking distance of the karaoke venue. I was grateful for the ability to at least be in their home, though that only helped dissipate the loneliness a little.

Given the size of the town, and the fact that college wasn't in session, I figured the pool of karaoke lovers would be thin and the bar wouldn't be crowded. The place was in the middle of a residential area and looked the part. Bright-red front door, flower boxes, and paned windows. I overheard one guy at the bar, drinking a Coke, telling the bartender he "didn't know whether to knock or ring the doorbell" in order to come in. The menu listed choices you might find in an aunt's kitchen: basic sandwiches, fish and chips, and nachos with real cheese melted on top (none of that stadium "cheese" nonsense). Simple fare with homemade flourishes. The beer selection provided craft options as well as the regular American offerings, but I ordered a Labatt's to celebrate Canada Day. As I sipped my beer and looked around, I saw a place where everyone felt at home and seemed to know each other.

The bartender let me know karaoke was set to start at 9 p.m., but the KJ didn't arrive until 9:20. He wore ratty jeans with a "my friend went to XX and all I got was this t-shirt." His fake tan and botox gave his face an artificial boyish glow. His overall demeanor read desperate used-car salesman. When I dropped off my slip, he flashed me a stretched grin and introduced himself as "The Real McCoy." His songbooks advertised himself as "The *Genuine* Real McCoy." My gut said to stay clear of the guy.

Meanwhile, the place began to fill up, and soon it was packed. I was dead wrong about karaoke fans in this small historic town. I observed a cast of characters from all walks of life. Men in dusty red softball uniforms propped themselves up against the bar and ordered pints. A sixty-something group of four dressed in biker gear occupied one table near the front: their leader was a man in full leather, a white mustache, and a skinny ponytail. A woman in a patch-riddled Canadian tuxedo burst in and yelled "I'm here" to the entire bar before she joined her group. A girl in a squeaky voice asked for a "flat" beer, meaning no foam. Her friends mocked her terminology. Both the younger and older groups talked about their high school days in a cross-generational nostalgia. (My heart grew when I heard everyone call everyone else "honey"—customers and servers alike.)

A guy two stools over noticed me taking notes and asked if I was writing a novel. I told him about my quest. "That's very unusual," he replied, and told me he'd just stopped by here after spending the day at an Italian festival; he was from a small town outside of Florence (his accent checked out). I overheard a young woman say, "Drink first, then sing. Very important." She then moved from her table to sit in the chair between me and the Italian, cutting the two of us off from further conversation.

While there were several people in the bar, it wasn't that loud or energetic. McCoy announced it was a slow night because of the holiday weekend, but it was busy enough that I had to take a long way around to get to the mic when my name was called. For my first song, I sang "Run to You" by Bryan Adams, in honor of Canada Day, and found myself holding back notes a bit. I could have done better if I had let loose, but my performance was good enough to generate applause—the loudest coming from the biker table. The Italian said my voice had "presence." He had moved to the stool next to mine while I was gone. He added that he liked karaoke because it's "homey. It's relaxed and comfortable. Not like a nightclub . . . 'homey' is the only word I can think of."

We talked about singer-songwriters, and I found myself having a hard time coming up with any—my brain was in some sort of weird fog. The Italian put forth the theory that a good song had to have a good story behind it. To that end, he wanted me to sing "Piano Man" or a Harry Chapin song like "Taxi" (he didn't like to sing, he said, just to listen). While I agreed those songs were excellent stories, I let him know they were too long and slow for karaoke; he didn't agree, simply because he would want to hear them. I couldn't argue with that.

Though there was a mix of ages in the bar, the music selection was mostly older stuff. A young man in a backwards baseball cap and reddish blond beard sang Frank Sinatra. A clean-cut skinny guy sang the Beatles. There were some older crooners who got up to sing Tom Jones and Dean Martin. It was a step back in time. I put in "Crazy Little Thing Called Love," and when it started to play it was the wrong version—not Queen at all, but more of a big band/swing rendition. I didn't sing the beginning, confused at what I was hearing, so the crowd began to sing, helping me as if I were stuck. I wondered if I should ask for the right version but decided not to, and started to sing. The crowd stopped their support, though I wished they had kept going; I liked the idea of a sing-along. I told McCoy about the version issue, and he disagreed with me—his database said it was Queen, so it must be Queen. But he held my hand and apologized. I let my hand lie limp in his. Not much later, McCoy wandered over and told me about the place: it'd been around since the 1950s, and used to host union meetings. It was now owned by the high school principal. I tried to distance myself from McCoy, but the place was packed, and McCoy had other ideas about personal space. He moved closer to me, handing me his card and allowing his hard-on to press up against my right knee.

As the clock struck midnight, the bar owner/high school principal started passing out free shots to those he knew—which seemed to be everyone but me. There's something about the midnight witching hour when a bar's tenor shifts. It can go dead; it can peak into a frenzy, as it did at Otter's; or it can turn into a complete drunken mess, as it did here. While it felt somewhat lonely to be one of the few without a free shot in front of me, I wasn't interested in drinking more, knowing it was best to keep my wits about me even though I wasn't driving. A few more rounds of free shots came and went, and drunk people became drunker. Men who could still focus started staring in my direction, seeing me as a fresh specimen, a single female never touched by anyone in the room before. I felt the creepy realization that happens when you're a woman alone in a room full of drunk men—it's no longer a matter of *whether* something horrible will happen, but how and when. It's a shitty feeling, but one that needs to be heeded. It was time to go and accept the fact that for the first time on this trip, I faced the reality of not feeling safe as a single woman in a bar late at night. It sucked. Though I wasn't quite ready to leave, I was done watching the pick-ups, shots, and people getting ready to drive home when they shouldn't.

The beginning of the night had been great, when there were more crooners than belters, and the buzzes were quieter. Before the drunken performances of "Low Places" and "Paradise by the Dashboard Light." When the bar was a home, complete with flower boxes and a doorbell. I snuck out while McCoy was occupied with his job and people were leaning into each other for stability. I felt bad I didn't say goodbye to the Italian; he was a nice man.

CHAPTER 20

A CANADIAN INTERLUDE

July 2-10. 2016

I HID FROM AMERICA ON ITS BIRTHDAY BY SPENDING A WEEK IN Toronto with my aunt and uncle, hoping to recharge and relax after twenty-four days on the road. Meanwhile, my home country fell apart. Right after Independence Day, a stretch of violence so horrible occurred that it was hard to get up in the morning:

On July 5, Alton Brown Sterling was pinned down and shot several times at close range by police in Baton Rouge, Louisiana. He died on scene.

On July 6, Philando Castile was shot and killed by police in Minnesota during a routine traffic stop. His girlfriend and her four-year-old child were in the car.

On July 7, a man targeted police officers during a protest held in response to the killings of Sterling and Castile. Five officers died and nine others were injured.

Though I was grateful to be somewhat distanced from the

horrors of my homeland, my heart sank into my stomach—
staying there, bracing for the next act of hate. I read
everything I could about the violence, about racism, about a
nation falling apart. Article after article—I immersed myself
in the details, the analyses, and the reflections, in hopes of
finding an answer to it all—systemic racism, gun control, fear,
an America divided. Black Lives Matter was replaced by "Blue
Lives Matter" and "All Lives Matter." The more I read, the less
I believed in anything.

Still, I did my best to take care of myself—to process the
multiple layers of grief that built upon each other. I got my hair
cut (Molly would have approved of the layers, but rolled her
eyes at the new strawberry-blonde color), painted my toenails
bright purple, bought two new dresses at my favorite boutique,
and ate homemade Caesar salad every night. And yes, I sang.

CHAPTER 21

NEW YORK

July 11. 2016

I LEFT TORONTO REFRESHED, BUT ALSO WITH A HEAVY HEART. IT'S always hard for me to leave a city that makes me feel so alive, and it was hard to re-enter the United States after all that had happened. Each time I turned on the news, I listened in fear of another shooting, another retaliation, another act of violence perpetrated by fellow Americans on our country. The sterile drive of Interstate 90 added to my sorrows, even though I was excited to be on the road again. I had a lot to be grateful for: my car and I were fully rested, my cooler re-stocked with healthy snacks—boiled eggs, red currants, and carrots. I was back on my quest.

I arrived in Albany before Beatrice, a former student of mine, got out of jury duty. When we had first met, she was looking for an academic adviser for her internship at Cascade AIDS Project. Since I was the human sexuality instructor, it was a natural fit. Each week she would come into my office a little torn up and angry. Her job at Cascade was to hand out condoms where sex workers often hung out. That part of her job was fine. What she had a hard time with was when the kids—some too young for a training bra—would walk up to her table, holding the hand of an adult woman, and say, "Look! Free supplies!" It wasn't her place to report anyone, no matter how young; it wasn't that she could prove anything, and the condoms she distributed were available to anyone who wanted them, no questions asked. But I shared her inner torment as she disclosed her growing understanding of how men learned to pay for underage sex. Women of age would wander around the streets and offer their services, and then ask if there was "something special" a potential customer would want. And that something special—a child who knew what supplies were—would be waiting in a nearby hotel room. The children never walked the streets; that would have been too risky for all involved. So they hid away, waiting for men to abuse them, and there wasn't anything Beatrice could do about it.

That internship did little to scare Beatrice away from working in HIV education. Actually, it strengthened her resolve and drove her further into the field. Her next volunteer position was in Ghana, where she developed health curricula for women. A couple of years later, she worked in South Africa, distributing condoms and educational pamphlets during the World Cup. And now, in Albany, she worked for the State of New York, a place with one of the highest rates of HIV/AIDS in the US. I envied her career path—and truth be told, I could have done something similar. But back then, while Beatrice was handing out condoms to people in Portland, Oregon, I stayed within the safe walls of the ivory tower and merely discussed the actions she undertook. Back then, I didn't feel I had the time to volunteer. And when I heard about her overseas plans, I was living with a partner who hated to travel, and hated the idea of me traveling. I didn't have the guts to drop everything—relationship, job, paycheck—to do what I longed for, but only dreamed of doing.

I parked in Beatrice's neighbor's driveway, not hers—I discovered my mistake when a woman with a broad smile and flowered housecoat wondered what I was doing there, and then kindly pointed one house over. She told me her "asshole brother-in-law" needed to leave, and I was blocking his pickup. She then said that if Beatrice and I were going to drink wine in the backyard, to give her a call. I thanked her and moved one house over, signaling her two Labs—one yellow, one black—to start barking. I remembered meeting the yellow one as a puppy during office hours, when Beatrice would come by—the bundle of squirm at her feet as we discussed HIV prevention in Portland.

Soon Beatrice was home from jury duty (they acquitted), and minutes later her husband and daughter arrived as well. He barbecued out back and we caught up on life as Caitlin, the girl, demanded attention and admiration for flipping on the swings and watering the plants. The backyard was surrounded by tall trees and peace; a couple of rabbits carefully hung out on the fringes until the dogs took interest and took up fruitless chase, returning, panting, satisfied with their efforts. As we talked about our lives over the past five years, I could feel Beatrice's admiration for me, which I did not think I deserved. The student had far outpaced the teacher in terms of having her shit together. I was proud of her and her accomplishments, yet she seemed to think everything I did was far more interesting. Beatrice had a job that mattered, in the field I always assumed I would pursue. Instead, here I was, traveling and singing, and when that was done, there was no next step, no life goal still undone (except for singing in Alaska and Hawaii, of course).

Stomachs full with pork chops and corn on the cob, we set off to the city center to sing. Beatrice was the one who found this place; all my online investigating of karaoke in Albany had come up empty for a Monday night. Yet through her work connections, Beatrice found a dive of a gay bar that hosted karaoke to kick off the week.

New York's state capital is a gritty place. As we passed through the city university campus, Beatrice shared stories of murders and rapes. People were lingering about, sitting on stoops, walking in the middle of the street, hovering over each other on street corners, hiding whatever it was they were doing. There were iron bars on all the shop windows, except for the ones that were covered in plywood. Beatrice and I circled the block a few times in order to find the entrance to the alley parking lot behind the bar. It was well lit and out of the way of general street traffic, so Beatrice thought it was safest.

We used the back entrance and passed a red, carnival-style machine spouting out free popcorn. I had no idea how a buttery smell didn't dominate the place. In a glass wall case was an array of dildos of all different shapes and sizes—one brand offered a five-and-a-half-inch cock, a seven-inch cock, and an eight-inch dong. (I guess I now knew the difference between a cock and a dong: one crucial inch.) A few anal plugs, a harness, and a pair of leather cuffs rounded out the selection.

A genderfluid couple was twerking and grinding on the dance floor; one was wearing only a long grey t-shirt and pink jockey shorts. Beatrice said he was an "underwear boy." Common in Albany, underwear boys frequent gay bars and are tolerated by the city, despite their clear intentions to serve as not-quite-legal companions. In her work in the HIV/AIDS department, they even made special underwear for them to promote condom usage. We talked about how that probably wouldn't have happened if these barely legal youth had been females, servicing men in gentlemen's clubs.

More and more people entered the bar, and karaoke time drew near. The KJ stationed himself behind a large black podium and turned on a voiceover promising that this night would feature "the best karaoke in the Capital District." The stage filled up with lights and smoke from a rickety machine. Recorded applause played at the end of every song. Names like Craiggers, Barbie, Jamroc, Mystery, and LD scrolled along the screen as everyone waited their turn. A woman with bright-red lipstick and pale-blue eyeshadow made a dramatic entrance, covering her left ear to tune herself better as she sang along loudly with the performer on stage; it was difficult to tell who was holding the mic. When it was her turn to actually perform, she sang a passionate version of Radiohead's "Creep" that the bar appreciated, clapping loud enough to drown out the canned stuff.

A tall, mocha-skinned woman in a striped summer dress, backwards ball cap, and Keds wandered over to Beatrice and me to make conversation. She said she came here to "practice"—her goal was to be a songwriter, but she didn't feel she had the talent to sing her own stuff. She was wrong. Her energy, style, and vocal abilities were top-notch. I had no idea what it was that she sang, but it was good—slow, sultry, decadent. When it was my turn, she cheered loudly in between sips of red wine. My '70s and '80s song choices didn't quite fit in with this crowd, yet it was all good. Between the aspiring singer and Beatrice, I felt supported.

C H A P T E R   2 2

CONNECTICUT

July 13. 2016

IT WAS MY LAST DAY SOLO ON THE ROAD. THE NEXT MORNING, I would make the drive to JFK to pick up Dave, who would join me for the rest of the journey. The seventeen states I had traveled to on my own had given me a larger understanding of America, karaoke culture, and my place in both. They also had my parents worried. Though I am middle-aged, and had traveled to several different countries spanning several different continents, it was this American trip that had them most concerned: a woman alone in bars, in a different place every night, sometimes in a place where no one knew where I was. I found the idea of being completely unknown a little lonely but mostly freeing. I turned down my dad's suggestion to carry mace or some other weapon, as I wasn't sure of the legality of doing so in different states. It would have been more stressful for me to deal with that unknown than the unknowns of the places I was visiting. Plus, the idea of carrying a weapon made me feel more defeated than empowered.

My parents were worried about me for another reason: though I had a part-time job to go back to in the fall, I really wasn't sure where my career path was headed. I was growing tired of Academe, tired of chasing grant funds, tired of the politics and the egos and the entitlement of the ivory tower. Desperate to help and needing to control some part of my life, my dad encouraged me to meet with his old boss, someone he felt was well-connected in fields where I could thrive. I didn't feel I could say no, so I drove to a small, rich town off a Connecticut bay, and met a man I hadn't seen since I was a child—a man who, in my dad's eyes, could set me on track for a successful future.

Over homemade chicken salad with grapes and two kinds of deviled eggs, the man and I talked about German blue-grass bands, memories of the Berlin Wall coming down, our travels to Latvia, and old family friends. Conversations were plentiful but awkward; Dad's desperate attempt to help me onto the right path of a successful and prestigious career led me to a dead end; Dr. White had long since retired, leaving him enough out of the loop that he really couldn't help me beyond what I could research online. It wasn't his fault; it's just that networks grow quiet with time. Eventually we sat in silence on his veranda, overlooking the bay and yachts sailing by. The house, on the water down a private road, was modest and rustic, its kitchen tiny and closed in, with no room to socialize as someone was preparing a meal.

When his wife sat down to join us, the political discussions began, slowly, hesitantly, and at the expense of Dr. White's dignity. As his wife grew braver and more willing to throw out her anti-Hillary Clinton rhetoric, he sunk further into his white wicker chair. To her, Hillary was nothing but dishonest; none of her accomplishments mattered, she was nothing but a cheater and a liar. "She's such a bitch," she spat. "No one would ever be stupid enough to vote for someone like her who will ruin our country." Then her venting turned to how "universities teach Marxism," preventing any healthy dialogue among the best and the brightest. Dr. White muttered a request to end the political discussions as he grabbed another deviled egg. I tried to listen with an open mind and heart, but all I could hear was her entitlement.

In her eyes, Trump was going to save our nation from all that was wrong with it. I had no idea a system could feel so broken to someone who had experienced it so well, but she rattled off plenty of faults—high taxes, lack of safety, political corruption. As a privileged American, I, too, saw our country as seriously broken, but for very different reasons. Her concerns didn't address social justice or equality. She seemed to want even more than she already had. I had a hard time envisioning a political system that could offer her what she felt was missing. Yet her desperation, her visceral sense that the USA was failing was clear. I carefully questioned her opinions, and provided alternative viewpoints, but never turned the conversation into a full-blown debate. Eventually, our conversations returned to easier topics, and Dr. White sat up a little straighter, wiping sweat from his brow with a cloth napkin. A chipmunk ran across the patio. I got up to take pictures of the beautiful view, ensuring a shift in conversation.

When it was time to go, the wife hugged me tightly and for a long time, and whispered pleas in my ear: "I wish you well in your future. Our nation depends on your generation. I'm so afraid." I felt her fear through her embrace, electric waves of uncertainty pulsing into my core. I heard her desperation to make America "great again" in her shaking voice. For the life of me I still couldn't understand her perspective. I thanked her for the meal, shook Dr. White's hand, and briefly thought about how I would never see these people again.

On the relatively short drive to my hotel, I took the side roads after yet another morning on interstates—I think I counted five interchanges, signaling that I was officially in the densely populated East Coast, where a network of asphalt takes everyone everywhere. Unlike the small towns I'd driven through in the Midwest—towns of historical grandeur with home-life simplicity—these small towns promoted their wealth. As I skirted the coast, I saw yachts, and old-money mansions on large plots of land. Lawns were crisp green and neatly clipped, all shrubs sculpted to perfection.

An Indian woman wearing rich jewel tones lined with gold checked me into my hotel room. Behind her, I could see glimpses of her home and family. Ornate decor: pillows in golds, reds, and purples. A rich blue-and-red carpet. Two kids playing. Smells of turmeric and saffron. Their home, despite being on the premises, was so different from the motel itself, which was dingy and frayed but well-kept. But I guess that was the point: If you were going to live where you worked, you needed to differentiate it from the guests to save yourself, and make sure you didn't lose who you were in a place where everyone else came and went.

I called the karaoke bar and learned the place was closed on Tuesdays. I was grateful for my obsessive need to check and double-check everything, and instead spent the evening writing and planning my route. It was my last night alone, and I passed the time exactly that way, not even venturing out of the room for dinner.

I woke up earlier than usual, actually setting an alarm to make sure I would arrive at the airport in time to get Dave. Our communication was going to be limited at best, given his lack of a cell phone that worked in the United States. Just like in the "old days" we had to rely on the fact that we would both be somewhere around the customs/international terminal and somehow find each other in one of the largest airports in the world. I entered the throngs of people in their daily commutes to New York City. It would cost eight bucks to cross the bridge to get to the airport, and another eight to come back over. People cannot live in Connecticut and work in NYC unless they have high-paying jobs. No way any of the people who accompanied me this morning were driving to a job at a diner, a convenience store, or even to work in a residential treatment center or teach a room full of students.

The drive was fine for a stretch, and then I settled into a thickness of cars, each inhabited by one person on their phone, eating, or putting on makeup. This was the multitasking of those who felt there wasn't enough time in a day to take care of basic needs without doing something else. I felt sorry for them.

Then I felt a sudden *bang* as my body thrust forward, my seatbelt grabbing my chest, my chest grabbing my heart, as I was forced back into my seat. I had been rear-ended.

I screamed and punched the steering wheel, then pulled over. The other driver didn't. Fucking hit-and-run. There was no way I was ever going to find the perpetrator in the steady stream of cars. All I remembered was that the driver was young, had dark curly hair, drove a white Japanese sedan, and was an asshole. One of hundreds around me. Fuck him and this whole damn state. I felt foolish for believing in humanity while surrounded by a sea of Connecticut's Manhattan commuters.

I assessed my car's damage and concluded it was minimal—though there was evidence of impact, no one was going fast enough to inflict too much damage. So I kept on driving. My poor car had been nothing but gold, treating me with comfort and respect for my whole journey thus far, and now it suffered a dented bumper and scraped license plate. I had to get Dave; with no way to communicate what happened, and no way of finding the guy who did this, there was no point in waiting for police to take a report, and no point involving insurance. I kept on going, turning my Buddha's face to anger and continuing my screaming rant until I was done, letting my impressions of self-entitled Connecticut fester into a simmering hatred. Fuck him. Fuck the East Coast.

I parked in a multistoried structure and looked at my car again. She was going to be fine, I convinced myself, and I gave her a pat on the roof and expressions of gratitude. I started to breathe a little easier. I found Dave with no problem; he was sitting in the corner of the terminal, on the ground, with his bright-orange backpack, gigantic suitcase, mussed hair in dire need of a cut, and ill-fitting clothes that dwarfed his already smallish stature. Our meeting was an understated hug and peck, but that was enough for now. My nerves from the wreck, from my concerns of finding him, from wondering how I would feel with him around, dissipated completely. I felt soothed and complete now that we were together.

At the car, he crawled under the rear axle to make sure everything looked OK. I had booked a second night in the same hotel so I could sing in Connecticut and Dave would have somewhere to sleep right away. Tired from his twenty-plus hour flight, Dave was in no mood to play tourist in New York. Seeing Ground Zero and eating one of the world's best Reubens would to have to wait for another adventure. While dealing with the traffic getting off Long Island, my trip odometer rolled past 6,000 miles. 6,000 solo miles, and now companionship for the rest of my journey.

We passed back through the wealth of Connecticut—so many expensive car dealerships showing off their large inventories out front. Ferrari, Lamborghini, Rolls-Royce; the Mercedes dealership tagging along under the shadows of the true luxury cars. Dave and I agreed that the only time either of us had seen this many cars that cost this much was in Dubai—and even then, not in mass quantities like this, but parked in front of the fanciest hotels, or driving down the street in front of the higher-end shopping centers and clubs. This was richness at a whole different level—restored revolutionary mansions, no mix of rich and poor—just money as far as the eye could see. Everything was cleaner, more ornate, more special than normal. This was the picture of success that was given to me growing up in New Jersey in the '80s. But now I felt uncomfortable and angry. No one needs this much.

As we got farther from the Manhattan commute radius, the small towns grew more humble. Moss on the roofs of some houses, driveways with ruts. We drove through Stamford and I told Dave the story about how when I told people I was going to Stanford for college, many thought I meant here, and I let them. I didn't want anyone to know I was smart. (I still don't.) We got to the hotel and Dave proceeded to sleep for six hours, deciding not to join me for karaoke after all. I was a little passive aggressive and whiny, disappointed over changed plans. One last night of singing alone.

Negotiating downtown New Haven wasn't easy; Crown Street was closed for a block, so I had to circle around to find an open road to get to where I wanted to be. I did an excellent job of parallel parking and felt slightly smug about it. The area was sterile—new, shiny buildings and smooth, white sidewalks. Everything so polished to cater to Yale students and newly minted grads. I didn't see much of the other side of New Haven—the part that inspired the first-ever needle exchange program in the US. The part that placed New Haven among the cities with the highest crime rates. Instead, my time in Connecticut was all spent surrounded by the haves—the ones who turned the electric shock dial all the way up during Stanley Milgram's famous experiments demonstrating the power of obedience and deference to authority. If the rules work for you, you might as well play by them.

I walked down an unmarked alleyway and entered the bar. The place felt dark, cozy, and friendly. The bartender (white) and a band promo guy (African American with dreads) were the only two people there. Together, the three of us talked about beer, and the ins and outs of promoting gigs on social media. It was the first genuine kindness I had felt in Connecticut. I hung out for a while, expecting the crowd to build. The large stage to my right remained empty. It didn't look like anyone was considering a performance, and that was because no one was. I asked the bartender when the karaoke was going to begin, and he let me know I was in the wrong place. I finished my beer and went farther down the alley, somewhat regretfully, to where I was supposed to be.

The look of Karaoke Heroes was completely different from the first bar. It was light, airy, and made to look like a private singing room reminiscent of an Asian karaoke establishment. Comic strip images decorated the walls, and I took a seat in an orange plastic chair at a white plastic table. Silver pleather couches lined the walls, and there was a small raised seating area with light-blue chairs and silver ottomans. A group of women sat upstairs, behind a table full of empty Corona bottles and tall cocktail glasses. A couple sat at one of the tables in the corner with a tray full of beer cans. A few men weaved unsteadily around the bar, seeking purpose; one of them tried to hit on me and seemed visibly irked that I didn't care to engage. There was no stage area, so singers just wandered around the tables or stood awkwardly in the center of everything as people crossed in front and behind to get to the loo or order another drink. When someone was finished singing, they either put the microphone down on one of the tables or light-blue chairs, or stood around holding it until the next singer grabbed it.

To put in a song, I needed to go up to the bartender—a young tattooed white guy who gave zero fucks and who often wasn't behind the bar, or even in the room—and ask for a slip of paper. He gave one to me, but only after I had ordered and paid for a below-average, overpriced drink. After I wrote my song down, the bartender told me to put the small piece of paper by the unmanned computer. Eventually, he programmed my choice in and eventually it would show up on the screen— just the song title, no name. No KJ announcing when a song was over and who was up next. The karaoke order was dictated by a list of songs on a little screen that everyone needed to follow to see when it was time to go up and sing.

Because so many people were drunk, not everyone had an idea when they were supposed to sing. The women upstairs would see a song and wonder whose it was, assuming pretty much all the songs were theirs. They certainly dominated the singing that night, primarily performing classic '80s tunes. During their rendition of "Time of My Life," they attempted the *Dirty Dancing* leap to no avail (this was probably fortunate). Besides me, they also had to share the microphone with an amazing singer wearing a cap with a Superman logo, Superman t-shirt, and nerd glasses. Clark Kent in a sea of chaos. While he sang amazing covers of Muse and Queen, his hands shook the entire time. The tremors seemed uncontrollable as his microphone waved spastically and the hand at his side constantly hit his thigh. When he was done—after the applause, and after he had relinquished the mic—his hands turned steady again as he drank his beer.

The focus of Heroes seemed to be more about making sure patrons paid for their drinks than creating a community of song. The place lacked karaoke's fun and passion. Like the bar in Peoria, it was a place without a KJ to hold the evening together. All that remained was a bunch of disconnected people waiting their turn, drinking when they weren't performing to no one. Too bad the first bar hadn't been the right place after all.

CHAPTER 23
RHODE ISLAND
July 14, 2016

DAVE AND I WOKE UP SLOWLY, STEADILY, ENJOYING THE COMPANY of a shared bed. I wandered to the hotel lobby before I remembered the only breakfast they offered was stale doughnuts and cheap coffee; I grabbed the latter for Dave as he sat up and relished his regained ability to read the news on an internet uncensored by the government. The main headline that day was the attack in Nice, France, where an ISIL supporter drove a cargo truck into a large crowd, killing 86 and injuring hundreds of others. Adjustments back to one's home country—reverse culture shock—require adjusting beyond the simple changes of time zone. I remember coming back from the Middle East and immediately feeling overwhelmed by American grocery stores. The lights, the number of options, the wide aisles all so overwhelming that it took me months before I was comfortable navigating them again. But being able to read anything, anywhere, no matter how tragic, is immediately appreciated.

Our day was spent driving slowly over the back roads of Connecticut, where almost every house was painted white and adorned by a barn star. We stopped to walk around one small town established in the 1770s, admiring the churches and statues of Revolutionary heroes; Independence Day decorations still adorned the local library and old yellowed country store. Upon our arrival in Rhode Island, a large banner outside the local McDonald's advertised a lobster roll—an amusing offer we couldn't refuse. Fast food isn't normally something I crave, or even tolerate, but in this case it seemed to be more about the local culture than part of the generic global phenomenon. The roll itself wasn't that bad—real lobster, and lots of it—but the dry bread was too close to a generic hamburger bun to really make the sandwich authentic. We vowed to try the real deal when we got to Maine.

I was both grateful and surprised the karaoke started at 7 p.m.—I can think of numerous times, especially after a happy hour, when I wished there was karaoke that started earlier so I could maintain the momentum of a light buzz and transition into an early night of song. On school nights, waiting until 9 or 10 p.m. to start singing rarely makes sense for me. Dave and I arrived around six thirty and each ordered the five-dollar all-you-can-eat pizza special; the place was packed with others doing the same. Though the pizza was fair at best, Dave wolfed it down, happy to get any form of pizza after six months in a country with minimal cheese. A greasy pepperoni square simply doesn't exist in rural China. A family of six—parents, three kids, and Grandma—each filled their plates and took seats at a front table. After a few bites, they started playing a card game that looked like a cross between Harry Potter and UNO. A large fan blew behind us, creating an unbearable wind that blew my hair straight into my meal. So we changed tables to get away from its strength.

Our KJ that night was Timmy Tune, an older guy with excellent posture wearing a tie-dye t-shirt with a peace sign. Although I was the first person to put my song in, Timmy let me know that he was letting Bob lead off the show "because he helped carry the equipment in for me." Timmy proceeded to put singers into the rotation without any more requests coming through, placing each performer in the order they came through the door. Eight names scrolled at the bottom of the monitor. By seven on the nose, the show was ready to begin. Singers included older men, middle-aged women holding martini glasses, and a guy named "Bongo George," whose namesake lay at his feet. Even though Timmy tried to get him to play, the instrument remained untouched through the night. A developmentally disabled woman sang often; she had a decent voice, and used it to entertain the crowd with '80s female rockers such as Joan Jett and Pat Benatar. After every song by every performer, she walked up to Timmy to see if it was her turn again; everyone was very patient, except her caregiver, who seemed to constantly be wrangling her to sit down. She sang "Margaritaville" with the bartender, giggling at the end of the song when the lyrics called upon her to sing "It's my own *damn* fault." She looked at her caregiver and covered her mouth, the satisfied grin from using such language still showing through. The table that included a blind man and a woman with an oxygen tank cheered the loudest at the rebellion.

The most unanticipated singer of the evening was an eight-year-old girl in pigtails and a bright-green soccer uniform. With the support of her adult companion, she went up to Timmy Tune and carefully chose her songs. First, it was Taylor Swift's "Blank Space." The kid sang with confidence and sass, putting in a few dances moves and hip sways in between verses about playing the numbers game when it came to relationships. It was hard not to laugh, but I did my best. I didn't want to seem unsupportive.

I considered karaoke to be an adult activity—probably because I associated it with bar culture. Yet singing has no upper or lower age restrictions. Anyone with a voice can express themselves through song. I'm glad there are opportunities for younger people to sing karaoke now—both at-home setups and these public events I'm now starting to see more and more of. Whether it's because there are actually more of them, or I'm just starting to notice, I have no idea. The first time I noticed "all-ages karaoke" was just a few years prior, when I saw it advertised on the marquee of a Chinese restaurant in Portland. No matter. Because of these opportunities, I'm going to believe that for some of these kids, getting ahold of that microphone and singing their hearts out to Adele, Katy Perry, 5 Seconds of Summer, or whoever they are listening to that moment, is saving them from loneliness, and allowing them to hear cheers specifically for them. Every kid deserves to hear those.

I wondered how my life would have been different if there had been a chance for me to sing karaoke at an early age. It simply was a non-opportunity, like not being able to be melodramatic on Facebook about how misunderstood I was, or texting friends surreptitiously during class. But if I had been able to go to a place, get up on a stage, or at least grab a microphone and sing songs from *Grease*, or something by Pat Benatar or Laura Branigan (that is, the stuff I sing now, but when it was actually popular), and hear applause when I was done, I think it would have helped me. A lot. I was far from happy starting around junior high, and really struggling to fit in. I was embarrassed that I was smart, not quite athletic enough to be praised for my sports accomplishments, not pretty enough or something enough to be considered really datable. Maybe a formal singing outlet would have been that little push I needed to feel good about myself. Or maybe it would have just been another thing I would have criticized myself over, turning myself off to karaoke forever.

Later, the soccer girl got up to sing "So What" by P!nk. More lyrics turned humorous when sung by an enthusiastic, athletic child in whom I could see a younger version of myself. This time, she bounced up and down to references of losing her husband and drinking her paycheck.

CHAPTER 24

NEW HAMPSHIRE

July 15, 2016

N EW HAMPSHIRE SMELLED WONDERFUL—SHARP CLEAN AIR
punched with evergreen. Such a small state emitting a
large presence; it felt as though we were a long way from anywhere, even though Boston was only a couple of hours away.
We drove down small roads peppered with country stores,
farms, and forest. One small shop served ice cream, sold
canned goods, and featured a wonderful deli counter complete
with liverwurst. Dave bought a Budweiser and I had my first
pickled egg, bright pink from beet juice. It was delicious, and I
silently chastised myself for waiting so long to try one, its color
and inelegant title shaping my apprehension until now. This
trip was all about taking risks, no matter how small.

We scored one of the last hotel rooms near the karaoke
venue after several attempts to find lodging. It was double the
usual price. A friend of mine who had grown up near here
had warned me not to stay in New Hampshire on NASCAR

weekends—yet here we were, paying the price. We parked my car among a sea of large pickups and dented Buicks to rest up a bit before singing.

The dirt parking lot of our karaoke destination was full of motorcycles and cars with out-of-state plates. Outside, a block-letter sign on the door read "No Patches," a request to bikers to not show their gang affiliations. This bar was neutral territory. Inside, the décor was Boston-sports-meets-ski-lodge-and-wood-peckers—fittingly, since the bar was called Woodpeckers. An obese man played an arcade shooting game. The pool tables lay dormant. Lots of people were playing cornhole on the side patio lit with white Christmas lights. The taps weren't familiar: Switchback, Tuckerman Pale, Pig's Ear Brown. We ordered so-so nachos and listened to an acoustic guitarist; I felt bad for him, performing inside to no one. There weren't any speakers to pipe his voice outside. He wore a tattered brown leather coat and sang things I expected—James Taylor and other folksy stuff—but also did a cover of Blondie's "Heart of Glass," one of my typical karaoke warm-ups. I laughed to Dave that he was stealing my material.

Eventually the lonely entertainer packed up, scooping up the three singles that had landed in his guitar case. The KJ announced a Sam Adams giveaway raffle in order to entice singers, to no avail, but that didn't deter her much. Her serious hustling continued: "Ladies and gentlemen, all you have to do to win a prize is sing a song! You could win a bunch of Sam Adams stuff, including a table umbrella and a beer cozy! Sing a song and your name goes right here in this bucket!" She held up a silver pail with a few slips settled at the bottom. The drawing wasn't until 11:30, and I was already beat. So was Dave, but he had just flown from China. I had no excuse.

A guy in dark sunglasses and a black leather hat sat at the bar and drank water before he got up to sing "Rhine-stone Cowboy." I had read about these sorts of singers on the

Karaoke Across America message boards, but never really noticed them before: people who don't bother to buy anything from the bar but take advantage of the free entertainment. In online forums, KJs stressed the importance of actually buying something if you were going to sing. If a KJ didn't draw in paying customers, she wouldn't have a job for long, and you wouldn't have a place to perform.

When it was time for me to sing, I told the KJ to not bother putting my slip in the bucket; she slumped her shoulders in resignation, and I felt bad. Maybe I should have just let her believe I was going to be there longer than it took to sing my song and check New Hampshire off my list. As the KJ cued up my Bonnie Raitt, she looked over at me and said, "I can tell you're going to be good." I had no idea if she said that to everyone, but it helped me. I beamed at her encouragement, and found the strength I needed to uplift my weary voice. Off to the side, I saw the KJ grooving to my rendition, mouthing the words and closing her eyes as she swayed to its bluesy beat. I finished my song, and the KJ went back to encouraging others to sing, trying to tempt them into taking the stage with the allure of Sam Adams gear. This is the sort of place that seemed to have more vacationers and travelers than regulars, and I doubted anyone would ever be there to win that umbrella.

CHAPTER 25

MASSACHUSETTS

July 16, 2016

THE DEUCE CAME UP AS A MUST-SING-AT BAR IN MASSACHUSETTS when Dave posted a request for recommendations on Reddit. While he was in China, he let the hive mind of primarily young, white men know that his girlfriend was driving around the country with the goal of singing in the whole Lower 48 and was soliciting suggestions. Most of the bars mentioned were from either Portland, Oregon, or California. Between my place in Portland and Dave's home base in Sacramento, we had those covered, but the conversations were entertaining. What made a good karaoke bar in the eyes of Reddit users? Mostly large crowds (Otter's in Minneapolis certainly fit that bill) and good drink specials. Sometimes there was something unique about the bar or the clientele. For example, someone suggested a bar in Nashville because it was a double-wide trailer always decorated for Christmas. We put that on the list. Another bar in Los Angeles was mentioned because porn stars go there on their nights off. The Deuce's draw was that it was a fun, packed place with a history of catering to WWII vets and a working periscope from an old submarine.

Dave doesn't like to sing karaoke, though he did once when we were in South Korea, where karaoke is extremely popular. There, however, as in most of Asia, karaoke primarily takes place in private rooms. In Korea they are called *noraebang*, which translates as "song room." These places are rented by the hour by groups of people who either take turns singing to others in the room, or everyone joins in song together; there are even rudimentary musical instruments—maracas, tambourines, cowbells—so you can provide additional musical accompaniment. Many of the songs also have strange videos that play along with the lyrics. The videos often have nothing to do with the theme of the song, possibly because whoever was making them had no idea what the lyrics meant. Most of these videos were also filmed in the 1980s, so there are a lot of big-hair styles and acid-washed jeans. *Noraebangs* are also known as places where men can hire additional "companions"—beautiful young women who will sing with them or perhaps entertain them in other ways. So, there are several differences between the karaoke experiences of South Korea and America; what they do have in common, however, is their pairing with booze. Technically, in a *noraebang*, the proprietors are supposed to get the booze for you, but we decided to cut out the middleman by taking ourselves to the nearby 7-Eleven—yes, they have those in Korea—and smuggling cheap bottles into the private singing room ourselves. What resulted was Dave singing in some weird gravelly falsetto that in no way resembled his actual voice. It was also there that I learned that Air Supply is an excellent karaoke option.

The Deuce itself was huge—a large open space with dark green walls and Kelly green carpet wherever the dance floor wasn't. The dark wooden chairs had green vinyl seats, and the lighting was too bad for me to figure out if the round tabletops were black or a deep shade of forest. The kitchen was out of commission due to a water pipe that had burst way back in January. Our bartender, a lithe woman with short brown hair whom I'd pick first to be on my team in any fight, showed us local takeout options and told us she would get them to deliver here. To my surprise, Dave chose Chinese food; apparently you can't get General Tso's chicken in China. The bartender recommended we get our food from a "really authentic" Taiwanese/Japanese place. I ordered a shiitake maki because I wasn't sure how much to trust fish-based sushi from a generic Asian restaurant in inland Massachusetts, no matter how authentic. Our food came more quickly than I imagined and wasn't half bad; Dave was just happy his General Tso's chicken was indeed chicken (and not dog or cat, like he'd had on that tropical island where he lived in China).

There weren't many people in the bar—just me and Dave, the bartender, a guy with a large mustache shooting pool by himself, and an older man who looked like a Hollywood-cast "fat guy biker" drinking ginger ale, sitting at the corner of the bar. The bartender let us know Charlie, the biker, had had a stroke a couple of months before, and this was one of the only places he remembered now; it was, in fact, the third time he had stopped by that day. His wife sent him here as often as she could. The bartender then wondered whether it was going to be a "SSS—Saturday Shit Show," one of those nights when the forces aligned such that no one ended up coming out and the bar remained quiet all night. It seemed like that might be the case. We ate our food, and still no one came except for the KJ. *You, Me, and Dupree*, with Kate Hudson and Owen Wilson, played on the overhead TVs.

I handed the KJ my song choice, Chicago's "Saturday in the Park," on a slip, even though there was no reason to waste the paper. I'd never sung that song before, but as there was no one around I figured it didn't matter. She thanked me as she took the slip, but didn't cue it up right away. A bachelorette party appeared, and then something went down. I wasn't sure what, but apparently Charlie said something to the bride-to-be, who was wearing an actual wedding dress—something about her being a fool to wear all white. It was enough to chase the party out before the first song they'd put on the jukebox was over. The bartender shoved her finger into Charlie's face, and scolded him for chasing customers away.

"They were customers?" He truly looked confused, scanning the bar as if finally realizing where he was.

"All people who come into this bar are customers, Charlie," she declared. Her shoulders dropped. He pouted. She told him never to do that again, but I had my doubts. Ever since the stroke, she said, his filter was more than a little off. Moments later, a second bridal party came in, and the bartender shot Charlie a stern look. He didn't say a word.

As more people, mostly women, streamed in over the next thirty or forty-five minutes, the KJ finally decided there was enough of an audience for singing, killed the jukebox, and called my name. My experimental choice no longer seemed like such a good idea, but I sang it anyway. One woman made eye contact with me throughout the song, nodded her head to the beat, and flashed a big smile in my direction, letting me know someone cared, or at least was paying attention. It felt nice. It was also nice that the rest of the crowd seemed to treat me more as background noise than the prime entertainment. Hiding in plain sight is sometimes a welcome feature of a somewhat off karaoke performance.

By the end of the evening, it was pretty clear this was a lesbian bar: women holding hands, standing close, males few and far between. A large group of people wearing tiny apricot-sized hats—cowboy, fez, sombrero, firefighter—poured in. Everyone was female except for one guy, who wore a mini chef hat. The apparent guest of honor, the one wearing a tiny crown, asked the bartender to keep her present—an inflatable slice of pizza designed for lounging around in a pool—safe behind the bar. "Can I trust you with my six-foot inflatable pizza raft?" Her question and smile were sweetly flirtatious.

By ten thirty, the place was packed; another bartender was called in to help. It was apparent karaoke was a big draw, but at the same time it wasn't the main event. Lots of singers were queued up to sing, but no one seemed to listen. The talent overall was mixed. One bridal party mostly sang in pairs, and as the evening wore on they did their best to hold each other up, both figuratively and literally. It was a great crowd, but the system was cranked so loud I could no longer have a conversation with Dave; people leaned in and yelled at each other to compete with pool balls smacking, karaoke singers wailing, people laughing, glasses sloshing and clinking. When my name was called again a couple of hours later, I screamed my second song more than sang it, just to be able to hear myself. (Pat Benatar was better for that than 1970s Chicago.) I saw people bobbing up and down to my music as they chatted with their friends. At least it wasn't another Saturday Shit Show.

CHAPTER 26

MAINE

July 19, 2016

YOU HAVE TO BE TOUGH TO LIVE IN MAINE. SO FAR NORTH, BARELY attached to the rest of the country, Maine stretches up into seeming nothingness, its rugged coastline and ice-blue waves daring fishers to come out and earn their keep. A row of antique shops, tired from the wind and snow of winter and the endless baking of a sunny summer, featured pockmarked buoys, lobster traps, wood-carved men in raincoats, and other icons of the sea.

Yet in spite of all of this, or perhaps because of it, a summer in Maine is one of the most beautiful things America has to offer. The air has a clean, salty smell, and the deep ocean shines of sapphires. For this brief moment in time, a few months at most, "Mainiacs" are able to get outside; that is, if they can deal with the throngs of tourists.

Dave and I drove into a coastal town and managed to

squeeze my car into a small parking space, the lot monitored by an old man wearing a striped collared shirt from L.L. Bean, circa 1994. We walked to a yellow wooden shack adorned with red flowerboxes and ordered a genuine lobster roll: a simple crusty roll filled with nothing but lobster soaked in butter. One bite and its richness filled me. One bite and Dave concluded he really didn't like lobster; he took another bite just to make sure and handed me the rest. I simultaneously savored each bite and forced myself to finish it; there was no way this amount of lobster was going to be fed to the seagulls who milled about our picnic table, hoping for a miracle snack.

Our first stop in Maine took us past Portland, where I would sing the next night, to a small rural area where one of Dave's friends and her partner had put down roots. Stacey's double-wide trailer sat on an isolated piece of property, a place where the roads were inconsistently named and paved. After a few miscues, passing the same beaten houses so run-down it was hard to tell if people still lived inside or if the sea winds had driven them out, we finally identified the dirt path that was her driveway. Compared to most of the dwellings we saw, Stacey's trailer was a dream home—a mowed yard, flowerpots on the front porch, fresh paint reflecting the setting sun. Over a few beers and a view of fireflies, Stacey said she and her partner often played a driving game called "dilapidated or abandoned," in which each would guess whether a home was occupied or had long been left to face the elements on its own. It was a game Dave and I would adopt on our trip, even though we quickly realized that while it could be entertaining, it required us to ignore the potential suffering such a house represented.

The next day we arrived in downtown Portland in the late afternoon, just in time to sit down and grab a beer at a local pub. Inside, we settled onto our barstools among a mixture of tourists in bright pastels and locals in paint-splattered cargo pants. A man with a large afro and horn-rimmed glasses wolfed down a large bowl of stew. Dave and I talked to the bartender, who used to live in northern Maine, in a "town where there was nothing to eat, but I saw every star that ever shone in the sky." She said she was one of the few who had dared leave, even though there was nothing to keep anyone from going. No jobs, no people, no hope. "Then again," she mused, "maybe those were the very things that made people stay." I tried to imagine what it would be like to feel attached to such a sense of hopelessness.

Our karaoke bar was in the trendy area of downtown, at the bottom of a dimly lit staircase. Inside, the décor was dark lacquered wood and predictably marine, but with an upscale twist; tasteful stained-glass lighthouses, a large bronze mermaid statue. It was quite crowded, and many people were dressed up for the evening—even the men, who wore business casual, or the standard preppy Izod and pleated khakis my classmates wore in the 1980s. Drinks were served in clear plastic pint glasses. One guy humped a pole in the middle of the dance floor as he talked on the phone.

The KJ sat high up on a stage, tucked away in a corner behind a massive desk filled with a soundboard, computer, and monitor. A tiny woman in a tinier skirt and neon crop-top carefully positioned herself on a barstool next to him and leaned over, letting her long, black hair brush his shoulder and giving him a view of her slight cleavage. As the show began, the KJ announced that a woman sitting at the bar was moving to Portland, Oregon: "Let the Portlands unite!" I let her know I was from "the other Portland," and would be happy to lend a hand if she needed anything when she arrived on the other side of the country. The woman looked down at her drink and confessed she was really going to live in Cave Junction—a small town the entire length of Oregon away from Portland— to take care of a sick relative. Her ultimate goal, however, was to move to the city out west. She said she longed to be in a city, a place where she could feel "I'm from somewhere."

Noting the crowds, surprisingly large for a Monday night, I put a song in early so I could get into the rotation. My name was called almost immediately, and I climbed up onto the stage to sing "Call Me," then asked both the KJ and his companion for advice on what I should sing for a second song: Donna Summer's "Last Dance" or George Michael's "I Want Your Sex"; the KJ's companion suggests the latter and I complied. The KJ apologized that it might take a while.

I sat back down and enjoyed the spectacle before me. A lot of people here were pretty wasted, but the winner of the most-inebriated award easily went to a guy in a Tom Brady jersey. He was wearing a sling, and I'm sure the beers he was drinking helped wash down some painkillers as well. He spent most of the night wandering around aimlessly from one end of the bar to the other, occasionally stopping to hold onto a chair or one of the brass poles that decorated the dance floor. I was amazed he was able to make it up the stairs and across the stage to submit a song. When it was his turn to sing, he tried his best to perform the rap "California Love," but was simply too far gone. As the music played, he clutched the mic in both hands and stared out into the crowd, swaying to the beat—or perhaps it was just lack of balance. His mouth hung open as the words scrolled by.

A woman in a sexy blue polka-dot dress and shiny white pumps grabbed the mic from Tom Brady and did her best to complete the song. She was more than a bit tipsy herself. She sang words that at least matched the beat. During the chorus she would shove the mic in Tom's direction to give him another chance to sing. I'm not sure he realized what was going on, and he didn't seem to mind (or notice) the takeover. The woman continued to sing with increasing gusto and incoherence as her boyfriend danced solo. It was even money which of the three would fall down first; it turned out to be the woman, as she tried to hand the microphone back to the KJ.

There was line dancing to a musical interlude after every song. People filled the dance floor to groove to "Shoop"—karaoke-dance-karaoke-dance-karaoke was the pattern, despite the long list of singers. Still, the crowd seemed to want the chance to move. My wait stretched to well over an hour when the next drunken karaoke scenario brought me to tears. Five young professionals in short, tailored skirts or button-down shirts with khakis giggled as they got on stage to sing "Firework" by Katy Perry. The song cracks the core of my heart, the sting starting in its top left corner, moving diagonally and out as it pulses into a slow piercing ache throughout my chest. "Firework" was the song Molly's old college a cappella friends arranged and sang for her when they heard of her diagnosis. From all across the country, her friends learned their parts and recorded them, one taking charge and care to mix all their scattered voices into one call of hope. In that song, they let her know they saw her strength even when the rest of the world, including her own body, was folding on top of her—and even when we all knew, in the end, that Molly would be the one shooting across the sky, like a firework, leaving the rest of us looking up in awe at her light.

I sat at the table, on the other side of the country from home, the love of my life by my side, listening to a horribly off-key group of singers perform an overplayed pop song, and sobbed, unnoticeable because of the noise and darkness. I was in public but in my own private grief—until poor Dave looked over, understandably confused. I managed to blurt out "Molly's song" before making my way to the bathroom to wipe my face. I stared at myself in the mirror while taking deep breaths. I looked awful: mascara ran down my tanned cheeks, no longer framing my puffy red eyes. The other women in the bathroom ignored me; I'm sure I was one of many who ended up in here sobbing. I kept staring into the mirror, really looking at myself, assessing the pain in my eyes. I was okay—it was more a shock reaction than anything. This was my new reality. I would always hurt—though eventually less often and perhaps less intensely. But at that moment I was affected by a horrible song sung horribly—and that's okay.

If only Molly had been there so I could call her and laugh about it.

CHAPTER 27

VERMONT

July 20. 2016

M Y TIME IN VERMONT WAS SHAPED BY TWO KIND STRANGERS: Steve Hess, who runs Karaoke Across America, and Cowboy Jim, a retired army veteran who opened his heart and the doors of his local American Legion so I could sing. Cowboy Jim now spends his days living on the road in his RV, visiting all the national parks, singing in different states as it pleases him. Living with no set agenda, just like me. But the similarities ended there. After Steve connected us on Facebook, I learned about Cowboy Jim's political perspectives; I saw his comments about how Hillary was a liar and in no way fit to be president; I saw his concerns over out-of-control immigration, America's lack of secure borders, and the imminent dangers of ISIL. Karaoke allowed us to connect despite chasms carved out by our experiences and worldview. The previous spring, as I was planning my trip, he had messaged me as he and his RV were passing through Portland, hoping to learn the best karaoke spots in town. I suggested a few places and was truly disappointed to miss a face-to-face meeting due to a business trip. He messaged me to let me know he "surprised a few of your city folk" by singing country classics at one of my favorite haunts, the How Can Be Lounge, a Chinese restaurant in the industrial area of Northeast Portland, more known for hipsters and gospel singers than country stars.

This time our paths would finally cross; he was stopping through Vermont to help his mother run a bluegrass festival. Yet even when at his home base, he still opted to live in his RV, parking it in her driveway. He helped her with the cooking and cleaning, but preferred the familiarity of his RV because he said his mom wasn't too neat—as evidence, he offered the fact that she never cleaned the top of her fridge or microwave.

Still, his kindness overrode his need for perfection as he went out of his way to help both the music festival and me. He knew how hard it would be to find a reliable karaoke venue in Vermont, and wanted to help. We messaged back and forth about dates, times, and towns, and finally settled on a small town with a population just under 4,000, on a Tuesday night. I was grateful for the help he offered in setting up a venue, and excited to meet the paradoxical man with a wandering lifestyle and meticulous motorhome.

The American Legion was a simple concrete structure with a flat roof and large tank out front. A bald eagle holding arrows and ribbons adorned the building's façade, and signs advertising bingo on Thursdays and steak dinner on Fridays decorated the front lawn. As Dave and I walked in, we were met with the challenging stares of the bartender and some old men playing cards. To them, we had no business being there. Yet as soon as we said we were looking for Cowboy Jim, everyone relaxed their shoulders, smiled, and jerked their heads left in unison—telling us to continue on back.

The karaoke setup was in a large back room with white

folding tables and a dance floor. A crocheted American flag hung above the door between us and the bar area; a forty-eight-star version hung on the other side of the room. Jim looked up and smiled brightly, walked over from his audio equipment, and gave me and Dave firm, warm handshakes. He had a perfectly pressed appearance, and wore a cowboy hat and boots, and a crisp blue plaid shirt that matched his piercing blue eyes. He smiled the smile of one who lives the life he wants—relaxed, secure, free—and let us know how glad he was that we were there. I was, too.

Our host made sure we were settled at a table with a beer in front of each of us, and continued to set up his equipment. He placed a small binder at our table; it listed all the songs he sang, and stated at the top of the first page that he took requests. I thumbed through an impressive number of titles—mostly country and folk, with a bit of rock sprinkled in—and I could feel his pride wafting off the pages. Jim also let us know he was bringing his own singers to join us tonight—some from as far as forty miles north, and twenty miles south: we couldn't have karaoke without a party! Plus, he said, some of his singers would be mighty disappointed if they found out he had hosted a show without including them.

Slowly, Jim's fans started to come in, greeting each other warmly and with surprise. Jim had reached from far and wide to bring a community together, and I was touched witnessing the effort he'd put into making this all happen.

The group was small—about twenty or so—but everyone came to sing. So we did. Jim sang James Taylor's pensive acoustic classic "Fire and Rain" to start the show, and he was damn good. The selections from the rest of the group were mostly country (modern and old-time) but also featured Jimmy Buffett, '80s love songs, and even a rendition of "Hello Muddah, Hello Faddah," complete with interpretive dance moves and hand motions. During slower songs, a senior couple in checkered shirts and denim—they looked like they had come straight from a hoedown—would take the dance floor under the disco ball and hold each other, swaying gently. Throughout the night, Jim sang with a lot of people—in duets, as backup, or in supporting roles—but always by request. Once, a severely dyslexic man asked for his help reading the lyrics as they scrolled by on the monitor. Together, they sat on barstools and sang, Jim taking the lead, the shy man a tiny fraction behind.

When it was my turn to sing, I tried my best to find country songs I could make my way through and offered my sincere apologies to Dolly Parton and Patsy Cline and the group who had come to listen. I wanted to please this crowd and Jim—to show my appreciation that so many had come that night to help me fulfill my karaoke goal. While I realized they were all here because they loved to sing, and they loved Jim, I also knew that their presence here helped me do something that was important to me. I was grateful for their kindness. So I did what all karaoke singers do; I sang my song as best as I could, respecting the original artists and their greatness. I crooned "Walkin' After Midnight" with a slight twang and wistfulness, and shared my aching heart as I pleaded to Jolene not to take my man. I hoped my fellow singers heard my thanks that they had let me join their tribe.

Two toddlers took over the dance floor, ran over to the table where their parents sat and screamed, "Daddy, sing 'Let It Go!'" when they heard his name being called—he sang an unenergetic Billy Idol instead. Undeterred, the girls bounced and twirled to Daddy's music. Then it was Mom's turn. Her hair was brown, speckled with grey, and her sweatshirt—the same shade of hot pink as her older daughter's tutu—turned her skin an exhausted yellow. As Mom took the mic and began to sing Sugarland's "Something More," her kids clung to her legs, and she closed her eyes as she sang that there had to be something more than what she faced every day. She disrupted her own performance to call to her husband, who was too busy socializing to notice that their youngest one had run into the bar area. He gave half-hearted chase as Mom found her place and continued to sing.

A woman in Capri sweats and a shabby tank top sang a polished yet feisty version of "Black Velvet"—a song that causes most karaoke audiences to wince, and is often included on KJ lists of "most hated songs." On one of Jim's frequent visits to the table I shared with Dave, I commented to Jim on her amazing voice; he let me know she fronted a band. Jim played the role of gracious host perfectly, talking to Dave and me about the ins and outs of being a KJ: the rotations, mic adjustments, and what he does when singers bring their own discs (he hates that), or request a key change (he hates that, too). As the rocker began to fade out, Jim rushed back to his station and said, "The next singer is going to switch it up a bit with Garth Brooks." We were back to the country for a while.

Jim next called up a guy who had driven over an hour to come to sing. His nickname was DJ, because Jim had never heard him sing the same song twice—Jim would joke that the young man should have his own radio show. DJ had Tourette's or something, because when he was just sitting by himself he made strange, jerky, rhythmic hand gestures over his head, out of time with any music. It was hypnotic to watch, though I tried not to stare. When he managed to put his hands down, he repeatedly looked into his empty wallet, just to make sure nothing had changed. Yet when it was his turn to sing, there was a complete transformation. DJ sat perfectly still, his eyes showing confidence and joy. He was in the karaoke zone, focusing on the music and nothing else.

Amid the veterans, the families, the casually dressed locals, I was acutely aware of being a stranger in their space, and outside of a few times I talked about song selections with some of the women, I experienced one of the few times I've been at a loss for words. Did anything else connect me to these people, outside of song? (And even that was a stretch, given my lack of knowledge about any country genres.)

I have no idea what my Vermont experience would have been like without Steve Hess and Cowboy Jim. There still would have been amazing scenery, delicious beer, and maple syrup tasting. I still would have visited the Ben & Jerry's factory and learned about Vermont's best-kept secret, the maple creamee (soft-serve ice cream flavored with pure maple syrup—it's life-changing). There would have been karaoke, probably somewhere in one of the larger towns, and most definitely not in an American Legion decorated with so many variations of Old Glory. I probably would have sung with fellow Bernie Sanders supporters (for the first time since I had begun driving, Trump signs did not dominate the political sign landscape), as opposed to singers who needed to be imported to make an evening. I'd be hard-pressed to say that such a hypothetical evening would have had the same community and friendship I felt and still feel. Both of these men who I had met online made Vermont about more than singing; they made it about people going the extra mile for a stranger.

PENNSYLVANIA

July 30, 2016

AFTER ANOTHER BRIEF DETOUR THROUGH TORONTO SO THAT DAVE could meet my family there, our drive through Eastern Pennsylvania was one big political ad; signs supporting local judges, council members, and representatives littered the sides of the roads. The number of Donald Trump signs wedged into the lawns we passed was rivaled only by the number of Confederate flags; the two often correlated. A few households stood out in their support of Bernie Sanders. Not a single one had a sign for Clinton, though there were several making statements against her: "Killary for Prison" seemed to be the most popular. It was hard to believe that a mere one hundred miles away, in the same state, HRC was accepting the Democratic nomination that very day in Philadelphia. The other news dominating the airwaves was about the increasing protests bringing awareness to police brutality around the country—the most recent case being the shooting of Charles Kinsey, an unarmed man who was taking care of an autistic adult outside of Miami. He was lying on the ground with his hands in the air trying to show his patient how to obey the officers when he was shot dead.

At the bar in the small college town of Bloomsburg, several people were sitting at the picnic tables outside, smoking cigarettes and drinking beer. Inside, several others were vaping, giving the place a smell of apples, musk, and artificial vanilla. Our six-dollar pitcher was served along with two glass mugs grabbed out of the standing cooler. The younger patrons were served their beers in plastic cups. It was announced that the UFC fight was going to start in ten minutes, so all interested in watching needed to move upstairs. Cover charge for that was ten dollars; karaoke was free.

The rules in karaoke usually go unspoken. Here, the KJ rattled off an extensive list: Respect the equipment, singers, audience, and world at large. Don't bang on the microphones, clap near them, or swing them by the cord. Don't heckle singers, or give them a hard time; support everyone who gets up on stage by clapping. Don't use your time on the stage to make fun of your friends, or heckle anyone in the audience. Don't change the lyrics to songs to make fun of or disrespect people because of their nationality, gender, or sexual orientation. That last one took me especially by surprise. While some of the rules seemed to make sense if the KJ was used to a large crowd of overly drunk college kids who might be a bit rough on the equipment, needing to tell people not to disrespect others hurt my heart. The way he rolled off the list of restrictions so smoothly and automatically suggested that he did this regularly and out of necessity.

Singers were ready right at the 10 p.m. start, the list of names began scrolling at the bottom of the six monitors distributed across the bar as soon as the first person was called. A handful of performers in, the KJ got back on the mic with more instructions on how to put a song in—either via a smartphone app or at the kiosk to his left. He announced that new singers got added to the next rotation; old ones kept their spot, and could fill in their song at any time before their name was called again. The KJ lined up his defense before the first accusation of unfairness was struck. While I had some admiration for his transparency, I was also sad that he felt he needed to run it this way. All these rules also made me wary that I was going to mess up in some way.

I didn't feel like downloading the app, so I went to the kiosk. As I was pondering my first song choice, a man who made up for a lack of hair on top by growing it long in the back sang a country tune; despite this lead-off, I looked around the room and didn't peg the place for a country bar, given the generally young thrift-store/Old Navy fashion crowd, and opted for the '80s instead. I had to press on the touchscreen quite firmly to get it to work, and even then needed to blow hot air on my fingers to make them warm enough for my choice to register. I found myself both liking the computer signup strategy for its fairness and hating its depersonalization. I prefer the connection I can make with the KJ when I turn in a slip of paper. Maybe the KJ wanted to shield himself from the singers as much as possible because of all the rules he had articulated.

As I continued to sign up, the screen told me, in bold block letters, to put my first name and last initial into the monitor or I wouldn't be called up. I obeyed and typed in "Kristi G;" as I watched other names go by I saw I was the only one with a last initial. The regulars knew which rules were okay to break, and I felt a little more relaxed knowing this place wasn't as strict as my first impression. Still, the first time I got on stage, the KJ reminded me about handling the equipment properly—not to bang on it, how to sing into the microphone by holding it closely to my mouth, but not screaming into it. I figured he did this to anyone who was new, as I saw him go through the motions with others as they got on stage, but it wasn't universal. I kept quiet about how this wasn't my first rodeo. After I sang "Voices Carry"—echoey sound effects enhancing an otherwise mediocre performance from my perspective— a young blonde came up to me and said, "You have such a beautiful voice," and gave me a hug. I found the human connections here after all.

For the most part, despite (or perhaps because of) the rules, everyone at the bar behaved—except for a pair of young men doing their best to get through "Sweet Caroline," who clearly forgot about the "no clapping on the mic" restriction, banging to the beat of "ba, ba, ba" during the song's infamous chorus. As they finished, the KJ snatched the mics away from them as quickly as possible. The singers didn't seem to notice as they stumbled back to their table and their beers. One of the guys chugged the remains of his Bud Light tallboy and promptly spewed it back up across the table. His friends mopped it up with a roll of paper towels conveniently placed on the table. He seemed unfazed.

When a woman named Bobby Jo was called up, no one moved. Then, her partner walked up to the KJ and whispered into his ear. As he pulled away, bringing the mic back to the bar table, the KJ told the audience that normally people aren't allowed to sit and sing, but since Bobby Jo was still recovering from knee surgery he was making an exception. I guess he didn't want anyone else to get ideas about wandering around the bar while singing—a shame, because I enjoy a performer who can work a crowd like a lounge singer from time to time.

I could never quite get a sense of the vibe here. It didn't seem as though anyone was really listening to the other singers—instead, they were talking amongst themselves, vaping, or otherwise waiting for their turn. Then again, sometimes people did sing along, in a mumbly sort of way, fading in and out of attention that was divided among friends, song, and drink. The only time the bar went silent was when Jack sung. Jack was in his 70s and wore a black baseball cap, a red plaid shirt, and jeans. He brought his own disc to sing Sinatra tunes, and with the first note of the song introduction, people dropped everything and paid attention to his cracking, heart-felt voice.

CHAPTER 29

NEW JERSEY

August 3, 2016

I SPENT MY ENTIRE CHILDHOOD IN A SMALL TOWN IN NEW JERSEY, about thirty miles outside of Manhattan. I went to the same public school system there from kindergarten until high school graduation. I spent every summer at one of the two man-made lakes I could easily ride my bicycle to. When I was younger, this place was idyllic—a safe neighborhood small enough to get around on one's own as a kid, during a time when such things were allowed. I could walk the quarter mile up the hill to my best friend's house. We could ride the back roads of town to the cigar store and buy twenty-five cent candy bars (twenty-six cents with tax), go swimming, or just stay at her house and play endless games of Monopoly in her parent's blue-and-green carpeted library.

Then puberty hit, and with my onset of adolescence the small-town options I found so freeing as a kid became stifling. Everyone knew who I was and what I stood for: I was a good girl, a smart girl, an athlete if I was lucky. I wasn't someone who boys asked out; I wasn't someone who got invited to parties when parents went away for the weekend. It wasn't that I was disliked—people from all cliques and grades thought I was fun and chatted with me during the school day at our lockers, passed notes with me during science class, laughed with me in the locker room as we got ready for softball practice. But the bottom line was that I wasn't one of the chosen ones. I would never be popular, and that hurt.

I'm not sure when I became completely unhappy, but it happened. I wasn't so much sad as completely empty. I didn't have the energy to care much about anything until it was time to apply for college. Then, I did everything I could to get the hell out of Mountain Lakes, New Jersey. I wanted out of the place that had treated me well, thinking that somehow escaping this town would change everything. And, in many ways, it did. When I got to college on the other side of the country, I reinvented myself, picking and choosing the parts of me I liked (very few) and tossing away the reputations others had given me. I drank, smoked, hooked up, and skipped classes, yet somehow found the drive and luck to graduate. Visits to the place I had grown up in were few and far between; I often used the distance as an excuse to not go back for holidays and summers, but the truth was I had no desire to return.

But now I was back, showing Dave the place that had nurtured me at first, then betrayed me by not allowing me to grow.

Driving around the neighborhood, showing Dave the lakes, the cigar store, my old house, my friend's house (her parents still live there), I was embarrassed. Embarrassed by its wealth and bucolic setting. How could life have been so challenging for me in a place so perfect? The houses were huge—Dave noticed it right away, and I cringed as we passed countless three-story dwellings with gigantic, perfectly groomed yards. Was this really where I had grown up? Was I really that rich?

In a way, yes, I was. But I also remember needing to put out pots to catch the drips every time it rained in our three-story stucco. And how, on especially cold winter nights, I could see my breath as I went to bed, despite the radiator clanking, doing its best to provide warmth. But my mother always put food on the table, and I always had new clothes at the start of the school year, whether they were purchased at a store or made by my grandmother. I was able to save up enough money from working at my mom's catering business to buy a '79 diesel Rabbit. The only suffering I experienced was inside my own head; I lacked for nothing materially, but emotionally was a whole other story.

We drove down the small winding street where I once lived. My house was the first one on the right, and though I recognized it immediately, it wasn't the same. The new owners had cut down the trees in the front and painted the exterior from a generic off-white with drab brown trim to a buttery sunshine with Kelly green. Those sorts of updates are to be expected, but what I couldn't understand was the fact that they put on a huge addition out back, replacing the wooden deck my Pappa had built with more square footage. It was already a five-bedroom, three-bath house when it was built in the 1920s; it had a full dining room and living room and a separate TV room. Why the hell did anyone need more space? Yet I knew this was the trend in the United States. I saw it all the time in Portland, and on the many shows I watched on HGTV; a family of four wanting 3,000 or more square feet of living space. The era of the McMansion—new construction taking up an entire lot at the expense of a yard or trees that could fill a neighborhood with clean air—is going strong. My hometown was no exception; big houses renovated to be even bigger. As someone who has grown to crave less space and fewer possessions—feeling the relaxation and bliss of simplicity, loving the fact that everything I needed for the next few months was with me in my two-door car—I felt out of place.

When we got to one of the lakes, I was pleasantly surprised, for it had escaped the progress the rest of the town had been submitted to. The docks were still small and worn. The snack shack was still a small hut painted white with green trim. Canada geese still crapped everywhere. Here was the place I had grown up in. Dave and I sat on a bench (that was new), and looked out at the still water, and it wasn't until then that I realized there was something different—there were few others with us. It was late afternoon, and when I was a kid in the early eighties that was peak lake time; actually, any time it was daylight was peak lake time. Every summer, every day, kids would get up with the sun, eat a hurried breakfast, and then go down to the lake. All we had to do was pass a swim test—swim around the buoyed perimeter of the swimming area, tread water for two minutes, and then swim back without being winded—and we could go to the lake without parents, high school lifeguards instead being responsible for our well-being. But today, there weren't that many kids around, and those who were there had parents with them. I guessed the rest of the kids were away at camp, or perhaps inside the air-conditioned additions of their homes. As Dave and I walked back to the car, I said goodbye to my small town; though it was still here, it was a distant memory.

The karaoke evening was more about reconnection than song. I had messaged many old friends who still lived nearby. That number was surprisingly high—many of my classmates had chosen to return to this area after college. It was a Wednesday, so a lot weren't able to make it out to a bar on a weeknight. We still managed to fill a large table to create a gathering that could have happened yesterday or forever ago. I knew from Facebook posts and tentative conversations that the political beliefs among us differed widely. Our gathering was more like the Breakfast Club—a group of teenagers from different cliques bonding together over detention—than a group of friends reuniting. Back then, we were jocks, brains, burnouts, and the lonely, and our differences morphed but remained as stark: Two long-standing couples, one covered in tattoos and dealing with grandparenthood, the other more clean-cut, whose first was going to college. A classmate who loved Mountain Lakes so much he became its mayor, and a man reluctantly coming back to help his family rebuild after the death of his father. A pharmacist. An older sister who was proclaimed "the best babysitter in the world" by another at the table.

I sang "Long Train Runnin'" by the Doobie Brothers, because of its energy and era, and my table erupted in applause. I felt warmed by such authentic support; no matter our differences, we cared for each other in a way only people with shared experiences can. Later in the evening, the KJ wandered over to our table and passed out microphones as he cued up "Piano Man"—a song typically seen as the death of karaoke due to its length and repetition. Yet here, tonight, this song could not have been more perfect, and somehow this KJ magically knew—knew we were sharing memories, knew that this was our song. Perhaps it was painful to the rest of the bar (my condolences to the other patrons), but for us, that tune was a bond. Billy Joel was a mainstay of our past—his roots were just a short distance away, since he was born in the Bronx and raised in Long Island—his lyrics often referencing a particular East Coast grit. But the significance of this song in particular was more than that: one week before our high school graduation, a classmate who was known in our small town for being the best piano player for miles played that song in the auditorium—as good as Billy had ever played it. All of us sang together. The entire class: jocks, brains, burnouts, and the forgotten. I focused on a particular verse all those years ago—the one about a bartender struggling with life, knowing he could shine, be adored, if only he could escape. I sang because I hoped that I was living that man's dream; my ticket out of Mountain Lakes, New Jersey, was punched in the form of college on the other side of the country. At the time, I believed it could only get better from there.

That night, thirty years later, people from my hometown were together again. Everyone at our table sang at the top of our lungs as the KJ accompanied us on his harmonica. Those who normally shied away from the microphone and stage, and those of us who embraced the spotlight joined equally. This time, different lyrics stood out for me—in that moment, I was in the mood for a melody, and I was feeling alright.

CHAPTER 30

WEST VIRGINIA

August 5, 2016

I WAS LUCKY ENOUGH TO BE BORN INTO A FAMILY WITH A DECENT amount of money, food on the table, and my own room so I could focus on my homework. My hometown had an incredible public school system. Not everyone has that, of course, and even those who do aren't always treated the same way—gender, race, class all play a role in how we are (or aren't) taught the skills needed to succeed. But I have no idea who I would have become if I'd grown up in West Virginia, a place that seemed to offer so few opportunities. Its median income and rate of college graduates are low; its poverty rate is high. The state's long-established reliance on the coal industry—both economically and culturally—is threatened on a regular basis. The land, while beautiful, is so hilly it makes it hard to grow any substantial crops, so an agricultural economy isn't an option. On our drive across the state, I see fresh fruit and vegetable stands advertising the sale of produce from Ohio, next door.

Dave and I turned on the radio and heard local stories updating the safety of the tap water in certain areas; contamination had been detected in May and no news coverage led us to believe the matter had been resolved. As we pulled into a 7-Eleven to pick up a couple of gallons of spring water, I saw a young woman in a neon pink "Guns and Buns" tank top, examining the fifths of Bootleggers—a dollar ninety-nine each and available in raspberry and grape flavors. We continued our drive, passing through small town after small town infested with Trump signs, "Hot Spots" (places with internet access such as restaurants, gas stations, and stores), gentlemen's clubs, and bars promoting wet t-shirt contests. Grocery stores were few and far between. John Denver's promise that West Virginia was "almost heaven" was a distant memory, if not flat-out false advertising.

We arrived on the western edge of West Virginia after two days of driving—not the most efficient route, but we had trouble finding a karaoke venue elsewhere in the state. Once again the karaoke network had treated me with kindness in helping me locate a place to sing. I first met Bo online through Karaoke Across America, and he reached out to let me know his schedule of upcoming events. The only one I would be able to make was a Friday night—so 554 miles from my New Jersey hometown, it became our next stop.

Bo was waiting for us when we got to the Elks Lodge. So was his assistant, Samantha, and his mother. Bo and his mom wore matching t-shirts sporting his karaoke business logo. She had no teeth, and was not shy in pointing out this fact to Dave and me soon after we shook hands. Not to worry though, she said, as her dentist was simply on vacation, but it did require her to pass on the corn on the cob that came with the Elks Lodge Friday-night steak dinner. Bo was kind enough to treat both Dave and me as his "honored guests" for the evening. After we ate, talk came easily, and it was hardly small. Dave

157

and I learned all about Bo's mom's history with men. We learned how her first husband cheated on her with another man. (This was why she didn't go to Bo's shows on Saturday nights, but went to all the others; she didn't want to run into the bastard.) The other man had a black book of more than 500 other men he had "done—including the sex positions and everything and the fact that he ain't never used a condom."

"Thank the Lord," she continued, "all my AIDS tests came back negative. I tested myself for eleven years before I was satisfied I was clean." She married again, but that husband soon became an ex as well, abandoning her in Mexico when they were both truck drivers. He was apparently now married to a white supremacist. His two "mixed" daughters from a previous marriage didn't speak to their daddy anymore but still loved her, Bo's mom said—showing a picture of a lovely teenager who apparently had been only two pounds when she was born. Neither of these men was Bo's father—that man lived in Florida. Bo's mom had been only sixteen when Bo was born, so it didn't make sense to get married.

Bo was equally forthcoming with his story. He told me he had the best job in the world because he got paid to party. His oldest son's friends thought he was the coolest dad, which made him proud. Bo had two teenage boys and a younger daughter who lived in Kentucky; his daughter had won a "cutest baby contest" several years back. That title now belonged to his eight-month-old son, he boasted, showing a picture of a chubby boy with an electric, toothless smile. His girlfriend had entered her older child into the contest some years ago, but didn't win—so Bo concluded it must have been his genes.

Like his mom, Bo's story wasn't without its challenges. A marine, he told us he wanted to quit smoking, but cigarettes really helped him with his PTSD. He also wanted to get off his pain meds, but without them the injury he had sustained during his service got in the way of him being able to play with his son, and sometimes caused him to lie awake all night. Bo said he knew what it was like to go without his pain medication, because sometimes his supply went missing. His friends would often steal his pills out of the console of his truck; he never wanted to leave them just lying around the house. "I'm too nice and people know where they are when I give them rides." He shrugged his shoulders and hung his head, as if there was nothing that could be done.

Bo and Samantha opened the night with a double-shot of Creedence Clearwater Revival. Two lights and a disco ball made a crazy display of color that reflected off the "Don't Tread on Me" sign on the wall over my head. After she sang, Samantha slid over next to Bo's mom and put her head on her shoulder. With jewelry in her eyebrow, lip, and tongue, Samantha looked a little out place at the Elks Lodge, which seemed to cater to a less edgy clientele. Her long skirt and denim vest softened her look.

"Mom, can I have a ride tonight?"

"Sure, honey, why?"

"Because I don't want to go to jail."

Samantha launched into a story about how her wallet had been stolen so she lost her driver's license, debit card, and credit card. She implied that she knew who the culprit was.

"She's a slut," Bo's mom replied as she kissed her on the forehead.

"I used the C word on her."

"Sometimes you just need to do that." Bo's mom gave Samantha a squeeze.

I sang Fleetwood Mac's "Rhiannon," and the crowd whooped with delight. Bo's mom said my voice brought her to tears, it was so close to the original. A man named Jonathan, who looked more Manhattan than West Virginia with his shaved head and horned-rimmed glasses, told me I should sing professionally or at least enter contests. The praise felt good, but misplaced; it does every time. More precisely—I hear praise and believe it, but then, as soon as I hear a recording of my voice, I think people are crazy. Bo tried to erase my self-doubts by buying me a shot. The herbal Jägermeister went down easily, and I was left feeling I might not be such a bad singer after all. This was a good thing, for it was time for Bo to record me for his You-Tube channel; he recorded people every week, at every show, yet somehow I felt special that he'd chosen me for that night.

While I knew the number of people who would actually listen to the video would be small, I didn't like the idea of my voice leaving the walls of the Elks Lodge. My insecurities resurfaced, and I wavered between playing it safe by choosing more Fleetwood Mac or going big; Dave encouraged big, and Queen's "Somebody to Love" was recorded. I love pouring myself into this song. Freddie Mercury had one of the most outstanding voices ever recorded: his range, his passion unparalleled, every note sung with such intensity. In my rendition that night I did what I could, but gave myself too much pressure; I sensed every missed note, every missed opportunity to amp it up a bit. Despite all the flaws, I had a good time, and awkwardly waved at the camera when I was done. The patrons cheered yet again, and the one black man in the whole place yelled, "Who let the dogs out?"—which seemed to be his signature phrase for a job well done. His friends encouraged him to actually sing that song, but he said no way, claiming his soulful voice was reserved for smoother tracks from the likes of Tracy Chapman and R. Kelly.

Bo called up the next singer, who was nowhere to be found. He wandered around the lodge, yelling "Theo" into the mic, with lots of reverb. He looked in the men's room. He looked in the women's room. He asked outside each restroom door—whether designated for men or women—in case he was pooping. Theo eventually showed, coming from outside after smoking a cigarette, or something else. His friends referred to him as

"Japanese," which I took to mean his eyes got small when he was high on something. The one black guy was then called "Black Japanese," to which he responded "only when I'm high," laughed and referred to himself as "Blackenese." I was reminded of Jimmy Walker on the old 1970s game show *Match Game*—the token person of color being made fun of openly, playing along.

At 11 p.m., we stopped for the traditional Elks toast:

> You have heard the tolling of eleven strokes. This is to remind us that with Elks the hour of eleven has a tender significance. Wherever an Elk may roam, whatever his lot in life may be, when this hour falls upon the dial of night the great heart of Elkdom swells and throbs. It is the golden hour of recollection, the homecoming of those who wander, the mystic roll call of those who will come no more. Living or dead, an Elk is never forgotten, never forsaken. Morning and noon may pass him by, the light of day sink heedlessly in the West, but ere the shadows of midnight shall fall, the chimes of memory will be pealing forth the friendly message—TO OUR ABSENT MEMBERS

I bowed my head and thought of Molly.

Bo and I closed the evening with the duet, "Stop Draggin' My Heart Around." We listened to the song once on his phone while he smoked out front. Bo let me know that normally he opened and closed the show—but this time he was granting me the honor of ending the night together. Our performance was great at times, shaky at others, but always fun. I find I feed off the energy of others as they sing, and there's no stopping my smile when I hear another person harmonizing with me. As our host wished everyone a "safe way home," people came up to the front and hugged me goodbye or shook my hand and wished me well. I wished everyone well, too, knowing that it was so much easier for me to fulfill these blessings to be well than anyone else there that night.

CHAPTER 31

MARYLAND

August 6. 2016

DAVE AND I MET UP WITH HIS LONGTIME FRIEND, BRAD, AT A brewpub outside of Fredericksburg, Maryland. It had been ten years since the two men had connected, and they had a lot of stories to share and times to remember: Stories about being roommates and barely getting by in a small apartment in San Francisco. Stories about repo-ing cars in some of the more unsavory neighborhoods in Oakland. Other stories you tell when you can't remember a time when you weren't connected.

Brad was accompanied by his wife of fourteen years, Stacy, and although I had just met the couple that evening, I immediately felt at ease, completely relaxed and drawn into the company over locally brewed beer savored outside on a shaded patio. Brad's beard, which hadn't been trimmed since Obama first took office, revealed his relaxed yet defiant nature. Stacy's smile, bright and genuine, was the same whether interacting with me or our server, making us both feel like the most important people in the world. I've enjoyed almost all of Dave's friends as I've met them over the years. Reconnections have happened in Sacramento, Portland, Oman, Vietnam, South Korea, and now Maryland. Wherever Dave goes, he makes and keeps friendships.

We ordered pizza—negotiating toppings took mere seconds—and talked. And talked. Some nights aren't really meant for singing, and it was hard to leave when the time came, but karaoke duty called. Brad and Stacy began their hour-long drive home to their two teenage kids. I was sad to see that part of the evening end, especially knowing it would probably going to be another five years, if not more, before Dave saw his friends again.

The karaoke bar smelled like fish, which made sense since it was hosted in the back of a seafood restaurant. The formal dining area was closed by the time we got there, and we made our way to the back area, where the show was already well underway. A blonde woman wearing a blue college lacrosse hoodie and holding a Bud Light Lime was singing "Black Velvet." Dave ordered a Yuengling; I settled for club soda and lime. There was horse racing on the television with wagering instructions scrolling beneath. I sang Bonnie Raitt's "Something to Talk About" because it was fun, easygoing, and not a huge challenge for me. Minutes later, Dave and I looked at each other and realized the evening had been full enough. We got back into the car and checked off the Maryland box of my karaoke goal, knowing the priorities of that day extended beyond the microphone and into reconnection and friendship.

CHAPTER 32

VIRGINIA

August 7, 2018

D AVE AND I WALKED LESS THAN A MILE TO REACH THE KARAOKE venue. There, we would meet a friend of mine, April, I hadn't seen since high school. Back then, she had been my "little sister" on the soccer and softball teams, two years younger and full of athleticism and enthusiasm. Our night stroll through Alexandria, Virginia, was delightful—cicadas calling me to join them in song, the weather warm without much heaviness. The cobblestones that made up the sidewalk were uneven and I was certain that many women stumbled and sprained their ankles on a regular basis here thanks to a combination of high heels and cocktails. Even sober in my relatively sensible wedge sandals, I sometimes had a hard time keeping a steady path.

The Olympics were on the bar TV, coverage alternating between swimming and gymnastics. I thought about how Molly and I always used to watch the games together. Every four years, whether in summer or winter, there was always an open invitation to sit on her couch every night for the sixteen days of sport. Sometimes there were snacks, sometimes wine, sometimes both, and occasionally neither—but there was always her company and the competition of the Olympics. Always the joy of seeing winners' eyes light up through tears, and the support of other athletes around them even as they conceded defeat after years of practicing, all for a few minutes—a few seconds—of time in the spotlight. During the Olympics, everyone seemed to support each other no matter where they were from or how fierce the rivalry.

As Dave and I focused on the TV from a wooden booth across from both the screens and the karaoke stage, April arrived. While it was easy to recognize her, she had become a different person outside. Her formerly short brown hair was now long and dyed blonde. She wore glasses, and the athletic build I recalled from our youth was hidden by time and inertia. She looked tired. It was both hard and wonderful to see her, though throughout the evening I realized that the sports and community that had brought us together when we were young just weren't there anymore. Conversations were stilted—we talked of jobs, social lives, living in the DC area—and seemed to drop off after a few sentences, each topic tossed across the table between us until it fell onto the floor along with some bar napkins and stray French fries. Talk picked up a little when it turned to music and what song I should sing. Together, we settled on "Walk Like an Egyptian," a song released my senior year that evoked shared memories of getting ready for practice in the locker room, boombox playing upbeat tunes that got us fired up to work hard. I'd never sung it before, but it seemed fitting for the night.

I introduced myself to KJ Jerry, a lanky white guy dressed in a button-down plaid shirt and crisp, dark jeans. The large bar looked empty, but there was already a list of names scrolling across the monitors. I handed my slip to Jerry and told him about my journey. He took my small piece of paper, eyes locked on me, wide and pleading: "You're living the dream." As we talked about the states I had been to thus far and compared notes about singing in unfamiliar bars, a young man named Davis came up to put in his song and joined in our conversation. When he heard about my quest he agreed with Jerry: "Singing karaoke across the country? Right now, I can think of nothing better to do with life."

I sat back down and enjoyed the combination of music and Olympics. Song choices focused on classic rock and adult contemporary. For the first time since I'd started this journey, I noticed that singers were racially diverse. This was not surprising given the location—just outside our nation's capital, in one of the larger cities in the US. I hadn't really thought about the intersection between karaoke and race until I started this trip.

As I observed the various patrons across the bars of America, it was clear that the vast majority I encountered were white (the place in Detroit being a notable exception). Remembering each state, each bar, I could recall persons of color individually: there were so few that it was easy. At first, I wasn't sure if whiteness was a phenomenon of karaoke, or if it was simply a matter of me spending most of my time so far taking the northern route across the country, and then driving up into New England.

The lack of diversity also could have been a coincidental byproduct of the bars I chose, those I found online and in the Karaoke Across America database. Was it possible that the bars in whiter communities were more likely to have an online presence? With few exceptions, most of the karaoke bars I had been to in Portland were pretty damn white.

That made sense to me, because Portland is one of the whitest larger cities you will ever encounter. I had always attributed the lack of diversity I saw when I was out singing to where I lived, not to karaoke itself, because the farther north I traveled in the city, away from the too-polished downtown, the more I found myself surrounded by people who looked different than I. One of my favorite places to sing in Portland—How Can Be, a divey Chinese restaurant with karaoke nightly—was located up north among truck stops, trailer parks, and some industrial buildings. There, you never knew who you were going to sing with: an elderly Asian man sipping a drink by himself at the bar; a small group of hipsters on their way to bigger and better evening activities; a lesbian couple singing a couple of tunes and sipping strong drinks; a multigenerational birthday party of mostly African Americans, many dressed up, some working the dance floor in support of anyone singing a song with even the slightest hint of a beat. When I was lucky, everyone would be there at once, combining fashions, song choices, and chatter into one burst of color—a Jackson Pollock painting of chaos and cohesive beauty. How Can Be is now closed—a strip club named Desire has since taken its place.

Back in the diversity of the Virginia bar, Jerry took the mic again. Though I was confident my name would be called, I noticed Jerry sang twice before some (me included) had sung once. On one level this wasn't a big deal, as there were only about eight singers in the rotation, but I found myself irked by the lack of professionalism. Except for taking on the role of kicking off the show with a song to set the mood of the night, KJs aren't supposed to put themselves first; KJs are there to let others have their time on the stage. While I understood that in order to be a KJ you probably enjoyed singing too, on a busy night it was up to the KJ to take a back seat, perhaps taking themselves completely out of the rotation in order to give others a chance to shine. Yet here, Jerry inserted himself in the middle of the rotation throughout the night, singing whenever the mood struck him. By the time we left, he had sung five songs while no one else sang more than three. My annoyance increased slightly when Davis was called up before me, despite putting his song in after I did, to sing Paul Simon's "50 Ways to Leave Your Lover." He kept the microphone in the stand as he leaned in to croon in a rough sexy voice.

Finally, my name was called. I gave my maiden voyage of "Walk Like an Egyptian" my full attention, losing my place a couple of times during its fast-paced lyrics and struggling with where to take breaths. Overall, I concluded that my performance wasn't too shabby. The pace was fun, and the light-hearted lyrics about waitresses, dropping drinks, and punk bands made me smile as I sang.

When I was done, I left the stage pleased, and vowed to add the song to my repertoire. I returned the high-fives I received as I made my way back to my seat; one guy held my hand a little too long, though, and I needed to tug free as I passed by. April congratulated me on a job well done, and that stroke to my ego allowed me to feel a little more connected to her the rest of the night.

One of the best singers I've ever heard sang in Alexandria that night. An older African American woman in a bold red dress and conservative pearls took the microphone and sang "I Never Loved a Man"—and she *was* Aretha. You didn't even need to close your eyes to believe it; her confidence, presence, and vocals were all part of the transformation. When she was done, I went up to her and told her how amazing her voice was, and she thanked me warmly, grasping both my hands and looking me straight in my eyes. I realized it was the first time I'd ever gone up to someone to compliment their performance; people had done it to me, and I'd found it hard but also thrilling to appreciate the compliments. Being the one to praise another felt odd; it was more difficult than I imagined. I was nervous it would be seen as insincere, or that the recipient would feel as awkward as I did. Yet I knew how much

I appreciated hearing the cheers, and realized that it was well past my due to pay it forward.

I needed no help choosing my second song, "Summer of '69." It was another song from my high school days, and I sang it for April and for my softball team from long ago. As I sang, I pictured her, me, and at least three other players crammed into our coach's dark green Camaro as we drove to practice. All of us had screamed the lyrics at the top of our lungs as our heads stuck out the windows and sunroof, insisting that those were the best days of our lives.

I didn't get as enthusiastic a response from the bar as I had with the Bangles, but I didn't sing that song for the crowd; I sang it for an audience of one.

CHAPTER 33
DELAWARE
August 8, 2016

I WOKE UP SICK, COUGHING AND NAUSEOUS. I FELT THE FATIGUE OF the marathon. Day to day, the trip had been relaxing, but it was also an endurance test of small stressors: finding venues, scheduling, constant driving. Compared to the daily grind of most people, I was highly aware of how little life was asking of me this summer. Yet still, on this particular morning, my body failed. I was tired, or maybe actually sick. Or maybe the strange mold on the hotel bathroom door had invaded my lungs.

Or maybe my sickness was resurfacing grief. For the past two nights, Molly had been in my dreams. We weren't doing anything special, just sitting in her living room or walking in the sun. But in those dreams, she had been healthy. She had her hair, her laugh.

Despite feeling ill, I still woke up with an intense desire to sing. The focus of my journey remained strong. I had considered the idea when I started that, although I would most certainly finish, there would be times that I would be singing out of stubbornness rather than desire. That hadn't been the case thus far, for each karaoke venue had affirmed my joy of singing. I hadn't felt the pangs for "home" at all, but perhaps that was because I didn't really consider Portland my home. Yes, I had a house there, but home was something completely different. Home was a safe zone, a place of comfort, the room I visited when I wished to isolate myself from everything. On the road, my car was home. My songs were home. Dave was home. I didn't need anything else.

We spent the day driving around Delaware, a state for which I had few memories or preconceived notions. For me, Delaware was a wallflower, a state without reputation. Dave and I poked our noses in overpriced thrift stores, bought blueberries and snap peas at a local farm stand, and ate homemade pork-and-cheese tamales in a hole-in-the-wall bakery in a strip mall in Georgetown—population just under 7,000. The young man working the counter had moved there so that his father could open a restaurant in this "city"; while I quietly questioned that term, Georgetown did have a DMV, a small airport, and a technical college. Given what else Dave and I had driven through in the past couple of hours, this was the most congested place for miles.

Rehoboth Beach was our karaoke destination. Before this trip, I had never heard of it, but it was a major tourist destination on the Atlantic Coast. Our first indication of its popularity was the price of our lodging: Our motel a few miles up the main road, away from the ocean and excitement, was $139 a night—one of the most expensive price tags of our journey. When we checked in, the person at the front desk said that rooms would be going for less than fifty bucks starting in October; no one wanted to be near the ocean when the weather turned cold. Around dinnertime, Dave and I drove down to the water. The downtown area by the ocean was packed with ice cream and pretzel shops surrounded by store windows displaying cheap t-shirts and inflatable rafts. Storefronts were painted in a variety of pastels to complement the yellow sands and blue sky.

Our first stop was Dogfish Brewery, known for making some of the best beer in the US (at least Delaware was known for something). The place was more than packed and getting a table would have taken almost two hours, so the hostess suggested we fend for ourselves at the first-come, first-served bar. So we stalked fellow tourists lingering over their last flat sips of foam until they vacated their seats, allowing us to slide right onto the deep-red barstools, still warm from the asses of strangers. My East Coast upbringing made such assertiveness a natural and necessary tendency, for we were surrounded by others who were used to being pushy to get what they needed. We indulged in anything we couldn't get in a bottle somewhere else: beers that, because they were aged in bourbon barrels, tasted more like cognac than lager; seasonal IPAs highlighting the tastes of summer with subtle fruit and lighter hops. We drank more beer than I would have had on a typical night, but the luxury of experiencing Dogfish at its source made it totally worth the expense and brain cells.

Full of delicious beer, we walked back to our coveted parking spot; as stalking drivers paused in false hope at our approach, Dave was quick to shake his head at them while I re-fed the meter. It took a while for us to find the bar in the small tourist center, even though we had its address and our phone GPS switched on. We ended up circling around small side streets with shops featuring seashell jewelry made in China and refrigerator magnets with crabs letting you know the surf was up.

We found our destination more out of process of elimination than actual map reading—there were only so many streets we could wander up and down. Inside the bar, the crowd was a mix of ages, but leaned toward middle like us. This included the KJ, a frazzled-looking woman with straw-textured blonde hair thrown back under a clear-green visor and into a messy ponytail. She wore off-white shorts, a neon pink Rehoboth Beach t-shirt, and no makeup—giving off a vibe of "fresh off the beach and I'd rather still be there." I walked up to her and introduced myself, letting her know about my quest. She couldn't have cared less; to her, I was just another tourist on another work night. It must be hard living and working in a tourist town, the faces in a bar always changing, making it difficult to foster a sense of community or familiarity. Instead, every day, you are surrounded by people like me, who are simply passing through—looking to grab a drink after a long day on the beach, and soon to disappear. Whether any of the tourists who were there that night were looking to sing would be anybody's guess.

The KJ opened the show by warning us that the mic and speakers were a bit on the fritz. She didn't sing a song to start us off, leaving that honor to a guy who sang a nostalgic Neil Sedaka song. Still not getting a good sense of the night and the crowd, I played it safe and put in Fleetwood Mac's "Dreams," a song that came easily to me and was soft and easygoing enough to let conversations flow over it. As I sang, I noticed the tech issues, my voice fading in and out over the speakers—but I still managed to connect with a table of four sunburned women who were slightly older than me. As I sang to them, I felt my voice becoming as seductive and smooth as Stevie Nicks's in the original recording and got the sense that, despite the blasé attitude of the KJ, that night was going to be a good one.

Though the crowd packed tighter and tighter into the bar as the night wore on, the list of singers remained short. As I got up to put in my second song, I encountered a man who looked to be in his seventies trying to put in request for the Rolling Stones, thinking someone else would then sing it for him. The KJ managed an overly polite smile bordering on a smirk and informed him that wasn't how karaoke worked—that the singers themselves pick the songs they want to perform. The man looked startled. He was a true newcomer to my world; I had no idea such folk existed. A tad crestfallen, he turned to me and asked if I was going to sing the Stones. I tried to let him down easily, apologetically explaining that the Stones aren't really a band I can do justice to. He replied, "Well, shit biscuits." I didn't want to disappoint this newcomer to karaoke, so I asked if there were another artist I might be able to sing for him instead; he requested ABBA, as he and his wife "just love that band." I obliged. I scribbled down my song, gave my slip to the KJ, and awaited my turn, more excited for it than usual.

The old man returned to his wife, leaned into her, and pointed at me. They both waved, and I waved back. For the next few songs, the man contributed to the positive energy of the place. He became the first to applaud, and started to dance along with the performances, dragging his laughing wife along for the ride. His dancing was contagious, and soon several in the bar—young and old, male and female—joined them on the floor. He remained the only one to tug up his shirt to reveal his hairy grey chest, however.

As the night continued, the song choices encouraged everyone to move, the lyrics growing flirtier with every singer. A woman in a very short skirt with a slit up the back strutted her stuff as she sang Madonna; one of her friends threw a dollar at her in approval and she tucked it into her bra. A man growled a version of Joe Cocker's "You Can Leave Your Hat On" while performing a mock striptease to a whooping audience. A wonderful rendition of Frank Sinatra received equal attention, even though the dancing slowed a bit as everyone drew closer; the song seemed to provide more of a break than a disruption to the pace of the evening.

I sprang up as my name was called. As the first few bars of the disco tune "Dancing Queen" were played, the bar erupted and the dance floor filled up even more. Because there was no stage, I was immersed in a sea of dancers. I basked in the bliss of happy people around me. The energy mimicked what I had experienced at Otter's in Minneapolis, and in some ways it was even better: it never got to be too loud, too crowded, or too stimulating. As I finished my song, the old man hugged me and thanked me for singing ABBA for him. His wife smiled, but stayed silent.

In this tourist town in an under-recognized state, karaoke magic blossomed without any regulars, without many singers, and without a charismatic KJ. What it did have was a whole lot of enthusiasm, fueled by a bunch of people high on vacation, led by one who had discovered the magic of karaoke later in life. I hoped this wasn't the old man's last karaoke experience, and that one day he would sing the Rolling Stones himself, to an equally appreciative crowd.

CHAPTER 34

WASHINGTON, DC

August 11, 2016

THERE WAS A VIBE OF PANIC IN THIS CITY—OF PEOPLE WORKING TOO hard to live too hard, of people desperate to move ahead in an image-infested web of bars and professional gatherings. Young people trying to act older, more responsible, trying to demonstrate that they have "promise." No matter where you were or what you were doing in DC, it seemed like you always needed to be "on"—for who knew who you were going to run into and where and what that might lead to. In DC, people don't seem to live in the now, but in the world of possibility.

Dave and I had agreed to grab a drink with some friends of mine after they got off work, and as soon as we got to the place, we immediately knew we couldn't afford it. A host wearing tuxedo slacks and a dark-blue shirt accompanied us in the elevator, up to the rooftop bar. The doors opened, and it was clear Dave, my friend Tom from college, and I were the only ones there not in perfectly pressed professional clothes. How everyone managed to look so put together after a hard day's work in the DC humidity baffled me. Tom's longtime partner and her colleagues were already seated among empty food plates and glasses of melted ice. Many in our party had bright-red faces from a combination of alcohol and sun, and a bossa nova band under a bright white tent provided musical entertainment as we looked out at a skyline view of silver and black.

Beyond labeling everyone as "professional," there was no way to tell who made up the crowd in this popular rooftop space; Democrats, Republicans, lawyers, ad execs, politicians; they all looked the same, and none of them looked anything like me. Dave and I sat off to the side of our group and mostly kept to ourselves. We each ordered a well gin and tonic, hoping they wouldn't break our limited budget, and for once I was grateful for a place so busy that getting the drinks took a while. Our server never came by again to see if we wanted another round, and that was fine by us. One mediocre drink each, with minimal service, and we each put down a twenty to cover the bill. It was time to leave and sing, hopefully in a place that was more my humble style.

We walked from the rooftop of a high-level office complex to a bar in a basement of a Red Lion Hotel, making our way down a dark and narrow hall past the hotel business center. Bingo! Recessions, voted the best dive bar in DC, had a décor of off-white faux rock walls; the basement-tile ceiling was falling apart and full of water stains. Counter to the street-level intensity of everyone rushing, their phones glued to their ears, we were far enough down and out of the way that I got no cell service (though it was possible to connect to Red Lion business center's wireless). None of the televisions featured the Olympics. Instead, the two large screens broadcast an NFL preseason game and the Canadian Football League. Recessions was showing the Montreal Allouettes vs. the Edmonton Eskimos over women's gymnastics and historic swimming moments by Michael Phelps and Simone Manuel—the latter became the first African American woman to win an individual Olympic gold in swimming that night. I immediately felt relaxed.

The karaoke started at 7:30, and was already underway by the time we arrived. The KJ sat behind the largest TV, the one showing the CFL, and was barely visible to the crowd as he announced both the next singer and who was on deck. Within minutes of our getting there, a young bearded man got up to sing "Bohemian Rhapsody," and invited anyone to join him— so I did, after ample encouragement from my friends, and a friendly beckoning from the singer. He took lead and pointed to me when he wanted me to sing, which was primarily during the high notes out of his range; I complied. The song is infamously long, and the singer acknowledged this by referring to different parts as "chapters" to keep the audience engaged. Overall, I found the performance extremely fun and just as surprising. First, rarely do I ever hear "Bohemian Rhapsody" sung in karaoke, and if I do it's at one in the morning, not just after eight. In fact, one KJ in Toronto whose show I attended had it on a list of songs which, you had to pay *him* fifty bucks to sing. (I'm surprised more KJs haven't adopted this practice. Other songs on his list were "Paradise by the Dashboard Light" and anything by Celine Dion.) Second, I have never witnessed a time when a karaoke singer actively encouraged strangers to join them on stage. Of course singers often come up in pairs or even small groups, and it's very common to have people sing along from their chairs. But usually a stranger accompanying someone's turn on stage violates a fundamental rule of karaoke. Yet there, in a shabby basement bar in the heart of DC, I was singing one of the most dreaded karaoke songs known, with a man I had never met. And it went just fine.

I stood in a line to drop off my first solo song. It took me a while to decide on something, because my first choices weren't available. I looked for tunes by Styx and Soft Cell and found neither artist in the book. I asked the KJ if he had them in his collection anyway, and he said no—if it wasn't in the book, it wasn't there. Tom had quickly found a selection, and sang "Jumping Jack Flash." He brought it some high energy—gesticulating like Jagger himself, taking long strides, bobbing his head, and shaping his mouth as large as possible. A tall, broad white guy sang "Gangnam Style" in Korean, and took up the entire stage dancing. My performance of Blondie's "Rapture" paled in comparison to these performances, as I have little outside my voice to offer as entertainment. This time, however, I did my best not to look at the monitor, and focused on the audience instead, trying to make eye contact, smile more, connect more to the community around me. Even though I knew the song cold, not relying on the screen made me nervous. The scrolling of the words as I sing usually brings me security, like a nightlight.

Two women got completely lost during their song and just stood in the stage area, swaying back and forth. A group sang "American Pie," another death song of karaoke. Their rendition was made worse by the fact that they didn't know it except for the chorus, mumbling words until they hit the familiar "Bye, bye Miss American Pie . . ." People tried to help by singing from their seats, but overall it was a painful eight minutes and thirty-one seconds. (But who's counting?) Next, a young man in an oversize navy jacket and shorts sang "I'm On a Boat," a parody song that drops the F-bomb every other line and had plenty of bleeps when it was featured on *Saturday Night Live*. But the common rule against swearing in karaoke didn't seem to apply down here, as there was no censor button in this basement bar.

Throughout the evening our group swelled to ten, as some of the folks from the rooftop bar joined us for one more drink. That drink was a twenty-eight-ounce beer named King Kong. Our table was full of hard drinkers, reflecting DC's high-pressure scene. Someone in my group told the KJ about my karaoke journey, and he called me over to tell me I was "living the dream." I couldn't disagree, but felt guilty admitting to a life of luxury and relaxation when I was surrounded by stress. When I told him I was from Oregon, he said it was an "honor" to meet someone from there, as he was a huge Oregon Ducks fan and it was *his* dream to visit Eugene. He avoided eye contact and his voice trailed off, as if he had shared a dream he didn't feel allowed to have. His friend, an Indian guy with horn-rimmed glasses and a half-empty King Kong, thought it was funny that the KJ loved Oregon so much: "It's not because you are black. You're just so straight! Why would you want to go to Oregon?" The KJ was Mormon, the friend said, and so didn't drink or smoke weed. He looked at me and asked sincerely, "Why go to Oregon if you don't do those things?" I had no answer, but I gave the KJ my Facebook details and told him to look me up if he ever made it out west.

As we chatted, a woman sang "Sweet Caroline." It was a horrible performance, musically, but the crowd eagerly turned it into a sing-along. The one with the mic continued to sing with enthusiasm, and friends danced and clapped alongside her onstage. It was a great example of how, in karaoke, people are genuinely rewarded for doing something they are horrible at. A different singer brought another set of interpretive dancers as he performed "Don't Stop Believing"; the bar continued to join in. Our large group helped wind down the night with an all-out participatory rendition of "Time Warp" from *The Rocky Horror Picture Show*. Mics were shared, parts distributed, and everyone danced.

The karaoke stopped at midnight, which is a typical weeknight bar closing time for downtown DC—probably to make everyone go home and sober up for their next demanding day. Dave and I went back down the hallway, past the Red Lion business center, back up the stairs, and returned to the streets of DC. In just a few hours, the intensity of the city would return. But for now, it was quiet in the humidity; windows were dark, and we were among the very few still out—until the next morning, when DC would again fill with a desperation for success.

CHAPTER 35

NORTH CAROLINA

August 15, 2016

Dave and I spent a long weekend recharging with my brother, Rob, and sister-in-law, Seamane, at their house in Charlottesville, Virginia. It was there that we learned Seamane had had a biopsy to check for breast cancer. While part of me understood that I was getting to that age when more and more of my loved ones were going to fall victim to this disease, it was too much. I had just lost one best friend; it was far too soon to think about losing another. I kept this self-pity to myself, for it was helpful to no one, not even me. Yet I felt the fog of grief take over my brain once again. The four of us tried to distract each other by brewing beer and spending our evenings watching movies and ordering takeout. It felt nice to not be in bars for a few nights. I needed this respite of home.

Early Monday morning, we said our goodbyes, trying to hide our collective concerns. The drive out of Virginia began in its wine country—rolling green hills, vast white-mansioned estates, and fences purposely unkempt to create a rustic feeling. Horses grazed on lush grass peppered with bright yellow flowers under a limitless blue sky.

As our drive continued, the scenery transitioned from majestic to hardscrabble. Four run-down trailers made up the homes on Little Heaven Lane. Impractical rolling hills, too uneven for farms or livestock, gradually gave way to tobacco farms and the occasional cornfield. Many of the fields were dry and frail. Houses displayed Trump signs and Confederate flags; one white traditional Colonial had a "Don't Tread on Me" icon painted on its side. A lone gas station was self-serve, but not automated for credit cards; I was surprised I was able to fill my tank before paying, and felt good about the trust in this community. When I went inside to settle up, I saw the gas station sold potatoes, cheese, and apples along with the obligatory malt liquor, cigarettes, and chips. Two Mexican workers filling their red pickup were already inside, cashing in their scratch-its.

I was singing that night with an old friend from Portland who had moved out to North Carolina for love. None of us from back west had met his wife, and I was excited to meet the woman who had captured my shy friend's heart. Our GPS led us to a brightly painted older home in the middle of Durham surrounded by an overgrown garden. I could hear chickens in the coop out back. The door opened, and though I recognized Adam right away—his short square build and unkempt beard still the same—he was a different man. The protective coating that had taken years for me to chip away at had melted away. In front of me was a relaxed and happy soul, settled comfortably into life. I breathed in his contentment before stepping inside. Arianna, his wife, welcomed Dave and me with warm hugs. Art from friends and family donned their walls. We sat in their living room, sinking into an old golden orange sofa, and petted the two pit bulls competing for attention with licks and whipping tails. The furniture was worn, but emitted a sense of warmth, not fatigue. Being there felt like comfort and security.

Adam and Arianna were eager to show us the town before we sang, so we first went out to a mediocre Mexican restaurant—one of those cheesy over-decorated and under-flavored establishments that dot the American landscape. Though I would have rather eaten at a taco stand—for a third of the price and all of the flavor—the company couldn't be beat. After our meal, we hit a brew pub—I continued to be surprised at how many craft breweries had appeared in almost every community across the country.

On our way back to the car, we ran into a skinny man with an impressively thick grey mustache. Adam had befriended him on his bus commutes. When he was not in jail, the man often camped out near Adam and Arianna's house. He had no home himself. Sometimes they invited him inside for dinner. Adam and Arianna asked him what had brought him to this side of the city. He looked away, and then at his feet, providing only a vague response. As he hung his head, the streetlight illuminated his neck tattoo: "Mama Tried."

The karaoke bar was situated among five hair salons, and across the street from a boarded-up building. We walked past several bikers sitting outside, smoking at a series of small black metal tables; mosquitoes were drawn to the lights over their heads. Inside, a large sign read "Bralie's: Supporting our community one family at a time." A large, shiny, cardboard "Happy Birthday" sign hung from a dark wood rafter that was collecting dust. There were pool tables, Skee-Ball, and pinball machines in the back room, with a large bar area showing various Olympic sports up near the entrance. The karaoke took place between them, on a small wooden platform set aside as a stage. People started to put in song slips before the karaoke began, but the number of singers never got too big. Arianna ordered a cranberry and vodka—a drink she called a "woo-woo"—took one sip, gasped, and said, "They are not playing." She only drank half of it before we wandered off to the pool table to play one game, badly; a couple of teams signed up to play the winner of our match, but we conceded and let them have a more competitive game.

Most of the crowd at Bralie's was in their twenties and thirties; it was getting harder for me to tell anyone's age as mine progressed. I knew we were quite a few miles away from Duke University's main campus, but it was possible some of their students were among us. A large group of people shared a round of shots and talked loudly after that, competing with the karaoke singers. The first couple of songs were rap/hip-hop, and I knew there was no way in hell I could choose a song that would fit in. When a group of young adults sang a few Backstreet Boys songs, my confidence to find something that fit in with the crowd diminished. My solution was to not even try; for the first time in a while, I just sang what I wanted. I was nervous when my name was called, and my experience went downhill from there. From the first few notes of Loverboy's "Working for the Weekend," I could already tell I was in trouble. The key of the song was wrong, and I didn't know enough about music to correct myself. I felt doomed.

I tried to fumble my way through the first few stanzas, but it was no use; I knew I was painfully off-key. I looked over at the KJ, pathetic and confused. She was sympathetic to both me and the crowd, stopped the song, and switched to a different version. I started over, feeling more than sheepish, embarrassed I was "that singer" who needed a different version of a song—a key change to help me through. I was given the chance to start over; I had never done that before.

The result was better for everyone. I sang on key with a more familiar backing, but left the stage as quickly as possible, to minimal applause—my friends being the unconditionally supportive exception. I asked the KJ what had happened. She explained that different companies have different versions of a song based on copyright issues, the quality of the re-recording, and other factors. Sometimes a song simply doesn't get recorded in the proper key by a certain label. I find this more than a little nuts, as the key of a song is, well, pretty key to the song. The version she went with initially was from an unreliable company.

I learned a few things from that experience: that I can't assume the key of a song, that I can start over if I really need to, and that it's okay to fail.

Arianna's name was called up next. She sang Adele's "Hello," and it was beautiful but quiet—sometimes hard to hear over the multiple conversations in the crowd. It was her first time singing in a year because of a rare disease, finally in remission after several months of treatment and fighting. Part of that fight included being diagnosed with a throat condition, and having a subsequent operation which almost caused her to lose her voice. I have no idea what Arianna sounded like before the operation, but her voice now was throaty and gutsy, yet restrained. There was a small plea for love in every breath: "Hello. Can you hear me?" I couldn't tell if her restraint was part of her artistic interpretation of the song, or her hesitance—a slow return of her voice·into the public light. Or maybe this is how she would sound from now on. What-ever the case, her voice reflected her story.

I congratulated Arianna on her performance, for both its sound and bravery, and continued to think about her experi-ence. She could have lost her voice. As in, no more speaking, no more singing. I remembered Molly slowly losing her ability to sing, and I regretted not telling her how awful it must have been. Among her friends, I probably had the potential to understand that best; Molly sang in a cappella groups and choirs, and along with the radio, with both formality and abandon. Losing that part of herself must have been a large signal to her that her life was ending. Soon after, her ability to sneeze, yawn, or laugh also became too challenging for her failing lungs.

I'm a total chatterbox. My whole existence depends on connections to friends, meeting up for coffee, talking over beers during happy hour. In my job, one of my favorite things to do is interview others, hear their thoughts on their work and its challenges, engage in conversations that allow me to dig into something that matters, or that help a community. In my work, I've talked to young people about the relevance of their sexuality education, to medical residents about the power of mentorship, to public health specialists about the importance of a closed-loop referral system to help people stop smoking. All of it is interesting, because I get to engage with people around topics that matter to them. Hearing the passion in their voices, listening to them wrestle with problems derived from thoughtful questions, and being able to probe further into understanding—without my voice, it would be impossible for me to participate in these conversations. Of course, not having a voice would also mean not being able to sing.

As I thought about these things, Arianna glanced in my direction, took a small sip of her woo-woo, and put her hand on top of mine. "Take every minute you can," she told me, "Appreciate what your voice gives you."

I think I do. I know I do.

CHAPTER 36
SOUTH CAROLINA
August 16, 2016

IME AND DISTANCE FORCED US TO TAKE THE FREEWAY INTO SOUTH Carolina. We stopped for fresh peaches along the way. The humidity caused my glasses to fog up as soon as I stepped out of the car. Compared to its neighbor to the north—or any other state for that matter—South Carolina was home to more churches and sex shops. Every few miles, we passed billboards reminding us of the legal drinking age. Other than that, the scenery was boring but green, dominated by deciduous trees. If you blindfolded someone and dropped them into my car, they would have been hard-pressed to know what state we were driving through.

We stepped into a true college bar, right across the street from Clemson. As usual, Dave and I got to the bar a little on the early side, though in this case "early" was hardly that—about 8:30 p.m. But the singing wasn't due to start until 10. On a bar post was a framed plaque from *Business Insider* proclaiming that we were sitting in one of the top forty college bars in America. It sure looked like it had seen a lot of action. The floors were worn, and every wooden surface—the bar, its columns, the tables and booths—were all packed with graffiti placed there with Sharpie, fingernail, knife, or pen. At my right elbow was a message in large black text that read: "Were [sic] those drunk bitches that signed a wall." The bathrooms were surprisingly classy: smoky grey tiles with a glass border and shining black sinks, like in a pristine modern bachelor's condo.

We were met by my friend from high school, Michelle, and her friend from work. Since our time together on the soccer and softball fields, Michelle and I had seen each other only once, at a reunion ten years before. There, I'd been surprised at how much we were drawn to each other, spending most of that weekend together. On this night, I was lucky she made it out to see me at all; she'd been struggling with brain tumors and was to have had her head cut open that day, and the unwelcome tissue removed. But the surgery had been postponed a week. It would be her second, and she acted like it was no big deal when I gave her a hug and thanked her for joining me under the circumstances. It was too loud in the bar to really talk about it further, and I'm not sure I would have anyway. I was worried.

Michelle was eager to buy us all a drink, and returned from the bar with a plastic pitcher of gin and tonics. On one side, the pitcher featured the bar's logo in dark purple; on the other was an advert for a DUI defense lawyer. Michelle gave off a kindness, a mellowing that was different from her high school ebullience; age, time living in New Mexico, and living with brain tumors had all affected her new sense of calm. Before, she had been the first one to cheer on the team, and could shout and whistle louder than anyone I knew. Back when we played soccer together, the entire team would try to match her volume and pitch as she showed off her talent for making eardrums shatter. The woman who sat across from me now, with her greying hair featuring a tail tapering off into a dove feather, had the same smile and same bright eyes, but a softer voice and slower gait. In our chatter, we didn't focus on the past, or on mutual acquaintances, but our lives as they stood now. We were enjoying the people we were now, not the ones we had been on the athletic fields decades before.

It was past 10, and the KJ showed no signs of getting started; he was calmly sitting at his desk, sipping a light beer. I wanted to wait until people started singing so I could figure out the style of music the bar would enjoy. Should I go more modern or country? Was this a place that loved its disco? I was adaptable, but without anything to go on, I was frozen in indecision. I deferred to Michelle for a song idea. She wanted to hear Pat Benatar, and so Pat Benatar it would be. I was called up at around ten forty-five, the first to sing. It was the first time I'd opened a place up—not even the KJ sang first. It felt weird to be the opening voice, a stranger in a strange land, out of my element on so many levels. I sang my song to Michelle, making eye contact, growling "Heartbreaker" and putting on the best rocker performance I could, closing my eyes during the high notes, raising a fist overhead; none of it was part of my usual routine, but it was fun to do. In response, Michelle whistled loudly, as if we had just won the state championship. Another state down—only sixteen to go. I got a sense that this was all really happening; my goal was within reach, and it excited me.

The second person got up onto the stage to sing Rush's "Tom Sawyer." The man looked exactly like a guy who would sing "Tom Sawyer." His twiggy arms and greasy hair thrashed about during his air drum and guitar solos. He thrust his hips through his tight torn jeans. He sounded great, and we all cheered loudly as he exited the stage flashing the sign of the devil.

Then no one sang. For a long time. The KJ filled the silence with his Pandora station. The skinny guy eventually returned to the stage to sing some Boston, and performed "beer guitar" during the instrumentals, strumming his bottle with all the enthusiasm of Tom Scholz. The mood of the bar had been set. I got up again to sing some more classic rock—this time "Separate Ways" by Journey, and I was all in. No note was neglected as I allowed my lungs to fill, then released each beat with the force of 1980s angst. Sometimes I held the microphone in one hand; other times I clutched it with two. When it was time to sing the final gasps, the desperate "NOOOOOOOOOO" that concludes the song, I dropped to my knees to plead to those before me. I don't think I'd ever had as good a time singing that song as I did then.

Slowly, other singers started to get into the action. There was some Backstreet Boys, just like in North Carolina, and some country selections. But mostly it was classic rock. For a while the playlist reflected a generic 92.3 radio station. It took me a while to notice I was the only female singing. Most of the singers looked like they were straight out of a fraternity, with careful haircuts, khaki shorts, and t-shirts ranging in degrees of snugness over their stomachs. I'd stereotyped karaoke as more of a female thing, but over the course of this trip I'd learned that that was simply not true. Lots of guys sing, and many times across many states I'd noticed that it was the guys, not the women, who dominated the stage. If you were on stage, if you were holding the microphone, you were asking to be heard. In that respect, maybe karaoke was more of a guy thing after all. Men are more conditioned to take center stage, take up space; men are allowed to be heard.

A country boy with a can of Busch Light took the mic and sang "Patience" by Guns N' Roses, with a Southern twang. He leaned on a tilted stool, ten-gallon hat pulled over his eyes, blond curls peeking through. He sounded good and knew it; I would have had a crush on this cowboy during college, admiring his confidence as much as his looks and voice.

There was a mad rush by the guys to put a song in as the KJ announced the last hour before closing. I was already in the queue, so I was quickly called for my last song, "Pinball Wizard." As soon as the song's title flashed up onto the monitor, a college kid stumbled onto the stage and asks if he could sing, too. "This is, like, my favorite song," he said. "Scout's honor." I'm sure I could have refused, but what was the point? I felt I had already reached my peak when I sang Journey, and what's a night of song without sharing a tune? So I agreed, and he smiled wide.

He tried to share my mic but leaned in a little too close, so I provided him with his own. As we began, I wasn't sure if he didn't really know the song, or if he was too drunk to sing, but I managed to put my diva aside and had fun sharing the stage. I understood why sometimes it might be more fun to sing with a friend or in a group. Sometimes being at the center isn't what matters. The song finished and my partner, beer still in hand, wavered as he struggled to stand. When he had found his footing, he announced, "We could go on tour. We've got something good here." I laughed and told him that sounded good to me. The cowboy looked at me and said, "*You* sang well." My inner crush-having college kid blushed.

We don't quite close down the bar, but come damn close. Michelle stole the plastic pitcher, stashing it under her shirt and proclaiming she was "preggo." We ran out the back door of the bar like kids. We were in high school all over again.

CHAPTER 37

GEORGIA

August 17. 2016

WHEN I ANNOUNCED MY KARAOKE JOURNEY TO MY FRIENDS ON social media, several chimed in to wish me their best, and some told me to stop by and visit when I was in their neck of the woods—but didn't offer any details. When Lynn said to come see her in Atlanta so we could go to Sister Louisa's Church of the Living Room and Ping Pong Emporium, however, I was *in*. Karaoke happened every Wednesday. With a church organ. I began planning my trip to make sure I hit Atlanta in the middle of the week.

I visited Sister Louisa's website to learn more. I read about its numerous awards—including being one of the "twenty-one best theme bars in America." I saw that it had been written up in *GQ*, *The Atlanta Banana*, and *The Wall Street Journal*. It had t-shirts, mugs, and hats for sale. While the place looked very impressive, it also made me hesitate; all this media attention made me think it was going to be a huge commercial enterprise. I couldn't have been more wrong.

Lynn drove us from her house in the outskirts of Atlanta to the southeast, taking us on a small tour of the city along the way. I saw that a cop had pulled over a car and the two African American occupants were waiting with their hands in the air. I got a text from Seamane letting me know she had Stage 1 breast cancer. I wasn't sure whom I was more afraid for: my sister-in-law or the strangers in the car.

Shaking my sense of dread, I walked into the bar and it instantly felt like my personal watering hole—the kind of place I would go to regularly just to grab a drink after work. Everyone has their holy place, their place of refuge, a place to go when nothing else in the world is right. For me, this was it. The dark, warm, old wooden bar was intricately carved. Above it was the establishment's own version of the "Three Kings": pictures of Elvis, Martin Luther King Jr., and Jesus. Opposite were tall tables alongside windows, so you could watch the rest of Atlanta go by; at this hour, many of those walking past were young couples dressed in bright colors and sharp suits, ready to dance. Some women's heels were so high that navigating the merest spate of gravel in the parking lot was a challenge.

The walls were packed with paintings from thrift stores and garage sales: sad clowns, children playing by a river, kittens with yellow saucer eyes, and of course Jesus—on the cross, playing with children, healing the poor. The art was poor quality, but what made it even odder was that each piece had its own additions: sayings written in bubble letters using primary colors, all religious. Or sacrilegious—the line was a fine one. A portrait of a woman with the caption "The taller the hair, the closer to God," a picture of the Last Supper with Judas asking for separate checks, one of Jesus tending to a flock of lambs with the caption "Jesus frowns on bestiality." The bar's flagship painting, captioned "Jesus loves a thirsty pussy," was available on a postcard that now hangs on my fridge with a "Pray for China" magnet Molly bought me years ago when she visited that country; she went during a huge trip through Southeast Asia, using her inheritance from her father's sudden death. She hadn't intended to add China to her itinerary at first, but decided to go because she was afraid that she would outlive the Great Wall.

An hour before the karaoke started we ordered house-made sangria and walked up the stairs lined with old album covers, some identical to those I had in my collection when I was young. I took a picture of one of Olivia Newton-John's records—an early one, from the 1970s, when she sang country. Dave, Lynn, and I sat on a plastic couch whose blue floral print matched my summer dress a little too well, and watched two guys play ping-pong. I was somewhat surprised by the intimacy of the space, given the bar's notoriety; upstairs there were only a few places to sit, the ping-pong table, and an area for the organist. Our couch was the prime seat in the house, comfortable and facing the stage. The organist/KJ, T.T. Mahoney, started setting up his instrument, an organ smaller than I knew existed, which was stored in a back closet. He placed it right next to a doll on a crucifix with a sign that read "Climbing the Ladder to Success." Then he placed a pulpit in front of the stage area. I grew even more excited.

T.T. was ready to begin, and turned to the building crowd: "Let's make some memories. I want to turn off all the other music in the world." Then he led us in a group meditation, which was a first (and only) for me in any bar. "Take some time to breathe into your core. Think about who made you mad today. Let that go. Stroke that person's face." I reached for Dave and stroked his sideburned cheek, and he responded by patting me on the head. "Relax your Kegel muscles" were the last words of the meditation as T.T. welcomed us to his 259th show, and opened up with the Smiths' "Heaven Knows I'm

Miserable Now." My smile was wide, my mind felt clear, and my heart was open. It was going to be a good night.

One person put in a slip. I waited for one more before joining in. The song selection was understandably limited, based on what T.T. could play. Still, I found plenty of appealing options to choose from, selecting an initial song that fit the religious theme. I had scanned the list and looked for something I knew really well, since I would be singing along with an organ—something I hadn't done since fourth-grade choir—and reading lyrics stacked in a disorganized binder. No monitor, no words lighting up in a screen as the song progressed—not even sheet music to follow the notes. But T.T. was always there to help any singer if they got lost—as pretty much everyone did. He helped us find our way.

When my name was called, I went behind the organ to a coat rack to pick out one of the many choir robes hanging there; I choose a deep red, and zipped it on. T.T. coached me through "Only the Good Die Young"; together, we established the pace of the song, which was followed by the intro, then a head nod from T.T. telling me it was time to sing about trying to win the affections (or at least the lust) of a Catholic school sweetheart.

I got lost a couple of times, and when that happened T.T. stopped and picked up where we left off. On this night, I was just like all the other singers, whereas usually I thought of myself as one of the more capable. Here, we all screwed up, we all lost our way, and we all knew it was safe to do so. At Sister Louisa's, all was forgiven. I had no idea how well I sang; applause was doled out equally. While a part of me cared, mostly I just had fun putting on a robe and belting out notes. I wanted to share this experience with everyone.

T.T. needed a rest from playing and suggested a group photo. Everyone on the second floor crowded near each other, except for one volunteer photographer. T.T. lay in front of the group, and the moment was captured. Then the music began again: "Keep those requests coming through the call center. If you don't, tiny menopausal ladies in pantsuits will jump on my penis—instead of my other organ—and it feels like crabs. So either you sing, or I get crabs."

A young man with blond curly hair and a British accent chose a dark blue robe before he sang "Milkshake" by Kelis, and the bar erupted in laughter at the combination of stately music and highly sexualized lyrics. As he sat down, T.T. smiled and said, "Never apologize for your art."

I went down the stairs to get us another round of drinks before singing my second song, "It's Raining Men." (Hallelujah! Amen!) The bartender handed me a button with Sister Louisa's slogan: "Fuck Fear." I pinned it to my wallet, next to my button that read, "I <3 Molly." The slogan fit Sister Louisa's perfectly; the place was all about taking risks. Its art and its karaoke style were risks. Every time someone donned a robe, they put themselves out there, and were most likely to fail—but we were all there to catch them. T.T. was there to guide us back to where we needed to be to finish our songs, and let our voices be heard.

I carefully walked back up the stairs, balancing three sangrias, and rejoined my congregation.

CHAPTER 38
FLORIDA AND ALABAMA
August 18. 2016

D AVE AND I BADE LYNN FAREWELL AND HEADED FARTHER SOUTH. I hit a wall, inexplicably feeling a lack of support despite a partner in the seat right next to me, going every mile with me. I felt responsible for his happiness, my happiness, yet unable to bring my A-game. Normally I was a go-getter and a motivator, but I found myself tired of planning—afraid something would go wrong and hold the agenda back for days. I had no reason to feel this way—it was just a floating feeling that got lodged in my heart and settled in as fear. It was weird to see my journey as hard, but it was. Somehow, driving across the country, which should have been seen as a vacation, was becoming a bit of a struggle, and for that I felt ashamed and unworthy.

Dave drove, and I stared out the passenger window at nothing in particular. I can't remember what there was to see, but I still recall the flat silence that filled my head and the space between us. In the late morning, we stopped at an antique market. Individual booths were filled with quilts, mugs commemorating events long passed, and guns. As we wandered through this collection of Southern minutiae, I found myself thinking that if I could sing in two states that night, we could get to my friends' house in Louisiana a day early. An extra day of rest, an extra day of friendship. I ducked into a booth full of shot glasses and spoons and began to research the possibility of a sudden change of plans, reinvigorated by the idea of breaking from my routine. I looked up websites, made calls, and saw possibility. Dave and I would dip our toes into Florida, I would sing a song, and we would drive a mere thirty miles to more karaoke in Foley, Alabama. The person on the phone in Pensacola said karaoke started at 8 p.m., which gave us plenty of time to do both.

As we crossed the border into Florida, all I saw were churches, and billboards letting drivers know about different churches hidden off the main road. I wondered how so many places of Christian worship could exist in such unpopulated areas, and understood the need for them to advertise to potential congregation members. I called the bar in Florida again to confirm the time, and a new person said karaoke started at eight thirty; rationally, I knew that the half hour made no difference in the plan, but my stomach seized slightly with the new information.

We arrived in Pensacola with hours to spare, and parked my car near Seville Quarter, a tourist trap conglomeration of bars and restaurants that had once been old warehouses. The façade was updated with soft green and grey paint, and electric lights made to look like nineteenth-century lanterns were equally spaced down the dark wooden overhang. It was here that I was going to sing at Lili Marlene's World War I Aviator's Pub. A valet/bouncer manned the door to the complex, and I asked yet again about the karaoke start. This time it was "eight thirty, possibly nine," with a warning to get inside by eight in order to avoid the ten-dollar cover charge. Another potential half-hour setback—and again the bubbling of a panic attack. Maybe spontaneity had been a horrible mistake.

A walk to enjoy the view of the Gulf of Mexico seemed like the perfect distraction. The salty air and seagulls settled my nerves as Dave and I walked out to the edge of a pier to watch the sun set into the calm Atlantic. Among the many boats docked along the way was a yacht upon which several young white men were drinking and laughing. A large "Make America Great Again" flag fell limp from the lack of a breeze. My nerves and insecurity from the uncertainty of the day transformed into anger. I wanted to scold the laughing men, who could afford to drink light beers from frosted glasses on a yacht in a harbor as the sun set. I assumed these men supported Trump in order to get more, but they clearly didn't need it. These men could support Trump because it wasn't *their* pussies he grabbed. I saw these men as among the privileged who liked their power and believed Trump would make sure they kept it. I tried to be more understanding of those who have different opinions from mine—to no avail. There are just some times I can't muster the open heart and mind it takes to understand those who perceive the world so differently.

Back at Lili Marlene's, I ordered a beer to calm my nerves and Dave got a Coke to help him stay awake for the drive to Foley. I asked one more time when the karaoke was supposed to begin. When the server said, "Ten—it's college night, and the kids don't really get going until then," tears automatically fell as my will shattered. I was sure that by the time we got to the bar in Alabama, it would be packed and the KJ would be taking no more new singers. The startled server quickly checked again with the bartender and was told 9. Dave looked down into his drink; I'm sure he wished there were booze in it.

Moments later, the KJ started setting up, and I felt brave enough to breathe. I got the courage to introduce myself to the

KJ, and explained my journey and that evening's atypically tight timeline. He responded with a smile, and said, "We'll start at 9, even if it's just you and me." I wanted to collapse under the release of my own doubts, but instead I continued to chat with the KJ as he set up his gear. He'd been hosting karaoke since 1980, when his equipment consisted of a tape recorder, a microphone, and sheet music. Over the decades, he had watched his karaoke business grow from a small gig in one dive bar in Sacramento to large-scale operations across multiple venues, hosting shows nightly in more elaborate spots such as large tourist venues and sports bars. His songbook had grown from a few hundred selections to hundreds of thousands. As our conversation continued, my mind settled and I felt excited about my two-states-one-night quest again.

My selection was queued up just a hair past nine, even though there were only five others in the bar. I saw the song title flash on the screen and began to laugh; in my stress and confusion, I had written down the wrong song—"One Thing Leads to Another" instead of "One Way or Another." I sheepishly asked to change the song, and the KJ complied. I'm not sure why I really cared; I've sung both before. Still, I switched the Fixx out for Blondie. As I sang, three bored looking twentysomethings stared at their phones. Normally I would have hated that, and a "Hey, I'm singing here" feeling would have crept up on me as I looked out into indifference—but that night I was happy and relieved to sing, even to no one.

When my song was sung, Dave and I thanked the staff at Lili Marlene's and sped off in the pouring rain, the windshield wipers moving as fast as they could, as water ran across the road in front of us. Though Dave's visibility wasn't great, the traffic was sparse, steady, and uneventful. We arrived at bar number two, in state number two, a little after ten. The line to sing was in the single digits. Getting myself wound up over nothing is annoying as hell, yet I can't do anything to stop it.

Expecting the worst and creating a potential disaster comes naturally to me.

Foley was purported to be a tourist town, but we couldn't see the beach through the black wet night, and nothing about where we were signaled vacation, even though it was still summer. The streets were dark and deserted, the buildings worn and tired. The bar was long and narrow, like a galley kitchen, and full of smoke. Two stocky men were singing a duet from their seats at the bar, beers in front of them, cigarettes resting in the ashtray. Both were wearing Confederate flag baseball caps, and half the pair was also wearing a black leather vest with a Confederate flag on the back, and a Confederate flag chain wallet was peeking out of his back pocket.

Dave motioned for me to take a seat at a table on the left, across from the bar. He went to get us a pair of cheap American beers, not wanting to stick out any more than we already did. Though we were dressed pretty generically—me in a simple polka-dotted dress, him in dirty jeans and a well-worn t-shirt—we did pull into the parking lot in a car with Oregon plates and a cartoon Buddha on the dash. And nowhere on our persons was a Confederate flag. We were strangers here.

As I waited for Dave to return from the bar, I read the collage of signs that decorated the wall next to me:

> You can't be old and wise if your [sic] not young and crazy first.
> The Smartest [sic] thing a man ever said was "yes, dear."
> This is not Burger King. You can't have it your way . . .
> A woman who is looking for a husband never had one.

Dave returned with our beers and pointed out his favorite:

> ASAP: As Southern As Possible

I took a long, deep swig and looked more carefully at the

company we shared. Everyone was white, and no one looked as though they came from money. A woman wearing a ribbed tank, her hair pulled back in a braid, flicked ashes onto the carpet beneath her stool; her male companion stared through the wall of booze behind the bartender, who sighed deeply as she mopped up spilled beer with a frayed towel. This was the sort of bar I thought I would see more of on this trip, but never did. This was the slice of America I assumed I would see based on all the Trump signs and flags I passed, all the trailers and Dollar Generals, all the closed-down stores and anti-choice billboards. I finish my beer quickly, put in a song, and got Dave and me a second round. I was carded, and smiled but complied; the guy next to me explained that Alabama had strict ABC (alcoholic beverage commission) laws when it came to serving. Bartenders were supposed to card everyone, no matter their age. I said that at my age it was nice to be carded, even if it was not specific to my looks. When I told him I was forty-seven, he thought it was funny that I was ten years older than he was. His red skin and heavy beard made us look the same age.

My name was called, and I walked to the front of the bar to sing. I tried not to look too nervous, but I was. I had chosen Juice Newton's "Queen of Hearts" for its country bent and '80s nostalgia. As soon as it started to play, people recognized the tune and their faces brightened. People tapped their feet on the barstool stoops and quietly hummed along, swaying their heads to the cute, friendly beat.

When I finished, I was met with generous applause and a handshake from the KJ, who asked where I was from. Dave got up from the table to join in on the conversation, and possibly act as a protector. When I mentioned my journey, the KJ was excited to hear we had chosen Foley as our Alabama stop: "Not too much happens here. Mind if I put it on my website?" I said I would be honored. He said he shared my dream to sing in all fifty states—but he was only up to nine so far. I assured him that we all start somewhere, and that someday he would have a chance to get on the road and sing across the country; his smile revealed a mixture of doubt and hope. As our conversation progressed, more and more people leaned in to listen; others asked where our next stop would be. When I replied we were headed to Louisiana the next day, a grey-haired woman several Budweisers into the night said to make sure "to call the Google" to check on the roads, as many had flooded during the night.

That night, I stood side by side with many people whose politics and life views I found unsettling—but to a soul, all were kind. They made small talk, filled me in on liquor laws, shared their dreams, and helped with mine. The bottom line was that everyone was friendly—and that unnerved me. These people were nice, but I also figured their niceness had its limits. We didn't talk politics; then again, maybe they would have been nice in those circumstances, too. I thought about my reactions to the young men on the yacht earlier that evening, and realized I knew no more about them than I did about those I had sung with. Maybe I could have listened to these folks from Foley explain why they were supporting Trump. Maybe they didn't support him; I honestly had no idea, because I didn't ask. I just assumed that anyone who had four visible Confederate flags on them wouldn't be voting for a female Democrat. All I knew about where I sang was that the KJ played fair when it came to the song rotation; I witnessed how the locals clapped for each other and me, a total outsider. Basic kindness existed under symbols of hate. I suppose this was as close to an epiphany as I would ever have on this trip, though I was smart enough to know that I wasn't transformed by the experience. A true change of heart and mind takes time, and my stay in Foley, Alabama was brief and superficial. But that night, amid the friendly chatter, applause, and helpful advice, I saw another side of the kind of people I often professed to stand against. That night I was reminded that humans are complex.

When Dave and I got to our hotel room, I took the advice of the drunken woman and "called the Google." I was glad I did. Sure enough, our planned route to get to Louisiana was closed; in fact, most of the roads were completely flooded.

CHAPTER 39

LOUISIANA

August 20, 2016

I N THE DAYLIGHT, DAVE AND I WERE ABLE TO SEE FOLEY, THOUGH we didn't drift down to the coast. Instead, we drove out of town through a series of thrift, pawn, loan, adult, Bible, and "fried chicken 'n biscuit" shops. Under the advisement of the bar patrons in Foley, we took a more northerly route to Mandeville in order to avoid the flooded roads along the Gulf. There, we would stay with some of my dearest friends since college, Geoff and Lisa, in their new home an hour outside of New Orleans. Just months prior, I had visited them in China, where they lived in Chengdu for three years on a work assignment. They had since been transferred back to the United States. Before that, I had seen them at Molly's house—after her diagnosis, and after her treatment had left her bald and frail, struggling for breath. When they said goodbye to her, everyone knew it was the last time they would see her alive. Even though Geoff and Lisa's belongings were still on cargo ships in the middle of the ocean, they were excited to host Dave and me, and I was grateful to see them again in such a short time frame, in such a different setting.

But first, Dave and I spent some time driving around Mobile, Alabama, struck by its beauty. As we made our way up and down its residential streets, I saw proud manors in white, yellow, and peach, surrounded by large metal gates and lush gardens. The majestic South puffed up, proudly showing its feathers. Even the homes in need of a new coat of paint appeared glamorous. At lunchtime we pulled into a local spot— it was packed with cars, always a good sign. Unlike the homes we had just passed, this building was in clear need of repair— a low-level concrete block in chipped green paint and with bars on the windows. Clearly it wasn't the exterior charm that had drawn so many inside. Still, the place was packed: state workers with badges still hanging around their necks, police officers, and retirees. A true community place. Lunch was had by grabbing a tray and walking up to the cafeteria line, where owners and staff alike were hustling and smiling, doling out food by the scoop, continually replacing empty dishes with full ones from the back kitchen. Sweat poured down the foreheads of both workers and customers. The traditional soul food options promised amazing taste and no hope of caloric restraint. Black-eyed peas that had been cooked forever in ham hocks were finished with just enough vinegar to brighten them. Greens cooked for two forevers were given just enough red chili to flavor, but not overwhelm. Ham hocks contributed their richness to the greens, too—everything tastes better with ham hocks. I shouldn't have, but I cleaned my plate. Looking around the room, I saw most had done the same.

Beyond full, we inefficiently crossed through Mississippi, a state yet unsung, into Louisiana to see my friends. (We'd pick up Mississippi in a few days, on a loop through the South after picking up our friend Russell, who was flying to Louisiana. A central California native who had lived in Oregon for a huge chunk of his life, he wanted to see this part of the country.) We listened to a local sports radio station talk about the merits of the University of Mississippi, Ole Miss, no longer allowing its marching band to play "Dixie" during football games. The hosts said times had changed; the composition of the football team had changed over the years, and there was no reason to continue to celebrate with the anthem of the Confederacy. While not calling race out specifically, the hosts managed to convey a clear message that a song like that had no place in the future of the university.

Several listeners called in to express their disagreement, demanding tradition be respected, insisting the song's origins had long been forgotten, and therefore had lost their meaning. To many, "Dixie" *was* Ole Miss, and to take that away was simply bowing down to the politically correct, who were being overly sensitive. In their voices I heard a mixture of disgust, disappointment, and anger. The hosts respectfully stood their ground, but allowed the conversation to continue. I was happy to hear those who thanked Ole Miss for eliminating that song from its repertoire, happy to know that my opinion was at least shared by a few folks who listened to sports radio in the Deep South.

As soon as Dave and I made it across the Louisiana border, Dave's priority was to find a drive-thru liquor place—not one where you drive your car into a bottle shop, pop your trunk, and drive off with a couple of cases of beer, but where you drive up to a window like any other fast-food place and order a drink. In Louisiana, that drink can have booze in it.

Within ten miles, we were able to fulfill our mission just outside of Bogalusa, a small "city" of just over 12,000, whose website boasts a "modern sewage disposal system that serves 100% of the city." The air was humid and damp, the trees dense and dripping; I don't think this place ever dried out. The drive-thru was on the left-hand side of the road, so Dave made a quick U-turn, pulling up next to a run-down shack with peeling white paint and bright blue and pink support columns. There, he ordered a hurricane—what else when you're in Louisiana? It was handed to him in a Styrofoam cup and plastic lid; the straw, still in its wrapper, was offered in a separate transaction, to abide by open-container laws. As we drove off, Dave took two sips of the red chemical syrup before declaring it undrinkable. One sip was enough for me. Every once in a while, Dave would reach for it again to see if it got any better. It never did.

By late afternoon, we pulled into Geoff and Lisa's new home. It was huge, located in a town my friends had chosen for its schools. Geoff met me at the door with a hug that calmed all the nerves I was feeling—and even those I didn't realize I had. He was one of those people who could make my life okay, no matter what was going on. And even though my life at that moment was blissful, the fatigue of travel had started to build, and all at once it melted away in his presence. Geoff then greeted Dave with a smile and handshake; it was their first time meeting, and I was nervous. Though Dave got along with almost everybody, this meeting was important to me, more so than the meeting of the parents. Geoff and Lisa were some of the closest family I had (and still are today).

Beers in hand, Geoff took us on the house tour. When I told Geoff that Dave and I could live in the pool house, which had its own bathroom and kitchenette, I was only half-joking. When Lisa came home from work, we headed to a restaurant where I had barbecued oysters for the first time. I vowed it wouldn't be the last.

The next afternoon, after a leisurely swim and general lazing about, Lisa, Geoff, Dave and I piled into Lisa's SUV, crossed the twenty-three-plus-mile Lake Pontchartrain Causeway (the world's longest continuous bridge over water), and headed to the Louis Armstrong International Airport to pick up Russell. Crossing the bridge, we could see the dark clouds over the New Orleans skyline hurtling towards us, and within minutes, it began to rain. Hard. Traffic began to build, as the other side of the bridge brought us into a mess of cars traveling to the Saints preseason game, and a few weather-inspired accidents. From the backseat, I saw a billboard that on one side featured a baby pleading, "Planned Parenthood, I'm worth more than the sum of my parts," and on the other, a Larry Flynt's Hustler Club advertisement.

We picked up Russell and headed to Bourbon Street. The clashing sounds of jazz, blues, rock, and mariachi from both inside bars and street performers filled the air with harmonious cacophony. There were clowns, people on stilts, clowns on stilts. There were people on the street begging for money and booze. We all paused to see if a mime and a drunk tourist were going to come to blows before we ducked into one of the many voodoo souvenir shops. Then it was time to sing karaoke. On Bourbon Street. On a Saturday night. The idea thrilled me as though I was preparing for a chance to perform at Carnegie Hall.

The Cats Meow (no apostrophe) is one of the most popular karaoke bars in the United States—which is not surprising given its prominent location on one of the most well-known nightlife streets in the world. It live-streams all performances on its website, and anyone knows that if you want to get a song in, you have to get there early and be prepared to wait along with all the other tourists and wedding parties, amid the smells of vomit and bleach. We made it ten minutes before the end of the happy hour, which advertised "3 for 1" drinks. We assumed that meant we would get three drinks for the price of one. What it actually meant was that each of us got three (watered down) shots into our gin and tonics. Such is New Orleans.

I grabbed the limited song list and made a choice quickly. On some level, there was no reason the choices should have been so restricted, but I gathered that was all part of the bar's image; by controlling inventory, there was no way a singer could bring the place down with a song that was either too slow or not well-known. The carefully crafted list consisted of nothing but upbeat classics spanning across the decades and across rock and dance genres, with a little country thrown in. There was something for every singer, and each song was for everyone. The Cats Meow was always packed, and those who ran the show there planned to keep it that way through careful orchestration disguised as a free-for-all party.

I yelled my song choice over the drunken crowd to the young woman who managed the rotation—she was dressed in ripped jean shorts and metal cat ears. She wrote my name at the bottom of a long list at her podium, and I returned to my company and drink to wait. Singers stared as the woman in cat ears wrote the names of the current and on-deck singers, as well as those in the hole, on a glow-in-the-dark board. If you saw your name, you needed to wait behind a velvet rope for your turn. The host of the show was an older African American man in a Superman t-shirt and bandanna. He entertained the crowd, encouraging people to dance on the stage to music videos between singers. The third member of this team was a mystery person, in a booth up above, choosing the dance tracks, queueing up the songs, and keeping the party going.

The performers were a mix of seasoned singers and drunken bachelors; talent didn't matter. The cheers were loud and alcohol-ridden for everyone who sang, and many on the floor crowded the stage, sang, and clapped along as they would at any concert. Though I had settled in next to the bar, away from the central action, the energy was infectious. I wanted to get on that stage and be the reason for the excitement. Finally, I saw my name in glowing green. I downed the rest of my 3-fer and took my place next to the velvet rope with a large brass hook to prevent soon-to-be singers from getting up on the stage prematurely. Then I was let in, the host holding my hand as I gathered my skirt, stepped onto the creaky wooden stage, and grabbed the mic.

I had chosen "Heartache Tonight" by the Eagles, for its loud, Southern vibe. It was a rock song that was also country—a song I felt everyone in the bar would know. Except me, it turned out. I confidently belted out most of the song with all the gusto and sass I could muster, and had the crowd going. Emboldened, brash, and proud, I skipped straight to the climax of the song, forgetting a verse. Oops. I quickly recovered with a shrug and a smile, and closed out strong, walking across the stage encouraging the crowd to sing along.

It was over all too quickly, and I reluctantly handed the mic back over to the host, who gave me a high-five as I was escorted to the other side of the rope, the other side of the podium, and back into the river of humanity that is Bourbon Street.

CHAPTER 40

MISSISSIPPI

August 22. 2016

THE FIRST PART OF OUR JOURNEY INTO MISSISSIPPI PROVIDED LUSH scenery and smells of yellow pine, but this soon transitioned into fields of cotton, dead corn, and soy. Lots and lots of soy. Rolling fields of soy interspersed with houses of varying levels of wealth.

Some houses—those usually at the base of larger farms or nestled into small alcoves—were two-story and pristine white. Others—closer to the road and without the cover of a tree canopy—looked like they were barely supported by their foundations. Tarps held on by rocks covered or replaced their roofs, and several rusted appliances were scattered out front. As we drove through these dilapidated yet occupied stretches, each as despairing as the one before, questions flooded my mind. Sometimes I would ponder them silently, sometimes I would express them out loud to Dave and Russell: Where do these people work? Where do they get food? How far away do they live from their friends? How many people live in that house? How do they pick up a welfare check? Cash it? Where do they hang out? In some locations, that last question was easier to answer: there would be a bar or two, and several churches on a small Main Street otherwise occupied by boarded-up shops. I never saw a bank.

There were few political signs on this leg of the trip. Maybe there was no one to persuade. Or perhaps no one here cared about politics. Mississippi ranks last in household income, with over 20 percent living in poverty (that is, earning less than $24,000 a year for a family of four). Under these conditions, I could understand the lack of enthusiasm for any candidates.

In Jackson, the state capital, we found ourselves driving on the worst roads I had ever been on. Potholes, rubble, and inadequate patchwork made for a bumpy ride for passengers, and a destructive one for my car. Dave entertained himself by playing slow-motion slalom to avoid as many potholes as possible. We passed government buildings on State Street, where the Department of Corrections building was much more impressive than the one housing the Department of Education. Several billboards advertising a suicide prevention program, Shatter the Silence, dominated the advertising. I wasn't sure if that was out of need, or a lack of competition from local businesses for the space. The car hit another bump and jolted me from my thoughts.

When we got to the hotel in Ridgeland, the pouring rain drenched me as I ran to the lobby and checked in. We had to park somewhat far away because they were repaving half their parking lot (it was too bad they couldn't fund actual road improvement) but considered ourselves lucky to get the last spot. After a brief rest, we saw that though the rain had stopped, the clouds remained threatening, so we didn't take the short walk over to the venue. It was just as well. Despite many phone calls, during which I had been assured that

Burgers and Blues would have karaoke, when we got there the stoned host mumbled he wasn't sure if they were going to have karaoke or not due to potential lack of interest. The manager was at Sam's Club, and he wouldn't know for sure until he got back. I looked around the room at the few customers, and made an executive decision: instead of taking our chances there, we drove back to Jackson, where we'd seen a sign for the Pig and Pint—an establishment that specialized in two of our favorite things. Regrouping there was as good a plan as any.

At Pig and Pint, the three of us split a heaping meat platter, and the greens were amazing. So was the mustard sauce. The bartender was eager to serve us the beers we would like, and so asked us our preferences and poured us samples. As we consumed our bounty, in relative silence outside of a few grunts of satisfaction and negotiations as to who would get the last piece of brisket, I searched for a new venue. The task turned out to be surprisingly easy, even on a Monday in Mississippi.

Our timing was perfect as we rolled up to the new backup karaoke venue—an Irish pub with little Irish about it except Smithwick's Red on tap, dark wooden walls, and Scotch eggs on the menu alongside fried pickles and fish tacos. The vibe was cozy and simple. The KJ wore tiny glasses and a Sesame Street t-shirt, and took a cigarette break on the balcony during almost every song. The book was inconsistently organized—alphabetically by last *and* first name. Selections were put in by scribbling on the back of a piece of bar tab paper. It was a basic eclectic system that got the job done.

The crowd was a mix of older African Americans and younger white folks. I heard the Red Hot Chili Peppers, Otis Redding, Garth Brooks, Reba McEntire, and Anna Nalick's "Breathe (2 AM)," which was sung by a gender ambiguous young adult in overalls. Everyone was pretty damn good except for a group of women who did their best singing Beyoncé. They had a good time doing it, and I had a good time listening to their laughter and gusto. I sang "Rhiannon" by Fleetwood Mac, because its pace matched the quiet of the evening, and I knew it was one of Russell's favorites. The microphone stand wasn't quite right, and when I put the mic away after I finished, it started to slide out, coming close to falling to the ground before the KJ leaned over to catch it. A patron instructed, "Stick it in, don't slide it," while making suggestive gestures to illustrate. Everyone laughed at the innuendo.

The last performance we heard, sung by a middle-aged man in a cowboy hat and checkered shirt, was "Live Like You Were Dying" by Tim McGraw. It was a sappy song that didn't exactly fit into the typical lighthearted karaoke spirit—but it made me smile and feel gratitude, as its poignant request was exactly what I was doing.

CHAPTER 41
ARKANSAS
August 23, 2016

OUR INEFFICIENT ROUTE THROUGH THE SOUTH CONTINUED. WHILE it would have made geographic sense to continue up north to Tennessee for the next stop, we instead headed west to Arkansas, to meet Anthony, who was free that night but was off on vacation the next. He was another singer I had met on Karaoke Across America, though his prowess took on a whole different level. He competed in karaoke contests all across the nation and the world. I'd seen signs for karaoke contests here and there around Oregon—bar marquees that would advertise fifty dollars, one hundred dollars, and sometimes higher prize amounts for winners. I had never participated in any of those contests, neither seeking them out nor shying away from them. The idea of karaoke as a contest—trying to sing one's best in order to be better than others—didn't appeal to me. Still, I was intrigued by the idea of someone who competed at such a large scale, so it was completely worth driving out of my way to meet such a man.

The trip to Little Rock also gave Dave a chance to reconnect with a friend. As soon as we pulled into his driveway, Dean opened his front door and waited for us alongside his girlfriend of two years—a woman he would marry the following summer. The couple made the three of us—Dave, Russell, and me—feel welcome right away. They showed us to our rooms and then into their sunken living room for conversation and dinner—all in preparation for singing later that night. We sat on old but carefully chosen furniture—gold velvet couches and broken-in chairs with large floral patterns. A makeshift stage—the focus of many jam session parties—was set up in the corner. Artwork of all varieties adorned the walls—pieces by friends and local artists, and from global travels. Three dogs lived in the porch area off to the side. They were quiet, for the most part, used to their separate living quarters—but they would occasionally erupt into a chaos of barking when a squirrel broke a tree branch or something else stirred their interest.

Dave had first met Dean when they both taught English in Iksan, South Korea, and played in Mongtooth, a band that boasted playing "3-chord drunk rawk" on its Facebook page. A year later, Dave convinced Dean to join him in Saudi Arabia, in a small city not far from Yemen, during America's takedown of Osama Bin Laden. Despite the severity of the situation—the evacuations, the slurs against American culture, the tension of war—their stories focused more on their experience making illegal booze out of fresh fruit juice and smuggled champagne yeast, on their lazy students, on their weekend adventures in the desert featuring armed and angry nomads, and on their memories of a handful of teachers who had gone mad under the stress of living in a country where they were hated. All these stories brought laughter to the point of tears—the kind of laughter shared by those who have bonded over adversity.

Jennifer was not only kind enough to feed us (she'd set up a taco bar in the kitchen), but also kind enough to drive us to Jimmy Ray's, a bar outside of any form of civilization, off a small country road nowhere near the kind of place I would expect to see a "karaoke bar and dance club." We pulled into the dirt parking lot next to a sign that said "Karaoke party: 8 p.m." and went in, escaping the Southern heat I was starting to grow accustomed to. With its black walls and floors, the bar was dark, except for a mirror covering an entire wall and a shiny suit of armor against one wall. Throughout the night, the mirrors' reflections confused me. I kept thinking the place was twice as big as it was, and found myself wanting to explore the other room that didn't exist.

We arrived before Anthony and his friends, but the bar was waiting for us. The bartender (she might have been the manager) ran up to me and gave me a big Southern hug. She said she recognized me from Facebook, and that she'd been dying to meet me. "Please plop your buns here," she told us. "The three of you should sit over here—what can I get y'all to drink?"

"Here" was a long, empty table all set up for a big crowd. A slightly smaller table full of older folks was already full; many of those seated wore cowboy hats. One guy was so tall he had to remove his hat and duck to get into the bathroom. The KJ, a perky woman with a sexy bob, had told these regulars to come early to get onto the list because the night was going to be busier than usual. Before I knew it, half an hour before start time, the line to sing was already eight deep, names scrolling along the bottom of a gigantic screen at the back of the stage. The old-folks' table skewed country all night—which was not surprising, given the hats. So I chose a song by CCR I thought would blend in with their set. I saw it as a good warm-up. I'd been thinking I wanted to bring my best tonight, or at least try a little more than usual. I cared what the champion thought of me.

He arrived just as the country karaoke was getting started. Anthony's introductory hug was warm and genuine, and I felt like I was going to be spending the evening with a long-lost friend. His dark, round face was that of someone who wore his emotions for all to see. There was never a question how Anthony was feeling: one look at his eyes, the shape of his mouth, the depth of his brow, and you knew whether he was joyful, frustrated, or in pain. I immediately liked this champion—another soul who had gone out of his way to set up a party for me, to help me with my quest—a huge act of kindness I simply hadn't been expecting when I started this journey.

Our table soon filled with Team Arkansas—seven singers, plus their coach and partners. As these folks filtered in, it became clear that there was another reason Anthony wanted to host a gathering for me; he wanted to show off his posse, a traveling group of highly talented singers who were preparing for the national competition in Seattle in less than two months. The winners—best male and best female—would represent the United States in the World Karaoke Championship. This was the same contest in which Anthony had received top honors two years prior. He was proud of this group. They were his family.

I was glad Dave and Russell had Dean and Jennifer to chat with, as the main thing Team Arkansas talked about was the competition of karaoke. To them, karaoke was a carefully crafted performance. These people practiced weekly, singing the same songs a thousand times, then a thousand times again, in order to master their performances. They focused not only on their vocals, but also on microphone control—bringing the mic close and pulling it away at the precise moments that would build drama in their performances. Each time they raised their hands, closed their eyes, or stepped toward the front of the stage was carefully planned. And as they practiced, with every move, beat, and note they considered the four criteria that judges would consider:

1. Vocal quality: the quality and mastery of your voice, including range and timbre;

2. Vocal technique: pitch, breathing, and overall vocal skill;

3. Stage presence: your charisma, confidence, and audience appeal (I know I fall way short here, doing little more than sway awkwardly during instrumental breaks); and,

4. Artistry. Anthony described this as "making the song your own."

While the first three criteria made sense to me as someone who had never entered a karaoke competition, I was surprised at the last one. Making a song one's own, to me, seemed to be the antithesis of karaoke. How was I supposed to draw people into my song if I was trying to change it, create something new? Where was the nostalgia, the shared experience, in that?

At that moment I was better able to put into words what I thought were some of the fundamental differences between singing karaoke and singing in a band. While in the latter I applauded originality—either through the introduction of new songs, or the reinterpretation of covers—in the former I felt differently. To me, karaoke was more like live radio, a bringing of the expected into an intimate setting. While the song choices would always remain a surprise, the backing track—which by default was identical to the original—and therefore the vocal performance should simultaneously send the audience back into their own memories, and also bring them together in the moment. When I was able to share something like that, I felt the joy of singing in a bar to a group of strangers.

Yet at Jimmy Ray's, among the competitors sitting around

me, karaoke was perceived differently. Anthony counseled that the most important thing about entering a karaoke competition was the song choice, and others around us nodded. But whereas I chose songs to fit in, Anthony and the others saw song choice as a way to stand out. The first way to set yourself apart from the rest was to care about the song. The biggest mistake was choosing a song based on what the singer thought others would like—because then, Anthony noted, the song wouldn't have passion, or his personal stamp.

What Anthony said made a lot of sense. I nodded in agreement—the student learning from the master—but I kept to myself the fact that I often broke this rule when I sang (as I had with my first song choice of that night). The deeper lesson was something I had been figuring out more and more during this trip. On the one hand, I knew I should sing what I wanted—for if what I was singing brought me joy, then others would feel that, too. However, it wasn't quite so simple. Part of my joy was also the shared experience—I was happier when I made others happy. There was no point in bringing a crowd down by singing a slower song or totally changing styles—no matter how I felt. Similarly, I wouldn't feel right singing hard rock in a bar full of senior citizens. As with so much in life, the trick was in finding the balance between self and others— the balance that made life wonderful. Karaoke wasn't about me—it was about us.

My name was called and I took the stage with an awareness that I was about to break this supposedly fundamental rule of karaoke. I sang my best Creedence to the rapt attention of my table. I knew these singers were curious about my performance, and I almost felt guilty for singing a song I didn't care about—a song that was just "for fun" and had no meaning. When I finished, I received supportive applause and high-fives as I returned to the table. Partly in self-defense, and partly to show I was listening, I let them all know that

that song was just an easy warm-up, and that my next song would be one that I cared about. Carlos, a karaoke judge with a large build and hair pulled back into a ponytail, asked what I liked to sing best. People ask me that question all the time, and I still struggle with the answer. I responded with Olivia Newton-John and Stevie Nicks, though I also conceded that Donna Summer was a hell of a lot of fun. I purposefully left out the one-offs like "What's Up" and "It's Raining Men," and didn't admit how much I loved to sing Queen's "Somebody to Love"—I knew I could never sing it well enough to confess it as a favorite among this crowd.

Carlos's eyes lit up when I mentioned Olivia, and Anthony butted in to request "Magic," while Carlos suggested "Xanadu." I "practiced" each for a couple of seconds in the bathroom, to figure out which one I wanted to sing. I focused on what I was in the mood for, and which one felt more settled and natural in my heart at that moment. I thought about getting a chance to sing "Magic," which can be a bit repetitive and slow, and that led me back to the point Team Arkansas was trying to make all night: sing what you want, when you want.

I walked up to the KJ and committed to the slower song, feeling a slight rebellion against myself. She shared that she hadn't made the cut for Team Arkansas; her voice had been off that night, and her energy low—it was not meant to be. Though she smiled, I could read the disappointment in her worried brow and defeated shoulders. I had heard her sing a bluesy number earlier, and she was damn good, carrying herself with confidence on stage, belting out notes with bravado. If *she* didn't make the team, who the hell did?

I was about to find out. The singers at my table had taken their time putting in their song requests, and were only now coming to the stage. At this point the list of those waiting for their time in the spotlight was more than twenty-five deep— the longest line of singers I'd seen since I had hit the road almost two months prior. It was then that I realized I had only ten more states to sing in. A rocket countdown before my mission was complete.

Anthony was first up, and performed "New York, New York" with more musical flair than Frank. He was serious up there—eyes focused, moves deliberate. He brought a finely choreographed performance to the stage, not merely a song. Others from the team followed in similar fashion, with everything from Radiohead to Bonnie Raitt to Josh Groban. The woman who had come in second at a national championship sang Adele to perfection. For her, the choreography was minimal—she sat on a stool the entire time. Still, everything about her movement—the angle at which the stool was tilted, every wave of her arm, the occasional closing of her eyes—looked as though it had been practiced. Each member of the Team contributed a polished performance. They'd clearly all been coached, like I've seen happen on shows like *The Voice*—only here in Arkansas the coaching was done by Anthony and a man named Bill, who wore a black ten-gallon hat and walked with a cane.

Since it was a party, we had cake—one chocolate, one lemon, both homemade. I had a slice of each. They were both delicious, though not the best when paired with beer; Dave had been buying pitchers of Dos Equis, each served with several slices of lime on the rim. As everyone ate, I looked around the room, struck by its diversity. While the table of older people (I placed them in their sixties, if not seventies) was white, our table was pretty diverse racially—and sexually, too. Seated with me were a hotel desk clerk, a nurse, and a high school career counselor. Some were in their early thirties, possibly younger. Others were in their fifties. I was surprised when a couple at the end of the table talked about being afraid Trump would be elected; they said they would move to Canada if that happened. A mental health nurse, meanwhile, was an avid Trump supporter, convinced he was the only candidate strong enough to fix the "ISIS shit" and get America "off its lazy ass" and working again. I was surrounded by the mix of people I'd been assuming I'd see at so many bars, and saw that the differing opinions were real. These people were all on the same karaoke team. This "family" had all the players that made up America.

As the time grew later and fuzzier (I'd had a shot of Jägey to go with my beers), the songs continued, and the conversations grew more serious. Anthony took a long drag off his cigarette and confided in me. He told me how a singing rival referred to him as a "Queer Nigger Hitler" because he bossed his team around. Sharing the story made him cry—some of his teammates gathered around him, while others steered clear. Carlos and a man who called himself Mr. Swoon put their hands on his shoulder and said, "At least Hitler was smart. Messed up, but smart." They admitted, though, that the other words were painful. The topic was dropped quickly after that, leaving me stunned and a little sick as I scanned the rest of the table, trying to identify who had said those words. I had my guesses, but never found out for sure.

Hours after my CCR debut, my name was called for my final song of the night. The peak energy of the place had long gone, as many had left and the attention of those remaining had shifted to their phones—especially Anthony, who had grown particularly quiet since sharing his story. I needed to sing for me, but I knew part of what I was doing was for the judge and coach—if they were even paying attention. My friends were, and they interrupted their conversations to hear my rendition of "Magic," as through its lyrics let people know that nothing would stand in my way.

It wasn't my best performance by a long shot, but my love for that song glowed inside me. I hoped my deep admiration for Olivia had shone through. Those I sat with were several levels above what I was used to hearing and performing.

Simply holding my own felt good enough. In my heart, I knew that for me karaoke was about the bar, not the stage.

It was time to leave, and I bought a souvenir t-shirt and hugged everyone who was still at the table. When I embraced Anthony, I knew I had made a friend for life. While I knew I wasn't a true member of this family, I felt I could pass for a second cousin by marriage. As the five of us walked out—the people who were my Team Arkansas—a woman wearing a red-sequined dress, feather boa, and pillbox hat called me over. Her hair was dyed pink, and her false eyelashes could be seen from a distance. I had noticed her when she'd walked into the bar several hours earlier—it was hard not to—and had kept looking forward to hearing her sing. She never did, and never intended to. She just wanted to dress up to go to a dive bar and listen to amateurs sing. For all I knew, she wore sequins to the grocery store. As I approached, she reached out to me and clutched my hands a little too hard. There were tears in her eyes as she told me how beautiful my voice was. "I got lost in you," she said.

This connection is why I sing.

CHAPTER 42

TENNESSEE

August 25, 2016

INSTEAD OF DRIVING THE 137 MILES TO MEMPHIS, WE DROVE THE 424 miles to Nashville, in order to sing at Santa's Pub. It was the place suggested to us by Reddit users, and was located in a double-wide trailer that was perpetually decorated for Christmas. When Dave had found a t-shirt for the place in a West Virginia thrift store, he bought it, and we made the commitment to drive the extra 212 miles. I'd looked up the place online to see what time things got started, and according to their website, there were a few things basic things to know about Santa's Pub:

> Santa's is cash only. (There's an ATM outside)
> Beers start at $2.
> Karaoke every night. It starts at 7 PM (9 PM on Sundays).
> Be nice.

At 8 p.m., we walked into a room of stale smoke. Outside, the double-wide was surrounded by a hand-built wooden porch in need of a new coat of stain; it somewhat obscured the mural of Santa riding a Harley. Inside, there were enough Christmas decorations to notice, but not enough to make a bold statement in the way you would expect at a theme bar or a TGI Fridays around the holidays. Colored lights hung around the edges of the trailer—a Santa or elf tucked away here and there among some old video games. Cans and bottles of beer were the only drinking options, and the food menu, consisting of a few microwavable items, was scrawled on a piece of paper and stapled to the wall.

Karaoke had started an hour before, but the only patron was a heavyset dark-skinned trucker with a beautiful, deep voice; he was singing a country music ballad. Next to him was a lanky KJ with long, dark, greasy hair. When the trucker finished, the three of us clapped, and he looked up and smiled before wandering over to the KJ; the two of them leaned in to the computer monitor, debating what to choose next. The trucker sang a couple more as we got some beers and settled in. After a few more tunes, he asked if it was okay for him to do one more before he had to hit the road; he had fifteen more minutes on his break and "singing is a good way to keep this trucker happy and sane." Unlike him, we had all the time in the world, so he entertained us with some Waylon Jennings; I sat back and relaxed, feeling somewhat envious of the apparent simplicity of his life. Of course, I had no idea what lay behind the peaceful melodies I heard.

After the bartender took a turn, singing something from a lesser-known country artist, he and the trucker discussed this hidden talent and other good country options to try in the future. It was clear the trucker wasn't in a hurry to hit the road again after all, as he refilled his soda before going back to the stage. He asked our table if we knew "Wildfire." Russell and I did. Dave shrugged his shoulders—his musical past focused primarily on punk rock and some alternative; mellow classics from the '70s were way out of his familiar zone. The trucker told the KJ to cue it up, and then let us know somewhat apologetically that he'd never tried it before. He chose the tune because it "makes me weep like a baby when I'm alone in my cab."

The trucker faltered a few times, but "Wildfire" caters well to a person losing his place. The whole effect was beautiful: a large tough man singing a song of loss and desperation imperfectly in a bar where few were there to listen. He hefted himself off the stool and declared his singing done for the evening. I figured it was my turn. I chose "Desperado" by the Eagles, another song about loneliness that blended into the evening. The trucker stuck around to listen, then shook our hands, and hit the road. His hand was at least twice as big as mine, but his grip still gentle. Dave, Russell, and I were the only ones left—outside of the people who were paid to be there. I mentioned to the KJ that he should sing more, but he said that the night before had been slow as well—he had needed to sing a lot then, so he'd be taking it easy now. This left me and the bartender as the only ones taking the mic. I put in another song, and followed up with another while I was there—my first (and probably last) karaoke doubleheader. I chose songs that weren't part of my usual rotation, and fumbled through parts out of unfamiliarity. It didn't matter at all. Sometimes, the safety and encouragement from a small group of friends and a few strangers is all you need to try something new.

During a break, the KJ and bartender talked about "the most hated singer in all of Santa's—which is saying a lot because we get thousands in here." The man was a dance instructor who would waltz with himself while others were singing, twirling around as if he had a partner. The bartender left his station to demonstrate—one hand holding an imaginary companion at the waist, the other in the air holding an imaginary hand. The dance instructor's daily outfit of suspenders (which the bartender always snapped after he served him a beer) and an old-timey newsboy cap bugged the bartender and the KJ. "Who the hell does he think he is? *When* the hell does he think he is? He'll sing 'American Pie' and sound like Kermit—and not in a good way." Yet, according to the KJ and bartender, he thought he was good and judged others as they sang—I think that was the key to their annoyance. Yes, the attention-seeking of the outfits and the dancing might have put them on edge, but those would have been forgiven if the man had been supportive of the karaoke community. Someone who broke the karaoke code of support had no business being in Santa's.

No one else came by except for a group of three women who stopped in when I was at the mic. They briefly exchanged words with the bartender and left—I had no idea what it was about, but Dave heard him say, "That'll be a $3,500 fine if you do that," as they stormed out the door. I had promised a friend I would sing Barry Manilow on this trip. Manilow's slow, melancholy lyrics rarely stand up to a night out on the town, and I knew many notes would be too low for my range. The overall effect wasn't going to be pleasant. Still, I took my promises seriously, and I saw this dare as an element of fun torture for everyone there. Also, I had a not-so-secret respect for the singer-songwriter. His over-the-top lyrics became poignant when viewed through the lens of his forbidden love for another man—something I hadn't understood until recently.

I sat on the stool, made sure my feet were planted properly, and apologized with a smirk for what I was about to do—a crowd, no matter how small, is rarely up for a moment like this. I sang and laughed as both Dave and Russell filmed me for proof of the promise fulfilled (and most likely later blackmail purposes). Of course, this was when a few more patrons walked in. They stood in the back near the bar to listen, heads slightly tilted in confusion. While it wasn't pretty, it was good fun.

As we got up to leave a bit later, one of the patrons was standing out on the balcony. He waved goodbye, complimenting my "bold song choice." I thought about explaining myself, but I just thanked him as we drove away.

CHAPTER 43

OKLAHOMA

August 28, 2016

W E DROPPED RUSSELL OFF AT THE AIRPORT AND DOUBLED BACKED
through Tennessee and Arkansas, making our way to
Oklahoma City. I felt sad. I was sad about my sister-in-law and
Molly and the fact that we had dropped Russell off at the air-
port. I was sad that our country was so racist, and that Donald
Trump had so much support out here.

Our drive took us through Arkoma, an Oklahoman town
named because one could look wistfully into Arkansas and
wish they were there instead. It was the starkest example of
rural poverty I'd seen on this trip. Houses and trailers were
so run-down that it was no longer entertaining to play "dilapidated or abandoned"—the game we had started playing in
Maine. Somewhat paradoxically, a handful of these homes
featured newer satellite dishes, and cars that cost more than
mine. The whole landscape made me recognize I had no idea
what it was like to live as these people did. I didn't grow up

poor. I didn't grow up rural. I didn't grow up conservative. Maybe the people who lived here were happy. Perhaps growing up here in a culture embedded with low expectations enabled one to express gratitude over simpler things, like a roof over one's head (even if it leaked), or food on the table (even if it wasn't fresh). Or maybe the reality was as I saw it through my privileged eyes: that everyone here had given up.

Nancy's Lighthouse, my karaoke spot for the evening, was decked out with lighthouse pictures, old window panes, Christmas garlands, and colored lights. A series of American flags hung from the ceiling. The chairs and high-backed bar-stools were from the Brady Bunch era, their wood carved into intricate floral designs and stained a dull brown. The patrons sitting on them looked like they had been there for a couple of decades, as they chatted over their highballs; cigarette smoke streamed between them. It took several waves and audible "excuse me's" for our server to notice us and reluctantly come over to take our order. He was a skinny young guy in jeans and an untucked plaid button-down shirt with eyes darting to and fro as if looking for a way to escape. After a good half hour Dave got his nachos and I had a plate of mac and cheese, though I'd ordered pasta salad. Our server sighed audibly when I asked for what I'd ordered, and stomped off without replying, eventually returning with a heavily mayonnaised pasta salad and a scowl.

The karaoke signups were via a kiosk situated behind the stage and KJ. It was an awkward setup—in order to put in your song, you needed to walk in front of someone as they were singing, then stand behind them while signing up. A couple of times there was a line three or four deep as background for the performance. While I was waiting with my choice, I read a large sign stating "No swearing ever." Underneath that was another, smaller sign, reminding me to tip my KJ. The crowd wasn't too diverse (mostly white and overweight), but the songs performed were. They included Blue Öyster Cult, Portishead, some traditional country, and a Natalie Merchant fest—first, a woman sang 10,000 Maniacs, and immediately after two other women who had been sitting next to each other chose back-to-back songs from Merchant's solo days—the optimistic "Wonder" followed by the more haunting "Carnival." Soon after, a man and a woman who didn't seem to be acquainted both sang Led Zeppelin selections one after the other. Before her turn, the woman yelled, "Here's some fucking Zeppelin for you," so I guess the no-swearing rule was just a suggestion. Indeed, as the one black man in the whole place sang Boys II Men's "Water Runs Dry," a big dude sitting at the bar yelled, "Oh shit, bring it!" Nevertheless, when it was my turn to sing Styx's "Too Much Time on My Hands," I decided to change the lyrics such that I didn't give a "dang" (instead of "damn")—just in case.

Though I had sung the song several years before in a basement bar in Oregon, and it felt upbeat enough to get this uninspired crowd going a bit—but not too rowdy for the older clientele in their Brady Bunch stools—my performance sat heavy in front of me. It failed to capture anyone's joy, including my own. My voice felt strained on the longer notes, my tone all wrong for the song. I didn't get that same forced nasal quality that Tommy Shaw pulls off so effectively. Instead I sounded more like I was whining about not being able to watch one more hour of TV before going to bed. As the last chord sounded and my song came to an end, I sat back down and took a large sip of my drink.

Our server, absent for most of the evening (at least to us; I never managed to order a second drink, as he was nowhere to be found), sang Everlast's "What It's Like," and a customer hopped up from the bar and approached the stage. While he sang, she stood in front of him and wagged her finger; he shrugged his right shoulder in response. She continued to bark at him. The server finished the song, passing by our empty glasses, still chased by the woman as he cleared a table and served a drink, never making eye contact with as much as his shadow. Eventually, the woman stopped her badgering, either giving up or satisfied that her message had gotten through. She never stopped her death-stare at the guy. Dave and I postulated whether the disapproval was because he should have been working instead of goofing off, because there was foul language in the song he chose ("get a job, you fucking slob"), or because the song contained an empathetic verse about someone choosing abortion. Whatever the reason, the quality of his service never improved that evening.

The Boys II Men fan then sang "Don't Stop Believin'"—or more accurately, he chose "Don't Stop Believin'" and relied on the crowd to carry the tune. After screeching the first couple of lines flat and strained, he faced the microphone toward the tables and encouraged everyone else to take over, allowing him to drink the two bottles of Bud Light he carried with him up to the stage. For the most part, the crowd obliged, but barely. Everyone remained at their seats, faced their friends, and sang, restrained, in between awkward laughs and sips.

A late-arrival party of three really big men sat at a table next to Dave and me. The one wearing a Judas Priest t-shirt looked like a love child between Santa Claus and a member of Duck Dynasty. His friend had a partially shaved head, and the rest of his hair was dyed a faded green. He drank an orange soda cocktail. The final guy had a t-shirt that read "Try Not to Suck." Dave and I didn't stick around to see if he followed his own advice as he took the stage. Instead, we walked out of the smoke and into a clear night. The weather had broken, leaving a cool breeze and a simple peace as we walked silently back to the hotel.

CHAPTER 44

TEXAS

August 30, 2016

BEFORE LEAVING FOR TEXAS, WE STOPPED AT THE MEMORIAL SITE for the Oklahoma City bombing, a reminder that we had been dealing with domestic terrorism for a long time, and that attacking our own was sadly not just a sign of current times. A chain-link fence that surrounded the lush grounds was stuffed with tokens left behind by visitors: a ratty teddy bear, keychains, pictures of loved ones lost. I had forgotten how many children were killed that day. Their pictures and toys, hung on the chain-link fence by loved ones, reminded me that protests against the government rarely hurt those in charge.

Driving out of Oklahoma, we saw a lot of dead armadillos, buzzards pecking on them at the side of the road. Carcasses in the middle of traffic didn't deter the snackers, who would patiently wait until the last minute before flying out of the way of a passing car—only to resume their meal moments later. It was beyond hot outside, and I was tired, so Dave and I pulled into a Taco Mayo for some caffeine. My Dr. Pepper came in a cup with a Bible phrase on it. We spent the next few hours passing churches, and billboards advertising churches. There was also a slew of PSAs encouraging people to stop smoking for all sorts of reasons—for their health, for their children's health, because it's expensive, because it pollutes. Otherwise, the drive was a whole lot of nothing. Between the lackluster evening at Nancy's and the dull landscape, I think Oklahoma was my least favorite state.

Our entrance into Texas was marked by a significant increase in speed limit. It was seventy-five on roads that had been cracked and turned to rubble by the heat and constant use. Signs warned us to slow down to fifty in school zones. African deer grazed in the distance (ibex, perhaps) and Dave commented that if he lived in Texas he would get a tiger and have a shit-ton of land. Radio listening consisted of "the cowboy hour," sponsored by the Beef Council; Christian bluegrass; and a call-in show where you could get advice from a lawyer. Money seekers included those who experienced a parking lot hit-and-run, a woman trying to collect $1,600 in back child support from her ex who was on disability, and someone hoping to sue because the water guy left the cap loose on his property and he tripped over it while mowing his lawn. The lawyer politely let that last caller know that he'd better get that taken care of before someone else tripped over it—it was his responsibility. I could hear the eye-rolls across the air as the lawyer calmly let each and every caller know that the likelihood of a case was slim. All the questions had to do with money—or, more specifically, how to get more of it.

A day later, Dave and I rolled into Austin, on our way to see my college friends Tim and Sofia. Sofia had three kids and chronic fatigue, so our visit to her house was brief. Their uncle had died unexpectedly the day before. Dave and I were warned that the house would be in "chaos." Yet as I entered

Sofia's house, everything was the same as I remembered from the last time I had been there—the chaos no more nor less. The kids were bigger, the cats were older, but the house was still a creaking, inviting mess, littered with books and food yet to be put away. I sank deep into a couch whose pillows hadn't been fluffed in years. Tim, Sofia's brother, arrived shortly afterward. He lived with his parents and spent his days doing odd jobs to help his family, and riding his bike; I couldn't remember the last time the man had had a full-time job. I would never understand how he managed to live the way he did, but he seemed happy. I wasn't sure what else anyone needed in life.

Our singing companion that night was a friend of mine from Portland who had moved from the Pacific Northwest to go to school and land a job in the gaming industry. We made it to Dan's and dropped off our stuff. Then the three of us walked to the karaoke venue, cutting through the wet grass of Dan's apartment complex before strolling down the neatly paved sidewalks. The night air was still heavy and hot, but its fresh, damp consistency felt good against my skin.

On our walk, Dave got a text from his sister. His mother, Milly Rose, was in the hospital after having what they believed was a stroke. After a series of texts—no conversation—Dave felt certain that everything was fine. There was nothing he could do anyway, being thousands of miles away—so he put his phone away and continued walking. I was more panicky about what the hell was going on. Dave had always been better at letting things go, trusting life and its unexpected turns as they unfolded.

Canary Roost was located in a strip mall next to a bakery. Inside, it was large, divey, and cool—thanks to a powerful AC system. The KJ was flocked by regulars who came up to give her hugs as they walked in. She stopped her setup ritual each time, using both arms to squeeze each person hard. At 9 p.m.

sharp she kicked off the show by announcing the drink specials for the next hour, and then launched into the slow-paced "Major Tom." It was an interesting choice as an opener, but her dramatic vocals carried us energetically into the night. Throughout the show, she wandered from table to table, downing bright green shots and chatting with the regulars. People would sit next to her at the controls while searching for a song—even putting on large headphones to preview potential selections before committing. I felt as though I was the only unknown singer, but that didn't seem to matter. While the KJ had friends and fans, there were no favorites. I was called when it was my turn, and was kept in the rotation when I didn't put in a song—the KJ even came up to me to let me know I was next with no song in the queue. Caught off guard, I put in a go-to to stay in the mix.

A woman lost her place while singing Pearl Jam and apologized mid-song for her botched performance. No one bailed her out by singing along, which surprised me; with this sense of community in the bar, I thought someone, if not several people, would have started singing to help her find her way back into the music. Maybe everyone knew her well enough to know not to do that. Her friend, a woman with pink and blue hair intermingled with her natural blonde, was next. Her powerful yet melodic voice belted out a glam-rock number by Poison, but it was her stage presence that made the performance. Her head thrashing, air guitar, and strong movements complemented her black tank top and tight, ratty jeans. Besides her and the KJ, though, the quality of the singing was way below what I'd grown accustomed to. Night after night, I'd enjoyed so much talent hidden in bars across America— amazing voices coming from the very young and the very old, the professionally dressed and the unkempt. When a person got onstage, their song choice, sound, and overall performance remained a mystery until the opening line. It was one of the many hidden treasures of karaoke.

Yet in Austin—one of the music meccas of the United States—the fun level was high, but the talent level was not. A young woman accompanied her male friends several times to sing songs none of them knew well; their laughter often obscured the lyrics. The singers by and large also chose long songs—during one stretch, there were five in a row that were each over five minutes long, with sometimes painful results. But the fun everyone was having on the stage—laughing and hamming it up—took the edge off a little. I chatted up the lost singer and the rocker, as their table was right in front of mine. They both agreed that Canary Roost was the best place to try new things—the KJ was super chill, and the crowd forgiving. The two of them had been coming to this place for a while, always challenging themselves with new material, knowing that nothing bad would come of a less-than-desirable performance.

Dave received more texts from his sisters about his mom's "stroke." The ER doctor conducted tests and more tests, and then some more to make sure. By the end of the night, a team of doctors was pretty damn sure it was lung cancer.

Over the next few days, as the diagnosis became clearer, I heard sickeningly familiar words—"Stage IV, non-small-cell lung cancer." Molly's lung cancer. Dave's mom had the same kind of cancer my best friend had died of seven months before. *Here we go again,* I thought. More tests, more unknowns, more watching someone you loved go bald, grow weaker, and then slowly fold into herself despite her struggles to remain present. Here came the decreased appetite, weight loss, trouble breathing, trips to the ER because you weren't sure how bad the cough was this time. The days the person spent sleeping while you read next to her because conversations were too taxing and she just didn't have the strength to do anything besides maybe unload the dishwasher as a special treat to herself—to show that she really could still do things. Resting after such a chore was totally normal, she would say, the same way it totally made sense that she needed to stop and catch her breath on the way to the bathroom. It was a big house, you know.

Here it came all over again—the fear, the aches, the awkwardness, the time running out, the death, the grief, the loss, the emptiness. It was too soon. Way too soon. I wasn't ready to lose someone else I loved.

When Dave got the texts from his sister—the texts about lung cancer—I wanted to leave the bar, vomit up the grief I had managed to push down along with the gin and tonics I'd been drinking. But he said we should stay, keeping the news between us; there was no reason Dan needed to know. Dave bought the three of us another round of drinks and stared down into his before taking large, life-stabilizing gulps. I walked up to the KJ and put in my final song—my choice based on loss, anger, grief, and Molly. It seemed fitting that I sing the song I hadn't been able to voice without crying since she died. Molly's cheesy, melodramatic song about heartache, regret, and being broken. My name was called, and I walked up, stunned. Then I took the mic and stared out into the crowd, tears welling up as I began to sing with all the strength I had. I poured my grief, my life, my fear into "Wrecking Ball" and allowed my pain to rise to the surface and into the bar.

I smiled softly but gratefully as others sang along with me from their tables. I didn't want to be alone, and I wasn't. The bar was with me as they wailed the chorus from their chairs, swaying back and forth and throwing their heads back to scream at the ceiling. Dave was with me even as he was forced to face a new reality. Molly was with me, singing through me, rolling her eyes at how seriously I was taking a song by Miley Cyrus. When I was done, people clapped, as they had for everyone. But at that moment my acceptance, my ability to bring joy to others in my time of grief felt vital to me. I heard some say that I "nailed it," and that my performance was "haunting;" I lapped up every validation. I went back to my lover and friend—my essence drained, left on the stage to dissolve into the next performer. I had been healed through song.

Dan, Dave, and I walked back in heavy, drunken silence. The grass was still damp, and its coolness felt good on my feet. On the guest bed was Dan's cat, Pippa, who looked exactly like my old tabby, Cyrus, who had kept me company throughout my childhood. Every night, Cyrus would jump on my bed for a final night's pet, her purr resounding in my ears. Then, when she'd had enough, she would jump down and go out the door. I never knew where she went.

That night, Pippa was my Cyrus, making sure I was tucked in safely, getting in some pets of her own, before leaving the room, and letting Dave and me fall asleep with his arm around me, no words exchanged, except "I'm so sorry" and "We'll figure out what to do tomorrow."

As I drifted off, I made the connection between Pippa and Cyrus and Miley Cyrus. I said goodnight to Molly and tried not to cry. It sort of worked.

CHAPTER 45

NEW MEXICO

September 2. 2016

WHEN A LOVED ONE IS DIAGNOSED WITH LATE-STAGE CANCER, IT doesn't change your life as much as splinters it into a million pieces that scatter far and wide, such that you have no control over anything, even the most mundane of tasks. The day-to-day steps you once counted on completely change. You need to learn how to exist all over again: how to wake up, how to eat, how to see the world. Dave bought a plane ticket departing from Denver, arriving in Sacramento. It was the cheapest ticket he could find on such short notice. It required us to cancel visits with high school friends, leaving unfinished business in Austin.

I'd finish my trip as I started it: alone. I tried to focus on the fact that I still had a few days with Dave before he left. Instead, I obsessed over how this had interrupted Dave's and my decision to live together, which we had made after finally agreeing that life apart was getting old. Just like that, we would be separated again. Our lives were shattered before we could become whole again. I felt guilty I wasn't considering the limited time he would have left with a wonderful, kind woman. All I saw was what it was taking away from me.

As we began the drive to New Mexico, I fell apart. I started shaking. I was drained, then sad, then empty, then fine, then broken. It was too much energy to tilt my head back to sleep, so I sat in the passenger seat and stared into nothing, and at nothing. We were nowhere in the heart of west Texas, its unceasing horizon offering an unobstructed view of loss. Dave would occasionally look over and put his arm around me. I couldn't think of anything better—except maybe that I should have been the one doing the consoling.

We talked about how he might want alone time depending on how his mom was doing—and I understood, but I hated it. Molly had just left me. Now Dave was leaving. Then his mom. I felt unwanted, though I knew I had nothing to do with anything that was happening. I was just stuck in the middle of some bizarre hell where everyone I loved was disappearing.

The drive was full of sky and scattered with pawn shops and storefronts advertising guns, deer processing, taxidermy, and churches. The land lay perfectly flat and dull in between. We stopped at a McDonald's for a restroom break; it blared conservative talk radio at its customers. A town bench in the public square told me to "Put my trust in God," and a church sign read, "Surrender your problems to God." I sank further down into the passenger seat, and into myself. Seamane texted me to let me know her surgery had been successful at removing her cancer. I sighed in relief, but wasn't sure if that was because of her news or because I was grateful I had lost the ability to feel. I wouldn't give up this journey, but its point was lost on me right then. As we crossed into New Mexico I realized I had forgotten to take a picture of a Texas longhorn.

We had passed so many over the outstretched miles. Another lost chance.

We spent a night in Roswell, New Mexico, as the distance to the karaoke venue in Santa Fe was too far to make in one day. Dave and I then spent our morning visiting alien museums and distracting ourselves from the current reality. An infamous motorcycle gang, Bandido Nation, whose motto was "We are the people our parents warned us about," joined us in one of them. Their eyes were wide in belief and excitement. We gawked at tourists wearing tinfoil hats. Everything about this town reflected its association with extraterrestrials and outer space: there was a mural of a mariachi band composed of little green men on the outside of a Mexican restaurant; mailboxes were painted to look like R2D2; the Arby's sign claimed to "serve aliens here." Without this tie to the alien world, there would have been no reason for Roswell to thrive, or even exist.

The almost 200-mile drive to Santa Fe, where I would sing that night, continued to emphasize the nothingness I'd been feeling. US Highway 285 went through what felt like America's version of the Middle East's Empty Quarter—endless, flat, and desolate, except for the homemade white crosses and faded plastic flowers laid along the roadside—reminders of fatal car crashes. There were so many that I lost count almost as soon as I started. I could barely read the names on most; the black paint left there to remember a particular soul had baked in the sun to the point of erasure. I had no idea if the loved ones who had created these memorials actually came back to them to pay their respects, or if they put them there more as a warning sign for the rest of us. Or maybe the memorials were there to remind us that we would simply never know when it was our turn to leave this earth.

I coughed up a lung on our way to karaoke. I was phlegmy and depressed, but I knew that once I got to the bar and started to sing, I would be okay. No matter how shitty my life was, I still had song. We pulled into Fiesta's in Santa Fe, and the parking lot was pretty damn full. We wandered to the bar at the back of the restaurant, where the KJ was setting up the fancy lights as preseason and college football played on the television screens. Vegas-style carpet in bright blue, red, and gold covered the floors, and a food donation bin sat next to the microphone stand. There was a line of five people at the signup kiosk—who knew how many had come before, but I knew enough to get in it as soon as I walked in the door. I'd figure out a song as I waited.

I stood behind a woman who couldn't spell "Bayou" and therefore was struggling to find the Linda Ronstadt song she wished to perform. I grew impatient and helped—not to be kind, but out of frustration. I sighed audibly as she failed to thank me and instead took up more time by signing up her girl-friend, who shouted her request over—too lazy to get out of her chair and do it herself. Behind me was a man with a long dark braid and inner calm, ready to put in his choice. Meanwhile, Dave grabbed the last table in the place, right up against the speaker. The clock struck nine, and the karaoke began.

This was a place where regulars ruled the roost. Names like Caveman, Disco Nanny, Ciro, Abe, Diva, Big Mike, and Cate Bell scrolled along the bottom of the monitor. My name didn't appear, and though I felt anxious about it, I tried to just sit back, relax, and enjoy the music. There were a lot of singers, and perhaps I was far enough down the list that my name wasn't showing yet. Plus, I'd had a rough day, and the singers here were amazing. A bald guy with a grey braid and thick glasses kept his hands in his pockets as he sang "Every Rose Has Its Thorn" in a droll twang that was slightly behind the beat, but still catchy. A woman in all leather sang "Natural Woman" while sitting down in a trance, bringing the entire bar with her. She was followed by a man who performed a song put in by request—a song in Spanish called "Volver Volver

(Return Return)" that had half the crowd singing, the other half in tears. A young African American woman crooned some Dixie Chicks and I smiled; I liked it when song choices broke stereotypes. Caveman sang Foreigner's "Cold as Ice"—another request. Everyone here knew everybody—it was one big musical family. Like the Osmonds, except less white.

After the woman who stood in front of me sang "Blue Bayou" and her girlfriend followed with some Janis Joplin, the man with the dark braid was called up. I'd been skipped over. I walked up to the KJ and asked where I was in the list; she looked down a long series of names until we figure it out. I was not only pretty far down, but my name was misspelled as "Krista" instead of "Kristi." Given that the "I" and "A" were nowhere near each other on the keyboard, I doubted this was my input error—instead, I concluded that the KJ placed me further down the list, behind her regulars, overriding the basic karaoke honor code of performing in the order in which you signed up.

Inside, I was seething—tired from my day, my year, my life—but to the KJ I managed to fake innocent confusion, and thanked her for showing me where I stood. I explained that I thought I had been skipped over completely, not seeing my name and all. Clearly silly old me didn't know how to use computers properly. The KJ looked at me, and suddenly became aware of my act. I had pushed my air of self-deprecation too far. I would have been fine—still annoyed but fine—with the whole situation if the KJ hadn't provided an excuse as to why I was so far down on the list. See, she over-explained, people must have gotten ahead of me by signing up on their phones. None of it added up, and the story wasn't helped by her defensive glare. I tried to take solace in the hope that I would soon sing in New Mexico.

After several more singers, my doubt crept in again. As more names scrolled by, Krista/Kristi was nowhere to be found, though I did see a "Kristine." I grew anxious again, but resisted the urge to follow up. When the name Kristine was called, I hesitated. The KJ looked over at me, stared, and repeated the name—louder, and with more stare. I leaned over to her and apologized for my confused look, but let her know she had gotten my name wrong again. She sneered, "Take it out on the song."

I did. I yelled "Jungle Love" as much as I sang it, managing to get a lot of smiles—even one from the KJ. Caveman joined me on stage to play some air guitar. All was right in the world again—at least for the next three minutes and nine seconds.

CHAPTER 46
COLORADO
September 4, 2016

 AVE AND I ARRIVED AT LINDA AND DEAN'S HOUSE OUTSIDE OF Denver, Colorado when the sky was black and quiet. A year and a day older than I, Linda had been a part of my life before it was possible to understand there were other people in the world. When I lived in New Jersey, Thanksgiving was always at Linda's family's house—the television set to the football games, the table set with a white tablecloth, turkey, and stuffing. Over the winters, our parents visited each other, and brought the kids along. While the adults listened to Neil Diamond and ABBA in front of a crackling fireplace, glasses of wine in hand, Linda, our brothers (also close in age), and I would play until we fell asleep upstairs; hours later, it would be time to go home. For more than a few summers, we vacationed together in Maine—on a remote island without electricity and plumbing, where the adults slept in a run-down house called "The Hilton," and the kids camped out in an abandoned chicken coop. We ate lobsters bought off the boat that took us to our summer home, and blueberries and mussels harvested from the land and sea.

All these years later, I was still friends with Linda and had since befriended her husband. Enough so that when we arrived at their house, Linda and Dean weren't home, but that didn't matter. They had opened their house to us while they were gone camping; that way we could get a good night's sleep before Dave left for California. The last time I had been there, I was experiencing a different kind of grief. Dave had split up with me a few weeks before, and I had run to Linda for solace. The breakup was unexpected, and for the wrong reasons—which explained our inevitable reconciliation a few months later, while I was in Toronto reconnecting with family and he was in South Korea teaching English. But at the moment of our separation, I was feeling lost, afraid, and confused. I needed a friend who knew me more than anyone. I had chosen to reach out to Linda—desperate for consolation, and for escape from the shock of loss where I had thought there was love. More than a friend, Linda was my sister. She took me camping that Labor Day weekend, letting me join in her plans with her husband and friends at the last minute. I had arrived at the Denver airport late that night, rented a car, and gone to her house. She and Dean had been asleep. That time, too, I had let myself into her home. Three years ago, a dog had greeted me at the door with a wagging tail and kisses. A cat jumped on the bed I was in, checking me out and letting me know I was in her space—then deciding it was okay and curling up at my feet.

The next day Linda and Dean had taken me to the mountains. I had nothing to camp with; they loaned me everything, from a tent to a flashlight. We spent two days and nights in seclusion—exactly what I needed, despite my lack of experience in the great outdoors. I had the right amount of company and alone time, and no way to check my phone. I was a little loopy from the rapid change in elevation—there was a 10,000 foot difference between Portland and the Colorado mountains—which served me well enough that I didn't even need booze to take the edge off the shock and weight I felt (though there was plenty of drink on this trip—more "glamping" than "camping," Linda said, despite the fact that we needed to traipse off into the woods with a shovel when duty called). We returned to Denver, where the bed and cat waited for me; it was only then that I knew I was going to be okay.

This time when I entered their house, Linda and Dean were camping again, as it was Labor Day weekend—exactly three years since my last visit. Three years, a mended relationship, and travel to nine countries since I'd last opened their back door and let myself in. The dog had passed from a heart condition, and the cat from old age. Dave and I slept in the same bed, with the same sheets and blanket. Home.

The next morning, the alarm went off far too early—in the dark, when it's best not to think of the hour or the reason you're vertical instead of horizontal. I was up to let Dave go. I drove him to the airport, dropping him off outside with the largest hug I could summon, trying not to betray my despair. I drove back through a slight rain—the windshield wipers could handle it, but did nothing to clear the water in my eyes. I changed my Buddha's expression from delight to confusion, and cursed it for not having an expression of sadness, or an option for feeling nothing at all.

I crawled back into bed. I was dizzy from a mixture of grief and altitude sickness. Breathing was difficult, my headache immense. I felt a blankness as I waited for a feeling—any feeling. Nothing came. Just as I was falling asleep again, my thoughts tumbled forth—an avalanche of thick lava, slow but unstoppable. Dave was currently airborne, off to Sacramento to be with his mom, who had been diagnosed with a similar cancer to Molly's. Molly was dead. Dave's mom would soon be dead. I would soon be done with my karaoke quest, and there was nothing after that. I felt angry. Without question leaving was the right thing for Dave to do, but I didn't like it. I didn't like anything. I finally fell asleep, and woke to the sounds of Linda and Dean returning. Once again, they were there for me in my time of heartache.

My friends were impressively energetic upon their arrival and suggested that the three of us go on an urban hike. Their rules were rather simple and delightful; for every mile of walking, there was a beer or wine stop. Dean reviewed a quick plan that would allow us to leisurely reach my karaoke destination, and Linda approved. We were off into the sunshine, into the city, into a day of friendship that would end in song. At each stop, each with a different beverage and seating arrangement—some open air, some shaded inside—Linda commented on how days like this make her life perfect. I agreed; walking around great neighborhoods with the sun shining warmly upon my back made the world a great place. For the first time in days, I felt everything line up.

True to plan, our last leg of the hike, now under twilight, placed us in downtown Denver, right by Coors Field. The crowds in the street were young and hip, dressed perfectly rumpled in vibrant summer colors. There were lines to clubs stretching down sidewalks, and packed rooftop bars all around us—but our destination was the emptiest bar for blocks. I guess no one wanted to sing on the Sunday night of a long weekend. We opened a heavy, dark wooden door, and there was no AC— maybe another reason this place was so deserted. Still, I fell in love with it right away. A group of black faux-leather booths and animal-print tabletops sent shivers of delight down my body and settled into my heart, right next to the spot reserved for Barry Manilow. Ratty wooden floors added to the charm, as did the Day of the Dead/vampire mural, and a caricature of a wizened old bald man showering under a can of PBR. Everything here was just as perfectly suited to me as the walk.

A few people were already singing in a rotation of three; I made it four when I chose my first song. The system was partially computerized, in that you went to the monitor to look up to see if they had the song you wanted to sing. If yes, you wrote it down on a Post-it along with your name and handed it to the KJ—a young woman with short hair and a ripped t-shirt, which screamed that she meant business. Across the stage was a commercially printed banner that listed all the house rules, which included:

Don't drop the mic;

Only put in one song at a time (the KJ emphasized this quite a bit while we were there);

Duets count as a solo performances;

No line cuts for anyone for any reason (among those listed: showing body parts, having a great personality, and going through a divorce).

When I got on the stage, I found the microphone firmly attached to the stand with duct tape (so much for the risk of dropping it)—the first time I would sing with a fixed mic. It wasn't as hard as I imagined; in fact, I liked it quite a bit. Somehow the need to stay planted in my spot paradoxically allowed me more freedom of expression. Since my hands were allowed to move, my face opened up, and my body followed. I sang Donna Summer's "Heaven Knows," recognizing that it reflected my current situation: a song meant to be a duet that I handled solo. A song about how life was not the way it should or could be.

The rotation grew a bit, but not by much—so I sang a few more songs while Linda and Dean delighted in taking pictures.

Some were of me entertaining a crowd of a few people . . . but most were of the animal-print tablecloths and artwork. I would have been just as happy if the three of us were the only ones there. That night, my friends were the only ones who mattered.

CHAPTER 47

WYOMING

September 6, 2016

I DECIDED TO DO THE 476-MILE DRIVE FROM DENVER TO ROCK Springs over the course of two days—for both relaxation and logistics. As I set out on this leg of the journey, I learned how to be alone again—my sunglasses and map on the passenger seat, sports radio and my thoughts to keep me company. Any detours I took—whether on the road or in my head—were completely up to me once again. I could have sung in Cheyenne—but I'd been there three years ago, the last time I stayed with Linda, when my karaoke goal was on a gradual (rather than deliberate) timeline. I wanted a different experience.

Finding that wasn't easy. Social media and the internet were coming up empty in my initial searches for a karaoke venue beyond the one I had visited before—and Reddit users weren't more helpful. I messaged someone I had been close to in college, and who had gone back to Wyoming upon graduation to start a music career. But he never responded. I didn't know if he felt karaoke was beneath him, or simply forgot who I was—I felt sad at the "official" letting go of someone in my life, even though we'd hadn't talked between then and now. My former friend was, in fact, a *former* friend, relegated to memories of goofing off in the back of class and cryptic notes of affection left on my dorm door notepad. But even the smallest of losses created a sharp ache in my heart as I was forced to solve this problem on my own.

I stared at a map of Wyoming. Since I didn't want to go too far north, too far afield from my almost-completed route, my choices were limited to Cheyenne and Rock Springs. I began committing my search efforts to the latter, since it was unknown to me. Finally, through creative keyword searches and a force of will, an option appeared. A Facebook message with the venue confirmed karaoke was on, and my destination was set. I had found a spot in Rock Springs to sing on Tuesday, and had two driving days to get there.

My first stop came quickly, as I wanted to have lunch with family friends, the Haswells, who lived just outside of Boulder. I had soup and a half sandwich in the company of Ellen, Linda (my second childhood friend of the same name, now living in Colorado), and Lisa—the mother and twin sisters at an outside table shaded with an umbrella. In their family of eight, three were already gone, the husband and two sons all dying in unexpected ways—heart attack, tragic accident, mysterious illness. The Haswells spoke of the two brothers comfortably, as if they were still alive. They were still part of the family, though it had been over two decades since either could have joined us. I felt comfort and relief in talking about those no longer with us.

I hoped that one day I'd be able to refer to Molly that way— but for now the mention of her name still brought heaviness mixed with awkwardness, as if I had admitted I still slept with a teddy bear. One mention of her name and people looked away, leaving me exposed and shamed. After an hour, or maybe two, Linda and Lisa returned to their respective jobs, and I hugged the mother, wondering if I'd ever see her again; it seemed unlikely. Our embrace felt like an unspoken final goodbye, a little longer and more gentle than one where we both said "I'll see you soon" or "Stay in touch." I thought about Dave's mom, and started to cry as I drove off; our parents were dying.

My afternoon was full of dry grass surrounded by barren mountains. The only color was an occasional red rock and the gold from tiny sunflowers that lined the roads. I found these flowers more beautiful than the big ones I was more accustomed to, a simple pleasure for the day. The roadkill in this region was coyote; the dead animals matched the ground, and even the road in some places. The AM dial provided me with sports, Spanish, and God; I welcomed the first as part of my journey again. Its monotonous and repetitive cadence was soothing, and as the broadcasters talked about Sam Bradford being traded to the Vikings, I wished I could ask Molly what she thought about her favorite team acquiring such a controversial quarterback.

The fact that the broadcasters were talking about the possibility of the Vikings being in the Super Bowl given the Bradford acquisition made me happy and sad at the same time. I was going to root for them this year, though Kaepernick's refusal to stand for the National Anthem—his way of taking a stand against the violence against his race—almost made me want to cheer for his 49ers. Almost. I decided I would root for the man, but not his uniform. My team loyalty would be to the Vikings.

I rolled into Laramie, Wyoming, where the Wild West was preserved for both honor and tourist dollars. Diners and used-car lots alike were decorated with cowboy hats and bucking broncos. Steak dinners were advertised on every restaurant marquee. Self-care at the hotel consisted of some treadmill time. My stomach was grateful for the simple dinner: a boiled egg, a piece of cheese, and a plum. I checked in with a few friends to let them know I was okay. At least that's what I was willing to admit—and when I thought about it, I found some truth in that statement, despite the fact that I also felt lonely. I was healing, and being alone helped that process. While I had loved my time with Dave, the nature of my trip had been changed by his company, his soul, and his larger sense of adventure. By default, I had less time for introspection—but I also failed to find the time for exercise and random walks through towns. I ate more, and less healthy foods—though by doing so I got to experience lobster rolls in Maine, barbecue in Mississippi, and hot chicken in Tennessee. Food is such an integral part of a culture, and indulging in it brought me closer to each state I passed through.

I was almost out of toothpaste—a signal that my trip was nearing an end. Then again, I wondered, does a tube of tooth-paste every really run out? Or do we just get tired of it and throw it away, deciding that the effort to squeeze out that last little bit is no longer worth it? In my hotel room, I turned off the light, feeling comforted in a strange place, alone for the first time in two months. I fell asleep quickly to the hum of the AC.

I woke up alone, which confused me at first—but then I remembered the circumstances that had lead me here. All of them. My love of song, my loss of Molly, Dave's mother's diagnosis, my desire to sing somewhere other than Chey-enne. It felt right. I went up through mountains, and my car's thermometer warned me that it was only forty-seven degrees outside; I wasn't expecting the temperature to drop that sud-denly, even though it was already a week into September. Yet, there I was—a witness to summer winding down. There was an actual chill in the air, and leaves were turning yellow. I appreciated how nature was so good at letting go, allowing trees to lose their leaves without so much as a wail or whisper of grief. I stepped outside to admire this transitional scenery of mountains and their dusting of snow, and then shivered and got back into the car. I hit Centennial, population 270—a stopping point for hikers and campers to get supplies before going off into the woods. There was no place to fuel up, however, and there wouldn't be for 140 more miles until I hit Baggs, with a whopping population of 450. Dixon, four miles earlier, stood at seventy-five.

My route eventually took me away from the mountains and returned me to vast, even landscapes of exquisite nothingness that stood alongside railroad tracks half-covered in dust. I saw a dead porcupine, and a mule deer walked across the road in front of me. I regretfully had to hit I-80 in order to make it to Rock Springs in time to sing, and the PSAs that dominated this part of the country encouraged parents to use the proper car seats for their children. The signal for the Denver sports radio station was loud and clear, and the host was Ed McCaffrey, former wide receiver for the Denver Broncos, and for Stanford University before that. I thought about how I used to drool over the then-young man in my psych classes—adoring his soft brown eyes, so perfectly covered by his floppy bangs. Now he interviewed a former Nuggets' coach who was spending his retirement supporting cancer survivors through proper medical care—both during treatment and after. How quickly we forget those who suffered after they are given the green light of successful chemo and radiation. "Congratulations!" we say. "The cancer is gone! Now you can go back to your normal life!" As if going back to a life before cancer is even possible. I made a note to be more mindful of how Seamane might feel when she was done with her treatment. I made a note about Dave's mom, too—though there I was less optimistic that there would be an "after."

Rock Springs itself seemed boring. My motel was in an

area that blurred into the rest of America. I passed a Taco Bell, a McDonald's, several gas stations, and a strip mall with a dry cleaner. The hotel clerk wheeled an oxygen tank behind her as she approached the desk to check me in. She handed me my key and let me know there was happy hour between five and seven in the breakfast room, and that as a guest I got a complimentary beverage. I had noticed the two taps as I was checking in and wondered if beer was served in the mornings in Wyoming. I guessed not. I headed over for a cheap G&T and watched cooking shows without sound on the TVs overhead. A few other stragglers were there, as it was almost quitting time. The server yelled last call as I stared into my half-finished drink. I was sure I could have gone up for a second freebie, or even thirds if I'd wanted. I hit the tread-mill instead—the server let me know that if their fitness room wasn't good enough, I could go next door to the nicer hotel and they would let me in. In terms of amenities and kindness, this was the nicest cheap hotel I'd been in since I had begun this journey.

I had looked up the Rock Springs smoking laws, and it seemed as though it was illegal to smoke in bars—but one step inside Killpeppers and I knew that wasn't the case. The air was dominated by the stench of nicotine, old and new. Tech-nically, this place was a "nightclub," with black velour-backed barstools and red velvety chairs on gold wheels at the tables. It was clearly a pool hall first, though, with all four tables in use.

Before getting there, I had texted a friend to express fear of going somewhere strange, of being harassed, of not being safe—apparently I wasn't as used to being alone again as I had thought. However, as soon as I took a seat at the bar, where the owner, a female, was running the show, I fell back into my sense of ease—my understanding that no one in a bar is there to cause me trouble. The bartender and I talked about hunting season (she explained that was why the place was relatively empty), cold weather (it had only just begun), and the kitchen opening up next week, while I sipped a gin and tonic no better than the one at the hotel. She then put on a Vikings sweatshirt, which opened the door for me to talk about the Sam Bradford acquisition. She wasn't Molly—not by a long shot—but just being able to talk football with a blonde female fan helped ease the loneliness.

The crowd picked up a little over the next half hour, and a regular kicked off the karaoke, taking the wireless mic to sing "I Wanna Be Like You" from *The Jungle Book* while simultaneously keeping his pool game going. He ended up doing both ineffectively. The karaoke setup here was strange—you could either stand on a huge stage (probably built for bands and the like) or face a monitor on the dance floor with your back to the rest of the bar. I reluctantly chose the latter, angling my body awkwardly so I at least somewhat acknowledged the rest of the bar. I sang my first song, "Free Falling," to a quiet audience, and left the stage to minimal applause—people there were more concerned with practicing for that weekend's big pool tournament than paying attention to (or participating in) song. It was the first time I had sung Tom Petty, and although the verses were a little low for my range, overall I was satisfied with the result. Tonight, there was no one to please but myself.

When I got back to my seat and my drink (the bartender had said she'd watch it for me), two women had taken up residence just next to me, despite having a lot of real estate to choose from. One was making goo-goo noises and rubbing the belly of the other, who was just starting to show signs of pregnancy. The pregnant lady laughed, saying she would be fifty when the kid was born—then she lit a cigarette and ordered a Sprite. A young man walked over and the conversation quickly jumped to the subject of oral sex; the young man claimed to prefer dick because "pussies smell like fish and look like cottage cheese." The older women let him know that if it looked like cottage cheese down there "then something is seriously wrong." He wasn't buying it. My company left for a bit, but their phones and keys remained on the bar, confirming my gut reaction that this place was safe after all, despite my initial reservations.

As the evening progressed, the KJ called out names of patrons and asked if they were ready to sing. Clearly the bar was full of regulars who either weren't interested in karaoke quite yet, or needed to be encouraged to sing. Some yelled back for more time, and others wandered over and chose a tune, interrupting their games. Everyone selected a slow song. Not what I would have expected here—heading into the evening I was pegging the place for upbeat modern country.

The first guy continued his repertoire of gravelly voiced songs by performing Louis Armstrong. The guy who liked dick—who turned out to be the pregnant lady's stepson—took a turn and sung "Stand by Me." It wasn't bad, but nothing inspiring. Mom disagreed with my silent assessment, and leaned into me so I could hear her over the music: "He has a beautiful voice. He's just not competent—I wish there was a way for him to be more competent." I thought I misheard her at first, but the repetition confirmed it; she was saying "competent" while meaning "confident," and while I nodded in sympathetic agreement, inside I was laughing smugly. The proud mom continued, "Such a lovely tone; I wish he'd sing louder. Dammit all to hell, shit." I felt warmed and tickled by her love and unconditional support of her adult child as she got ready to care for a new child.

Soon after, the woman's husband came up and slurred enthusiastically to no one in particular, "Why does Wyoming have wind? Because Utah blows and Nebraska sucks." He continued to talk about Wyoming to the bar in general—facing no one, focused on nothing. He referred to his home state as "God's perfect square"—then a "shithole," moments later. The dichotomy made perfect sense to me when I reflected on the state's natural beauty, juxtaposed with the cookie-cutter big-box stores that dominated this town. The bartender replaced his empty bottle with a new one, and asked the woman's husband how his granddaughter was doing; the girl was in a cast after a mishap on the jungle gym. We never found out the answer as he took a long sip of Bud before launching into a story about how he had dislocated his ankle several years before. After eight weeks in a cast, he had to scrape the dead skin off his heel with a butter knife. His wife wailed Lita Ford in the background.

I sang a second song, and then said goodbye to the bartender, throwing another couple of bucks onto the bar for the club soda she had given me on the house. I didn't say anything to the family next to me, and they didn't seem to notice me leave. A police car had pulled over some folks across the street, and arrests were being made as I headed back to the hotel. I was alone again in a strange world located in the heart of my own country.

CHAPTER 48

UTAH

September 8, 2016

I FELT A LITTLE OFF THE NEXT MORNING, WHICH ONLY MADE SENSE given my relative lack of dinner the night before, and the smoke from the bar clawing at my throat. My jacket smelled like stale cigarettes, but I put it on anyway to combat the morning chill as I headed to the motel breakfast room. This time, instead of serving booze, the room offered a meal designed for a hunter's appetite—faux omelets, questionable sausage patties, waffles, the works. Thankfully, I was also back in the part of the country where boiled eggs and yogurt were part of a typical morning spread; the land of biscuits and gravy was now thousands of miles away. As I headed out, I passed by a Starbucks and considered treating myself to a pumpkin latte to accept the fact that fall had come. Instead, I filled up my car at Cruel Jack's Truck Stop and took off into the morning sun.

The first leg of my trip took me through Flaming Gorge. I

stopped at every official viewpoint—and some unofficial ones as well. There were a few other cars and people along the way, but no signs of settlement in this protected land. No barns, no houses, no commercial enterprises; nothing but mountains and open space. I tried to draw some sort of conclusion about the relationship between the beauty of the terrain and the ugliness of the towns it surrounded. Instead, I spent the next few hours focusing on the present—appreciating the beauty around me as the mountains effortlessly shifted from brown to green to red against a cloudless blue sky.

I pulled into the hotel parking lot in Sandy, Utah, and was delighted to see that not only was my venue for that night a five-minute walk away, but it shared a parking lot with an Asian grocery store—the kind I frequent in Portland in order to make food shopping more interesting and to remind me of my travels to South Korea and Vietnam. I stocked up on snacks that would last a couple of days: dried tofu, coconut water, and mochi; before long I'd be arriving in California and reconnecting with Dave. I treated myself to an afternoon snack of a steamed pork bun—the perfect balance of salty and sweet, fat and carbs. The whole experience left me feeling slightly homesick for Korea, not Portland.

After eating, I wandered over to the karaoke venue, Club 90; a man stood on a ladder in the entranceway, hanging up a sign promoting the Pittsburgh Steelers and Coors Light. It was the first night of the NFL season, but it wouldn't be the same without listening to Molly go on and on about her fantasy team picks, none of whom I'd be familiar with. I asked both the man and the bartender inside what time I should return in order to get on the list; this would be my first and only live-band karaoke experience on this trip, and the website promotions and reviews encouraged people to arrive early in order to get a spot in the limited rotation. Both men and the website encouraged me to arrive ninety minutes before the band got going, and being the nervous Nellie I am, I obeyed.

I'd sung karaoke with a live band in Portland about fifteen years prior. Karaoke from Hell had been just getting its feet wet in the Portland music scene; back then, it and the concept of live karaoke were new terrain. The song choices were understandably limited and mostly revolved around classic rock (their website suggests this hasn't really changed)—a genre that's probably more easily pulled off by a live band than, say, hip-hop or dance hits. Also, there was no monitor with lyrics, no color-changing words to help you pace your song; instead, there was sheet music, on a rickety black music stand identical to the one I used in middle school band when I played the flute. In order to follow along with your song, you had to be able to read music and manually turn the pages as the song progressed.

For my first song with Karaoke From Hell, I had played it safe, choosing "Hit Me With Your Best Shot" by Pat Benatar. I knew it, and so did everyone else, so people could sing along. The song had no weird surprises, like a key change or musical bridge. I was shaky at first, but found my rhythm and happiness in the song's lack of coolness, and the rush of having an actual band behind me. I immediately put in a second choice, going bolder with *Jesus Christ Superstar*'s "I Don't Know How to Love Him," for reasons that are still unclear to me. Maybe it was because it was in my range and quite familiar to me. Those were probably the only reasons I needed. I gave it my all, wondering if anyone was listening to a stranger self-indulging in show tunes.

Apparently some *had* been listening, because when the song ended and I reluctantly left the stage, a few asked me what band I sang in; my heart, smile, and pride grew with that one question. I let them know I didn't sing in a band. That remains true today, but I did daydream about the possibility for a few days—until I recalled my inability to stay up late.

In Sandy, the cavernous venue was nearly deserted despite

the numerous and consistent warnings of the show's popularity. Still, I was glad I had come early, happy to grab a seat and watch the first game of the season along with a few other fans dressed in the appropriate jerseys. I had mistaken a heavyset grey-bearded man for a member of the karaoke band, This Is Your Band (TIYB), and started up a conversation, hoping to learn about live karaoke in the 2010s. Turns out, he wasn't part of the band. Instead, he was waiting for one of TIYB's members, hoping to talk about a song he had written. He offered me a seat, and sang me a song about wanting a more meaningful relationship, tired of the one-night stands and superficial bullshit that was offered so easily these days. As he finished, I found myself not wanting to engage in conversation; I felt sorry for this guy, and that put me on edge. Through his composition, I had learned too much about him, and too fast.

The band member arrived, and I was relieved. The two talked about the song, and the TIYB member, careful not to overpromise, offered the talents of a young female vocalist and some limited studio time, stopping short of offering promotion and connections.

TIYB warmed up casually while a roadie conducted an extensive sound check, hustling all over the vast room to make sure that you could hear from all corners, and that no feedback screeched in protest. More people arrived to claim tables, though they were hesitant to sign up. The extensive song lists lying on the tables were thumbed through and considered, but no one was willing to take the next action. The choices here were far more abundant than those from my live-band experience all those years ago, and I was impressed that a group could perform so many songs. Finally, one singer was brave enough to commit to a song, and the floodgates opened as people put down their names and selections on the handwritten list maintained by the owner of the bar and her friend.

By 8:30, the list was nearly full; getting there early had been the right call.

From the first note from the first performer, I fell in love with the energy of live karaoke all over again. When my name was called, I started to shake with excitement. As I got on stage, I was completely blown away by the fact that the lyrics showed up on a monitor at my feet. No sheet music, no rickety stand reminded me that I was anything less than a professional musician onstage with my fellow band members. I gave Journey's "Separate Ways" all I had. It was the same song I'd sung in South Carolina, but here I added extra flourish. Still, the experience was different beyond my extra enthusiasm. Here I was not alone on the stage. I had a whole band supporting me, sharing the experience with me. That night, I was part of a team. The pulsing rhythms and electrifying guitar riffs encouraged me to break my chains, completing my transformation into a rock star. The final note, the final wailing "NOOOOOOOOOO," perfectly articulated my reluctance to let someone else have a turn. I didn't want to get off this ride. I took a bow and exited stage right, where I received fist bumps from the crew. It was time for the next singer to shine.

CHAPTER 49

ARIZONA

September 9, 2016

I MADE THE TRIP FROM SANDY TO FLAGSTAFF, ARIZONA, ALL IN ONE day, even though that wasn't my original plan. There was just something inside that kept me going. I didn't care enough about the rest of Utah to stop to take pictures. Instead of opting for smaller roads as I had done most of the trip, I took the interstate for 150 miles. The scenery was little more than different shades of gold in the form of dead grass, mountains, and the baby sunflowers I loved so much. Off the freeway, I passed numerous signs enticing me to visit Bryce Canyon and Zion, but I didn't bother to stop, rationalizing that a few hours' visit wouldn't do justice to either. I admired their fiery red rocks from afar as I kept moving.

I passed far too many dead deer; their corpses affected me more than roadkill normally did. I wasn't sure whether to be alarmed by the fact that I was so touched that day and so blasé the rest. Over the past few days, I had seen live deer, antelope, and even a badger. Then suddenly the animal sightings turned grisly: crushed skunks pecked at by birds of prey, twisted deer covered in flies. Copious signs warned of their crossing—some even with blinking lights—but nothing seemed to do any good. I thought about how these animals were just trying to exist—to get from one place to another—when their lives were snuffed out. At least I hoped it had been quick.

I stopped in Kanab, Utah; as I got out of the car and stretched my arms to the sun, my legs shook beneath me. This is where I had planned to be done for the day, having put in 300 miles. The man behind the counter at the tourist information center didn't try to convince me to stay; he even reassured me that it was okay to bypass Bryce. He tipped his cowboy hat and leaned into me. I could smell the tobacco on his breath as he whispered, "I can sense that you have a different agenda today. It's not about Bryce for you; it's about getting to Flagstaff. We all have different goals in life. I think you know what yours is today."

I wasn't as sure as he was, but I felt as though I had been sent a message. From whom, I didn't know, but his words were enough to put me back into my car and keep driving. Before I left, I asked the man where he would stop—even if it was just for a little while—if he wanted to take in at least some of the beauty around here. Back in his role as tour guide instead of prophet, he suggested Horseshoe Bend: "If you're going to see one thing, this is it."

I crossed into Arizona. Again I grew weary, so I stopped in Page, hoping to find some singing there. After a brief internet search and a few phone calls, I had no luck and pushed on. Horseshoe Bend was only a few miles away, and I could use the small hike it would take to get there to see this marvel along the Colorado River; it would snap me out of my driving fatigue and make me feel slightly less guilty about bypassing all the other natural wonders on this leg. I pulled into a parking lot full of cars covered in desert dust. Signs warned of extreme heat, and to not embark on the one-and-a-half-mile journey without water. I looked around and saw everyone applying sunscreen, so I did the same, and brought my umbrella for extra protection. I had learned that trick when I was in Korea, and since landing back in the States I always wonder why Americans only use theirs when rain falls.

On my walk into Horseshoe Bend, I was surrounded by tourists; most weren't speaking English. Normally a crowd this size would have annoyed me, but I felt comforted by the foreign tongues. I got to the site, and was almost too tired to appreciate what I was seeing: a majestic rock hugged by a perfect semicircle bend of azure blue. It was breathtaking enough to allow me to briefly ignore all the selfie sticks. I preferred to capture the memory without me in it. Minutes later, sweat seeping through my sunscreen, I headed back; the return hike was more difficult due to the uphill climb and increasing heat. The workout gave me the shot of energy I needed to push forward and complete the final two-hour drive to Flagstaff.

I pulled into a McDonald's parking lot and stole their internet just as final fragments of sunlight were fading. I called Granny's Closet—the website claimed there was karaoke Friday and Saturday nights—and found out they only had karaoke that night, Friday. As I listened to the server on the other end of the phone, I realized this was one of the only places I'd never confirmed, and felt a rush of relief that I was here on the right night. The wisdom from the man in Kanab, my determination to keep going, and the hike to Horseshoe Bend had all been given to me for a reason.

I arrived at Granny's as a very young crowd started to pour in. I would have carded the lot of them, but I knew they were all legal; I'm just that old. I got a Coors Light and a songbook, and wrote out a slip, which was quickly snatched up by someone and brought to the front. I continued looking through the book, but I was only kidding myself; my exhaustion meant I was going to be there only for one song.

I introduced myself to the KJ—a young man in a carefully tilted grey herringbone fedora—and tried to glance subtly at his stack of song requests, to see if I could determine my place in the queue. I knew I would stay until my name was called, but it was going to be a challenge to keep my eyes open for the duration. I wasn't so stealthy after all; the KJ saw what I was doing and said I was fifth in line. Embarrassed at being caught, I mumbled an excuse of just wanting to make sure that my slip had in fact been turned in—a woman I didn't know had taken it from me, and I would have understood if she hadn't brought it up yet. The KJ said that Sherrie, one of his regulars, had taken it up for me, because she recognized me from before. I said she must have been mistaken, as this was my first time in Flagstaff—and I let him know about my almost-complete quest. While the boy did his best to feign interest, he was more interested in hearing my opinion of the show that night, as it was a "karaoke reunion" to which he had invited a bunch of former regulars. It took me a while to grasp the implication, but when I did, I laughed out of shock: the karaoke that night was a one-off. There were no more regular shows at Granny's Closet. Nothing short of fate had led me into this; I was giddy with gratitude and fatigue.

The KJ worked a two-microphone system, running a mic to the next singer as well as to the one on deck to keep things moving quickly. He even walked up to me to let me know when I was two away from singing. I wondered if he always ran such a tight ship, back when Granny's was a regular thing, or if his efficiency was due to the special occasion and larger-than-usual crowd. Sherrie opened the show with a passionate "Faithfully," full of vocal embellishments and clutching hands, reaching out to the audience in desperation. After her, however, the talent took a nosedive—the next few performers bombed their songs. A Goth gal sat at her table instead of taking the floor; her hoodie covered a lot of her face. People kept looking back at her as they read the monitor and realized she was woefully behind on her lyrics—lost in her place in the song, if not lost in her night completely. Yet when she was done, the applause was loud. This was karaoke's way.

My name was called and I stepped to the front of the room as the young crowd seemed to finally see me, a stranger, in their midst. The staccato intro of "Eye of the Tiger," the theme from *Rocky III*, began and I was relieved to hear roars of appreciation from a group who hadn't even been born when the song was released. However, on this night, I didn't sing for the crowd. I channeled Rocky's battle against both Lang and himself as I sang for Dave—he had suggested the song at least once when we had been on the road together. I sang it for his mom, who had decided to undergo a cruel treatment program to give her an extra six-to-twelve months of life. I sang it for my sister-in-law, who was simply too damn young to have cancer. And I sang it for Molly, who had always appreciated cheesy '80s tunes. Finally, I sang it for me—for driving over 500 miles, following a hunch, and believing in the pull that kept me going.

I didn't have a lot of energy behind my performance; I was too exhausted to offer anything beyond my strained but grateful voice. Yet true to the karaoke community, the crowd bailed me out, providing the boost I needed. The crowd sang loudly with me—an unknown face crashing their reunion—and clapped enthusiastically as I crossed the finish line. It was the perfect, victorious end to a long day.

CHAPTER 50

NEVADA

September 10. 2016

NEVADA WAS MY PENULTIMATE STATE—THE LAST ONE I WOULD visit on my own, before reconnecting with Dave and fin-ishing my journey in California. The morning brought me a new sense of grief. I recognized the need to move forward, and the fact that that I couldn't live this way forever—in my car, singing every night, experiencing karaoke culture across America. This grief was less heavy that the grief I associate with death. This grief, the one of closing a chapter to begin a new one (or perhaps to return to the old one) was more like heartbreak. My chest tightened, my stomach fell, and my hands shook just a little—frantically searching for something useful to do when there was nothing to be done.

I stared down the road, distracted by my racing thoughts; I wasn't quite ready to see what lay ahead. I thought about how every state—from the mundane experience I had had in Iowa, where I was the only performer; to the crazy night in

Minnesota, where the distinction between singer and audience collapsed under enthusiasm. I thought about the characters I had met: Gerald, the man in Illinois who serenaded stuffed animals; the woman who sang for escape in West Virginia; the KJ in Montana who had just lost her friend. I expressed gratitude for the chances I had had to reconnect with old friends in Indiana, New Jersey, and the Carolinas, and meet new ones in Vermont and Arkansas.

I had experienced more than I ever thought I would, traveling and singing across the country. Even though the goal itself—to karaoke in the Lower 48—seemed straightforward enough, my journey had been anything but. I learned. A *lot.* I grew even more. And while each venue had been unique, with its own clientele, ambiance, and bartenders, the karaoke itself varied little. The rules of karaoke were simple, yet complex: I sang a song that fit the mood, my mood, whatever mood, and people cheered, no matter how well I performed, and no matter how much they liked the selection. The crowd always cheered, for on that night, every singer was part of their community. No matter what was going on in the world, in a karaoke bar we were one nation under song.

The Nevada scenery that accompanied my thoughts was brought to me by historic Route 66, and featured several antique stores offering up pieces of farming history for sale in the form of rusted tools and wooden signs, and the tiny sunflowers I'd come to see as friends dancing in the breeze. I looked over and saw a horse rolling around in the dirt in pure delight; it was the first time I'd seen horses running, playing, looking happy. Before, I'd just seen them standing around, watching the world go by; it was nice to see them actually living. Along one stretch of open field, a farmer had placed a series of classic Burma Shave ads, each with a partial phrase, slowly revealing the intended lesson:

If daisies are your
favorite flower
keep pushin' up
those miles per hour
Burma Shave

If it weren't for the quality of the smoothly paved road, I wouldn't have been able to tell whether it was 1950 or 2016. I was grateful for this day that had no time.

I had reserved a room in a casino in Henderson, Nevada. Its tired sign strained to light the already-bright sky with red-and-yellow flashing lights. As the receptionist checked me into my room for the night, he looked at my Oregon driver's license and a half-smile cracked on his overworked face. He told me how he was looking to get the hell out of Henderson and move to Eugene; he even had a real estate agent helping him find a new place to call home. It's funny how some people dream of going to the place you had fled months before and now had mixed feelings about returning to.

I purposely chose to sing in Henderson, instead of Las Vegas. I had already sung karaoke once in Vegas in the early '90s and it was a disaster. I'm hazy on the details, as one is wont to be in the City of Sin, but what I do remember is that a casino bar was hosting a contest and I was inebriated enough to sign up. Back then, I had only participated in karaoke a handful of times, so I really didn't know how it worked— never mind how a karaoke contest worked, and never mind how a karaoke contest in Vegas worked. So my friends and I stood around in the packed bar and waited for my name to be called. It didn't dawn on me that even though I had put in my name, I didn't put in a song. That's because it was a "kamikaze karaoke" event, where a song is given to you at random—and there you are, on stage in front of hundreds of people at the

New York, New York casino, singing a song that you may or may not know.

When it was my turn, I saw the name of the song flash on the monitor, and my stomach went into knots. I didn't recognize the song, or the artist—"What's Up?" by 4 Non-Blondes. Fuck. As the first few notes played, I realized I was at least familiar with it, though I didn't really *know* it until the chorus kicked in. When that happened, I gave it all I had, hoping to make up for the fact that for the first couple of minutes I was mumbling a vague combination of words and notes. Then, when the verses began again, I resumed my quiet insecurity and swayed uneasily until the familiar chorus.

When it was over, I rushed off the stage, went back to my friends, and got the hell out of there. Despite my embarrassment, I learned the song was a good fit for me vocally, so I memorized the hell out of it, and it became one of my stronger choices. More important, I discovered that karaoke disasters are totally survivable. If I could survive being up on a stage in front of hundreds of people, swaying uneasily to an unfamiliar song, then I could fail in other ways and make out just fine. Friends will always be waiting for you when the mess is over— standing at the finish line whether you come in first or barely make it to the end.

I also sang in Henderson because one of my goals on this trip was to see "the real" America—take secondary roads, and go to different kinds of bars—and Vegas didn't really fit into that agenda. Sure, "real people" live and work in Vegas; they serve food, fight fires, and provide medical care. There are lawyers, taxi drivers, real estate agents, teachers, and shop owners in Vegas. But all the karaoke I could find in the city was in casinos or bars attached to casinos, and that wasn't the vibe I was looking for. I wanted to mingle with a more authentic, local crowd. I wanted to be among true Nevadans, not a bunch of tourists like (or unlike) me. The bar in Henderson, on the outskirts of Vegas, fit the bill perfectly.

The karaoke bar was a fair distance from the casino; nothing is close to anything in Nevada. The inside of the place matched its outside—dark wood, with antique barn and pioneer tools decorating every visible surface not already taken by neon beer signs. I had gotten there a tad early, hoping to watch some college football and grab a bite to eat before singing. Instead there was NASCAR on the TVs and no food served—which was odd for a place that was open 24/7. I ordered a pint of Rolling Rock; it was flat and sour, indicating that the taps hadn't been cleaned in months. The air was coated in a dense fog of tar—everyone was either smoking or vaping. I grabbed a seat at the bar, trying not to set myself in front of a gambling machine—I wanted to avoid its lure into bankruptcy, or at least the loss of a few bucks. This was no easy feat, as the machines lined the bar, with few spaces of reprieve in between. I guess some aspects of Vegas are present no matter what part of Nevada you're in.

A group of three people sitting a few stools over was chatting with the bartender; one of them asked what "suburb" meant, and the bartender replied, "It's a fancy rich town with lawns." I supposed that definition was as close to the truth as any. Then the KJ rushed in, hands full of gear and a face full of smile, and let everyone know he got a new special effects lightbulb to make the show more fun. The patrons responded excitedly, and many left their seats to take a look at the new feature. When it came time to test the wonder light, it literally took four people to figure out how to screw it into the ceiling fixture above the bar. Once that was accomplished, the rest of the patrons came over for an awe-struck inspection of this marvelous new addition to the place as it rotated around the small ceiling space above the bar, offering up red, yellow, blue, and green squares of light. I got the feeling this was the most exciting thing this bar had witnessed in a while.

The rush of novelty soon died down, as people returned to their seats and conversations. A new customer came in and asked for a Bloody Mary. The bartender looked confused and turned to one of the three patrons near me for help: "A Bloody Mary? Oh! That's vodka and juice," explained one. I guess the specifics of which fruit weren't important in these parts. I slowly sipped my beer, which tasted worse as its coldness disappeared, and continued to eavesdrop on the small world around me:

"I'm tired. I work five days a week and have a yeast infection."

"I was in her pussy when she woke me up."

"What happened to Chris?"

"He died."

"At least he didn't owe me money anymore."

A group to my right discussed who was and wasn't in jail that week. A woman sitting behind me covered an entire table with clean squares of tissue paper and spent the evening crafting tiny roses in red, baby blue, and yellow.

At exactly 9 p.m., the karaoke began. First up was the Flower Woman, who went by the name "Froggy." Froggy wore a t-shirt with her namesake on its front and green stripes down the sides of the sleeves. Perhaps she wore this same shirt—or something similar—every karaoke night. A quilted vest in a playing-card pattern completed her look.

As she was at the mic, singing a country tune about an auctioneer, a bearded man wearing a Hawaiian shirt and US Navy baseball cap came over to give me one of her light-blue flowers before launching into an hour-long monologue disguised as a conversation. He had a pronounced lisp, due to his lack of top and bottom front teeth. The mystery of his missing teeth was revealed quickly, as he started his conversation not by introducing himself, but by ranting about how his dentist screwed him over with promised implants and how he was now suing to get his deposit back. Then he launched into stories about winning karaoke contests in Redondo Beach, about the properties he owns, and about how he used to be a roadie for a bunch of bands: the manager of Fleetwood Mac had given him his first break. He name-dropped Don Henley, 38 Special, all the Beatles but Lennon, and others I can't remember. Adjusting his cap after every sentence or two, he shared stories of stars insisting on sleeping in tents, but being served food on silver platters, and of him carrying heavy cables through the desert heat for two miles to set up an outdoor show. The man honestly thought Paul McCartney was dead.

I got a few minutes' break from his chatter when it was his turn to sing. As he crooned "That's Life," full of lust and glee, my heart softened momentarily, and I could see why he was the winner of so many contests. While I found his stream-of-consciousness monologue to be more irritating than interesting at times, his stage personality was charming and larger than life. Froggy came up to me and made me another paper rose—this one red—as we listened. I now had a mini bouquet in front of me and I felt touched by its kindness.

The man returned to the barstool next to mine when he finished, and started to ask about me. I told him about my quest, how it was nearly completed, and he jolted back in surprise; he said he'd never heard of such a thing, and I could hear his wheels turning, considering whether he'd ever undertake the same quest. Sure enough, he began to share his thought process: He had a motorhome, but needed to fix it up. He had three properties, but wanted to sell them anyway and get the hell out of Nevada. I thought about my conversation with the casino/hotel receptionist and wondered if everyone who lived here wanted to get the hell out. "This could work," he lisped. "I can just drive around and sing in bars and see the country. It sounds like the perfect life." He slipped into some sort of dream world—one that I understood, and was about to leave.

I sang two songs, dedicated to the man in the Hawaiian shirt, and anyone else in Henderson, Nevada, who needed to hear them. The first was "Hold On Loosely," by 38 Special—chosen because it was one of the bands my companion said he worked for. The second, "Dreams" by Fleetwood Mac, also was inspired by his touring days, but the message ran a little deeper. I sang it for him, for the hotel receptionist, and for me—all of us who wanted out of our situations. We all wanted our freedom, and no one had the right to keep us away from our dreams.

Soon after, my body started to break under my hunger, the smoke in my lungs and eyes, and the fatigue of a long journey coming to its end. I thanked Froggy for the flowers; she hugged me and said to come back next week. I smiled without commitment and walked out the door, knowing I would never return.

CHAPTER 51

CALIFORNIA

September 14. 2016

I WAS UP AT SEVEN THE NEXT MORNING, AMPED AND ANXIOUS despite staying out late the night before. I still felt the smoke tightening my lungs and grasping at my throat. I knew I shouldn't be driving the 600-plus miles to Sacramento in one day, but I also knew I would. I left the casino, the machines quiet except for a few random noises emitted to lure potential victims. But the gamblers were all still asleep. I got into my car as my heart raced. My hands gripped the steering wheel as I took a deep breath, encouraging my mindset to transition from tortoise to hare. Off I went.

I barely remember my drive through the desert, except for the long stretches of road where I was convinced my car didn't even need a steering wheel. I also remember texting my brother during one of my stretch breaks, expressing my concerns and fears over moving forward with my life without all the pieces in place—Dave and I weren't going to live together as planned, and I was going to be facing two family members fighting cancer. He responded, "Life is closer to chaos theory than linear." Nothing could have been closer to the truth.

As I crossed into California, the Trump signs began to reappear, along with demands from farmers to make the state solve its water crisis—"No water, no food" and "Fix California's water"—as if any form of government had power over Mother Nature. The simplistic portrayal of impossible demands angered me, yet I tried to appreciate the panic of those who had posted the signs—those who would lose their livelihoods without lifted restrictions. I'm sure I had numerous other thoughts about politics, people, and my own life path as I drove the more than ten hours to get to Dave and his family, but as soon as I pulled into the Smith driveway, chasing away the chickens renowned throughout the suburb of Fair Oaks, all those thoughts vanished as I knocked on the door and prepared to face grief once again.

I wasn't ready. Milly Rose looked the same as when I had seen her last Christmas. Her dark, curly hair was still perfectly coiffed, her kind brown eyes framed with large plastic glasses. She got up from her computer solitaire game, and her hug was strong and full of love and life. I wasn't sure if her slower, more deliberate steps and her slumped shoulders were real or imagined.

I couldn't see the normalcy of the situation, despite the fact that it was right in front of me. Instead, I saw the future: the hair loss, the weight loss, the energy loss. I didn't have the strength to watch someone die all over again; it was just too soon. The healing I had done on my trip, comforting me lightly like a soft, loosely knit sweater, came unraveled as Milly Rose unknowingly pulled at an unfinished strand and left me standing, bare and raw all over again. The idea that I was going to finish my journey lost its significance as I tried to come to terms with this new battle. I collapsed, exhausted from a long day of driving, and emotionally drained by what lay before me. I crawled into bed. Soon after, Dave joined me, taking me into his arms. We held each other extra close.

I woke up next to Dave, and for that brief moment between sleep and life believed with all my heart that nothing else mattered. I just wanted to be in that space, pressed against his belly, his arm heavy on top of me, forever. Reality was quick to shatter this fantasy, as I heard Dave's mom struggling to make coffee. Where I wanted to be didn't exist anymore. Laying in that bed—the one Dave had slept in as a child, the one he was going to sleep in as he looked after his mother—I realized that technically, I could have joined him. I could have lived in the run-down house in Fair Oaks, California. I could have gotten a different job, a different life. We could have figured out how to make things work.

But I also knew the truth about me, and about us. I had an independence I couldn't shake; I knew that living in this home, so close to death, wouldn't allow me to heal. I heard the selfishness in my desires, and tried to pass it off as protectiveness, but I knew better. The reality was that I needed to take care of myself still, and had no desire to take care of another. I could have stayed, but I had to go.

My last hurrah—my final karaoke destination—was the Distillery, a bar that Dave had frequented back in his computer-geek days, before he began teaching overseas. He had always known there was much more to life than being a desk jockey—though he had also known that his friends, the ones he would die for, would always live in Sacramento. A few of these friends showed up in support of my final song, and to see Dave, whom they hadn't seen since he left for China.

The crew was more than motley. Jonathan was on mushrooms, yet still did his best to sing. It was clear he wasn't sober when he was called up to the stage, but I wasn't sure if people recognized the cause of his stumbling. For all they knew, it could have simply been his gangly tall frame and social ineptitude, or more than his share of beers. Kevin was hammered, already a bottle of wine into his evening, his eyes glazed over in friendliness and confusion. He had lost his ability to focus hours ago; another friend had to come pick him up so he could attend the celebration. Marletta, Dave's ex, was also there, sitting with a sense of inner peace that always made me feel welcome.

The rest of the crowd at the bar seemed small and uninspiring, but there was already a line of singers by the time I put my song in. The place didn't look packed, but it was a big space with long bar and several tables on either side of gigantic polished wooden support beams. Most of the time our group sat outside to smoke, leaving me and Dave alone at our picnic-like table, waiting for my name to be called. Every once in a while, Dave ventured outside to hang with his friends, leaving me alone. I didn't mind. This night was as much about him seeing his friends as it was about me finishing what I had set out to do. Besides, I appreciated the solitude, so I could reflect on this final moment. I don't remember what went through my head then, but I remembered feeling anxious, excited, warmed, and tired.

Somehow, as if summoned by an internal alarm clock, everyone managed to come back into the bar in time to hear me sing my own "Last Dance," courtesy of Donna Summer. I was more nervous than I thought I would be, despite the support of friends and the indifference of everyone else. I sang the first few notes with a sense of relief, and then a sense of disbelief—but both faded as I focused on the upbeat disco melody.

After three minutes and twenty-five seconds, the song ended, and my quest was complete. Though the KJ announced with a flourish that I had officially sung in all the Lower 48 states in one go—a statement greeted with hoots and hollers from my table, and a new round of drinks—I didn't feel much different. I sang a second song to normalize the evening, transitioning into a relaxing night among friends. But as I sat quietly, applauding the other singers for performances well done, I noticed that the joy that filled my body every time I sang karaoke was now bigger than ever—slowly rising through my core and into my head, and releasing into the crowd through a satisfied smile.

When it was time to go, Dave opened the passenger door of his large pickup truck, and I climbed inside. We didn't talk much on the ride back to his parents' house, instead enjoying each other's silent company. Home safe, we crawled into bed, and I once again pressed my backside into his belly, and his arm draped heavily over my waist. I looked forward to waking up in this exact position—the one that always felt right, no matter how much everything else changed.

ENCORE

I SPENT EARLY AUTUMN SETTLING BACK INTO A CITY AND LIFE without Molly. Though it would never be the same, I also knew Portland wasn't such a bad place to be. Dave, meanwhile, remained in Sacramento to care for his mother. She was undergoing radiation to zap the tumors in of her brain, and then would be prescribed a targeted pharmaceutical to prevent the cancer in her lungs from spreading. She would take this medication for the rest of her life, and no one had any idea how long that would be—until the very end. We lost Milly Rose in late July 2018. My world isn't as bright without her smile and hugs.

Of course, I kept on singing. On Tuesday, November 8, 2016, I was surrounded by fellow karaoke buffs at Voicebox, the private-room karaoke venue in Portland. Celebration turned to disbelief and churned into dismay as my liberal friends faced the reality of Donald Trump as our 45th president. Amid the tears, my friends sang "Canada" to the tune of "Panama," and "We're Not Going to Take It" by Twisted Sister.

They were part of a large portion of the country who was shocked over the results, but I wasn't that surprised. My journeys through various states—Alabama, Pennsylvania,

Oklahoma—all revealed to me that, to so many, this man represented the change they wished to see, the change they felt they deserved. In various karaoke spots in Arkansas, Missouri, and Vermont, I met people who supported our soon-to-be-president, and together we shared the beauty of listening to each other— not to our political rhetoric, but to our voices and cheers.

We are now told that we live in a country divided, but I don't completely buy it. I still hold out for common ground, for I have seen the communities in karaoke bars across America. I know in these places, alongside others who may think quite differently than I, there are pockets of joy to be found through song. Problems aren't solved, but we can still share space, have fun, and even support each other. It's a start.

I still have no sense of why I did what I did: why I drove 17,774 miles across America in ninety-nine days. Why I longed to sing karaoke in every one of the United States. My answer lay in the words of another. Author Elizabeth Gilbert, in a social media post, once said in response to a colleague who had asked her why, as a successful author, she felt the need to write and record a song:

> What is it for? I know more about myself than I did at the beginning of that journey, and that makes it inherently worth doing. It's for joy. It's for recognizing that you're not just here to pay bills and die. It's for trying something, it's for expanding yourself.

Gilbert was able to answer the question I had been struggling with ever since I took on my quest. After my trip, I learned no huge life lessons. What I did wasn't challenging, impressive, or noble. It wasn't the sort of accomplishment one receives recognition for. It didn't save or even improve lives. So, what was my journey for?

The answer, so simple, is about what often gets lost in our daily lives: I did it for joy.

MISSION ACCOMPLISHED

ALMOST A YEAR AFTER MY KARAOKE JOURNEY THROUGH THE Lower 48, in late August of 2017, I sang in Alaska, accompanied by my friend Margaret, who was excited to check off her own forty-seventh state (as a visitor, not a karaoke performer). We flew from Portland to Anchorage and sang in two places the night we arrived. The first was laid-back Al's Alaska Inn, bedecked in diamond-plate tables, floors, and walls. A dancing pole stood awkwardly center-stage, and was occasionally graced by a couple of women dressed in tight, shiny gowns, who accompanied a man with a black leather jacket and gravelly voice. The second venue, Mad Myrna's, required us to enter through a back alley and go through security, where my bag was searched and my body wanded. Inside were throngs of people, bodies sweating, voices yelling. I wondered if the security measures were due to the part of town, or if these were post-Pulse precautions—Myrna's was one of the few gay bars in the city (and probably in all of Alaska). I sang three songs that night, and state forty-nine was complete.

Soon after, Dave moved up to Portland, somewhat assured that the radiation had successfully fought back the tumors in his mother's brain, and that the targeted pharmaceutical was keeping the cancer in her lungs at bay. Seven months later, things began to shift again. Dave still hadn't found a job, and his mother started to lose weight, barely tipping the scale fifteen pounds lower than what her doctor recommended. Trying to soften her ice cream enough that she could scoop it, she would accidentally set the timer on the microwave for a full thirty minutes. When she fell, she couldn't get back up on her own. Dave and I woke up one Saturday morning, dark from Portland's overcast wintry sky, and he declared his intention to move back to Sacramento. A week later, in March 2018, I was in Hawaii to complete my quest.

My friend Kathy, the one who had welcomed me in Spokane when I began this journey, invited me to join her on a business trip in Waikiki so I could finish it. By 9 p.m., Wang Chung's was already packed with a mix of young gay men, a smattering of women, a few older couples, but no KJ. I gave my bright green song slip and a buck to the bartender, who punched in my selection. I sat down with a well-balanced lychee concoction and waited my turn.

My final song in my final state was Erasure's "Chains of Love," from 1988. The song was a bit too old for this crowd, but its lyrics, referencing a time of walking hand in hand, had grabbed my heart as I grappled with the most recent school shooting in Parkland, Florida. It had left seventeen dead and the country more divided than ever.

At Wang Chung's, there was no stage. Singers blended into the crowd of drinkers, dancers, and celebrators. And as I milled about the crowd, mic in hand, I realized that the time I was singing about still existed after all: it happened nightly, at any karaoke joint.

ACKNOWLEDGMENTS AND WHATNOT

SOME NAMES HAVE BEEN CHANGED, AND SOME HAVEN'T. IF A person wanted their real name used, I honored that. If they didn't, I honored that, too, and allowed them to choose their alias. For all the people whose contact information I didn't have, I changed their names. It was my intent to represent each person I met with accuracy and honor, and I apologize if anyone feels differently.

This book has one author, but a team of people behind it. I feel profound gratitude every time I think of all the help I received to make this work happen.

Thank you, Margaret Seiler, for your editing skills; Tom Doyle, for your continued advice and support through what you knew was going to be, at times, a painful process. I'm so lucky to have stumbled upon Inkwater Press, which has guided me every step along the way to turn my journey and Word document into an actual book. A special thanks to editor Andrew

Durkin for polishing my words; our collaboration has made me much happier with the final product.

Steve Hess, owner and master of Karaoke Across America—without your website and social media presence I wouldn't have found so many of the wonderful karaoke locations and met some of the warmest people out there.

Dave—without you I would have left many risks untaken, many sights unseen. I love you.

Thanks to all my friends old and new who opened their doors and hearts to a wayward traveler.

My heart glows when I think of all the karaoke singers who pour their souls into every song, singing to a room full of strangers—and the audiences who support them no matter what.

CPSIA information can be obtained
at www.ICGtesting.com
Printed in the USA
LVHW051112080523
746408LV00005B/526